*To all the people who feel that
massage is like art and who help others
live with energy, love, and a higher conscience.*

# CONTENTS

**Prologue** ..............................................9

## THEORY

**The Psychology of Holistic Massage**
The Seven Bodies.................................... 13
Essence and Existence ......................................... 15
The Seven Chakras: The Disks of Awareness ..... 18
The Seven Chakras ............................................. 21
How Energy Problems Somatize ........................ 25
Pain in the Body: Finding the Cause ................. 25
Principles of Energy............................................ 26
Touch ................................................................,,, 27
The Body. The Magical Creation ...................... 28
The Skeletal System ........................................... 29
The Circulatory System....................................... 30
The Nervous System .......................................... 31
The Muscular System.......................................... 32
The Internal Organs............................................ 33

**Principles of Each Method**
Shiatsu ............................................................... 35
Tantric Massage.................................................. 37
Reflexology......................................................... 40
Sensitive Massage .............................................. 42
What Does Each One Do and How Do
    They Differ? .................................................. 43
Practicing Holistic Massage ................................ 44

**The Therapist's Training and Wisdom**
Purification Program for Holistic Therapists..... 47
Sequence of Yoga Asanas.................................... 51
The Six Qualities of a Good Therapist ............... 59
Couples' Meditation .......................................... 60
Beginners and Professionals............................... 60
Spiritual Openness.............................................. 60
Do-In: The Self-Massage .................................... 61

**Elements of a Massage**
Physical Comfort................................................. 65
The Environment: Stimulation of
    the Six Senses ................................................ 65
Specific Oils........................................................ 65
Disorders and Their Treatments......................... 68

## PRACTICE

**Zen Shiatsu**
*Qi* Energy .......................................................... 74
*Kyo* and *Jitsu*: Deficiency or Excess of *Qi*.......,,,,, 75
Ways to Apply Pressure ...................................... 76
The Five Elements............................................... 76
Basic Shiatsu Techniques.................................... 77
Techniques for the Sacrum and
    Sciatic Nerve ................................................. 95
The Pain Relief Trilogy....................................... 101
Zen Shiatsu Points to Target
    Specific Problems.......................................... 102
Hara: Center of Vital Energy.............................. 103
Shiatsu on the Face and Head .......................... 104
The Keys to Zen Shiatsu .................................... 110
Working the Points on the Upper Back .......... 118
The Meridians and Their Points....................... 119

**Tantric Massage**
The Big Bang: Rain of Light on the Cells ........ 133
The Seven Principles of Tantric Massage ......... 133
1. The Principle of the Body ............................. 134
2. The Principle of Movement
    and Dance....................................................... 142
3. The Principle of Breathing ........................... 144
4. The Principle of Fire and Arousal ................ 146
5. The Principle of Pleasure and Love............. 148
6. The Principle of the Union between Shiva
    and Shakti....................................................... 149

7. The Principle of Silence, Ecstasy,
and Unity ....................................................... 152
Harmonization of the Chakras .......................... 154
Massaging the Chakras on the Feet .................. 162
Tantric Massage for Couples ............................ 170
Chakra Points on the Body ............................... 177

**Reflexology**
The Benefits of Reflexology in the Body .......... 179
Map of the Foot ............................................... 184

Foot Massage Techniques ................................. 185
Tips for before and after the Session ............... 187

**Sensitive Massage**
Basics of Sensitive Massage ............................. 190
Sensitive Massage for Different
Types of People ........................................... 191
Techniques for Different Personality Types ..... 195

**Epilogue .......................................................... 215**

# PROLOGUE

Completing this book gives me great satisfaction. It is a work that spans nine years of learning, studying, and teaching the art of massage.

At a time when our bodies are suffering from stress, poor posture, and disorders, this book offers a wise and intelligent perspective to care for our physical beings. It is for beginners in the quest for valuable knowledge, as well as for advanced professionals seeking to reinforce and learn new methodologies for healing.

Massage can be thought of as a lifestyle, where living is geared towards enjoying pleasure, comfort, and health as our most natural state.

Massage helps us discover that inside the body there are organs, muscles, bones, and more, but there are also emotions and feelings,

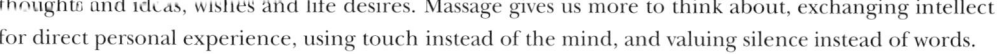

thoughts and ideas, wishes and life desires. Massage gives us more to think about, exchanging intellect for direct personal experience, using touch instead of the mind, and valuing silence instead of words.

Through this book, you will gain in-depth knowledge of important secrets about human beings, and you will be able to combine love and art with energy and wisdom. It is a journey through our holistic surroundings: body, energy, emotions, thoughts, and spiritual insights. It will inspire you to work with your hands and chakras, breath and soul, where the recipient and the giver are divine instruments.

Today there is huge amount of information available regarding spiritual paths, natural therapies, and self-knowledge techniques, and this book is written to get you to take the first step towards your personal evolution or give you additional ideas if you have already begun to move in that direction.

Throughout my travels and career teaching different paths of personal growth (such as yoga, tantra, massage, and meditation), I noticed that massage therapy is what gets most people's interest. And this should not come as a surprise given that many generations have been prohibited from learning through touch; children are often told "do not touch that." But now it is time for us to touch, feel, perceive, and awaken.

Massage is the contact between body and soul, it is a journey of transformation that goes from a state of tension to that of complete relaxation and, in some cases, astral experiences, and energizing the chakras.

I hope you enjoy what these pages have to offer; it is a pleasure to share this knowledge to enrich your life and that of all who give and receive a massage.

It is an invitation to travel from the hands to the soul . . .

GUILLERMO FERRARA, Barcelona, 2001

# THEORY

# THE PSYCHOLOGY OF HOLISTIC MASSAGE

Holistic massage is the union of four methods (shiatsu massage, tantric massage, reflexology, and sensitive massage) that aim to balance all aspects of an individual. This massage basically seeks to stimulate the recipient's physical being as well as their energy, emotional, rational, and spiritual being, because all these components are related to one another. In fact, holistic comes from the Greek word *holos*, meaning "total."

This effective therapy treats any type of problem because it focuses directly on energy. We are made up of energy, and when this vital energy is not flowing harmoniously, we have bodily pain. The vital energy, called *qi*, *chi*, or *prana*, is what keeps all beings alive on this planet. However, this energy can get blocked due to multiple factors, such as stress, poor diet, negative emotions, fears, bad habits, etc. Holistic massage can reactivate the flow of energy, providing balance, harmony, health and wellness.

This type of massage is not muscular (although it is applied to the body); instead, its primary focus is the psycho-emotional causes that affect energy, and then the physical body. Any illness, pain, or discomfort can be merely physical or it can affect the emotional or mental aspects of an individual. Holistic massage has the ability to soothe and harmonize to counteract the symptoms in the recipient's physical body.

By thoroughly studying human beings, you begin to discover the wonders of the body and its functions, the energy flows that feed it, the world of emotions, the labyrinths of the mind, and the desires of the soul. By touching the recipient with your bare hands, you form a connection that goes far beyond the physical realm. This connection takes you both into a spiritual, quiet, and meditative state.

I will describe the psychological basis for my work with holistic massage whereby you will be able to learn about your recipient's troubles so you can give them the appropriate treatment.

## THE SEVEN BODIES

Humans are not just physical bodies; we are made up of seven bodies with specific functions. These bodies are energy—different vibrations of awareness—and they work in teams: interweaving like the layers of an onion, exchanging daily awareness of each other.

These seven bodies have particular functions: the physical body, the energetic body, the emotional or astral, the rational, the spiritual, the cosmic, and finally, the nirvanic.

### 1. The physical body
It is the one that performs all actions, the ACTION. It is also the densest of all; therefore, it is visible to the human eye.

Many people are unaware that the wonders of the physical body go beyond what we can observe.

They do not know how many vertebrae are in their backbones, how many times they breathe per minute, how many liters of blood run through their bodies, nor how many miles of veins they have.

The physical body is a perfect creation. Its natural state is healthy and flexible, but that happens (usually) only during childhood, because later on the body becomes rigid and susceptible to diseases due to lack of "maintenance."

## 2. *The energetic body*

It is the body that contains the 72,000 *nadi* or energy channels called meridians. Just as blood flows through the veins in the physical body, ENERGY flows through the meridians in the energetic body.

The main meridians are twelve in total (six yin and six yang), although there are two other extraordinary points (conception vessel and governing vessel) that make up the microcosmic orbit and energy reserves.

This body absorbs energy from the Sun and Earth to ensure that the physical body receives vital energy (*prana*).

## 3. *The emotional or astral body*

This body resides in FEELING. This is where the seven chakras can be found, which are connected to the glands of the endocrine system in the physical body, and which are the basis of the psyche.

*Each chakra has a function and generates a basic desire:* material desire, sexual, desire for food, emotional, creative, intuitive and intellectual, and spiritual desire for unity with the divine.

When one of these desires is unharmonious or dissatisfied, the corresponding chakra gets overloaded with energy, creating an imbalance. For example, someone wants to buy a house (material desire) but is forced to wait because he does not have the money, so he may start eating compulsively due to anxiety (food).

Every day, we see how any given chakra can be overworked due to desires that cannot be satisfied. I will describe each chakra further on (starting on page 18).

## 4. *The rational body*

This body is made up of thoughts, ideas, projections for the future, past memories, calculations, intellect, beliefs, etc.

The mind, which is made up of THOUGHT, is a great mystery with great potential. And just as with our bodies, our minds differ from one person to another. It is precisely because we all have different ideas that bad ones set off wars, resulting in the deaths of many people.

The mind keeps people from relating to the soul's harmony; this is because beliefs make the person react instead of responding by conscience or personal experience. A misused mind separates people because it creates distance within the individual's own self. How many times does a person feel one thing yet think another? If we think differently than how we feel, then our physical body does not fulfill our action and we create inner conflict for ourselves. Conflicting energies in the body create pain and disease. If people listened to their soul and acted accordingly, if the spirit were to freely express and the mind were in the service of self, there would be no diseases or anxiety.

The mind has been overloaded with ideas that go against nature, the spirit is full of guilt and suffering, and the body has been flogged on behalf of the spirit. We need to devoid ourselves of negativity through silent massage. By using meditation that helps silence the mind, the heart and emotion will then open up, and the physical body will be able to relax, increasing vital energy. Holistic massage restores and harmonizes the energy flow by balancing the bodies and getting to the real root of the problem.

## 5. *The spiritual body*

Humanity is moving very slowly because of the conflict that exists between our minds and our emotions. We insist on meeting the requirements of the mind (while burdened by the stereotypes created by advertising), when the spiritual body can open up a vast field of perceptions and faculties.

The spirit is a plane of PERCEPTION and, as the soul's "shell," it manifests with great force while we undergo a massage, engage in deep meditation, or sleep. It can then push the individual toward new levels of insight.

## 6. *The cosmic body*

It is a much higher plane, but in fact, these last three bodies must be created, since they are like seeds that we need to care for in order for them to flourish in the soul.

The cosmic body merges the individual with divinity, granting access to the real, holistic world, where the dual borders disappear. There is no "there" and "here," but rather consciousness considers everything as One.

## 7. *The nirvanic body*

This stage vanishes the ordinary self into the infinite consciousness. It is the enlightenment of consciousness, a homecoming.

The Soul (*Lilah*) is now projected towards the eternal. At this level, learning is complete. In the words of Jesus: "My Father and I are one and the same."

### *Conclusion*

- Each body has a particular function, and they are all interconnected.
- Feelings and thoughts must work in harmony in order for there to be balance. Most problems or illnesses arise from the conflict between the two.

- Where there is harmonization there is also the possibility for consciousness to ascend into deeper levels of perception.
- Massage is a tool to access a holistic range of energies that come together in the physical realm.
- Every individual has to be observed as a whole so we can determine how they are energetically, emotionally, mentally, and spiritually.

## ESSENCE AND EXISTENCE

We each have a soul or essence, a divine spark that God has given us. We are a cell in a large body called the universe, cosmos, life, tao, or God. Our essence is the same for everyone, and the only differences among us are our bodies, emotions, thoughts, actions, and individuality; this is our existence. Our existence is a different adventure; it is how we express our essence.

Jesus, Socrates, Buddha, Mozart, Einstein, Osho, Dalí, Beethoven, Vivaldi, the Bee Gees, or Nino Bravo turned their physical existence into a beautiful manifestation of the universal essence; they flourished and left a great legacy of creativity.

Our essence is the same spark of a great fire, the same drop in a boundless ocean, a gift. For this gift of having a personal existence, we each have to pay back by doing something creative to benefit life, the divine plan, the evolution of the species.

Many people, however, do not care for their existence (which is an individual responsibility), and instead of weaving a beautiful personal history, they become lazy and forget that they have a gift.

Each one of us has a particular mission, but when we abandon our intended path, problems start to show up in our lives. No matter what it is that you do, you should be feeling it and enjoying it with your heart.

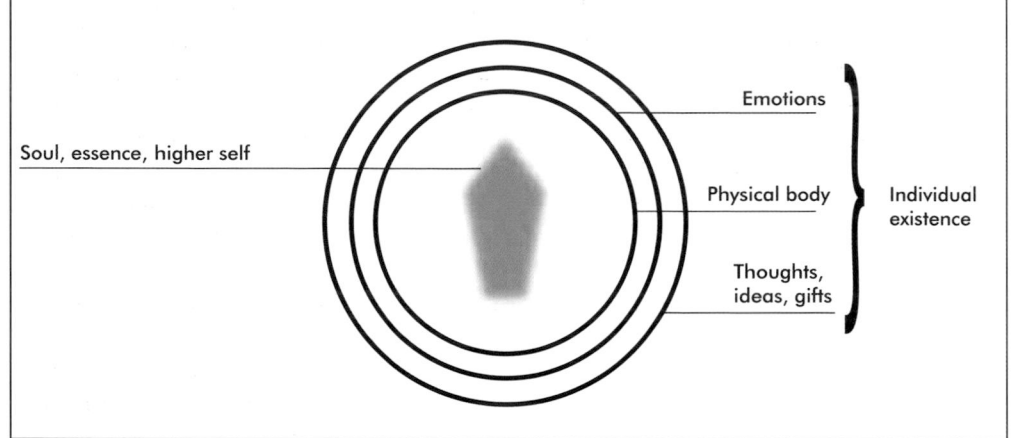

Throughout history we learn about the path of those who left a message; a mark that brings us beauty, pleasure, and transformation. Similarly, there are those who played a negative role. It is up to you to use your gifts for Good or get lost in the dark night of the soul. The soul is the raw material. Existence is your personal story.

The essence requires a physical body through which it can express its potential. A body with its own emotions, gifts, mindset, and habits makes up each individual's uniqueness.

At all times you should be aware that you are a soul, and you have a body with which you can express yourself.

### The origin of our internal conflict: To feel or think?

Our four bodies are the physical, the energetic, the emotional, and the rational. The remaining three remain in seed form, latent.

If the physical body acts, the energetic body takes prana, the astral body feels, and the rational body thinks, so what happens when you feel one thing yet think a different thing? There is conflict, and this conflict creates pain in the physical body (blocked energy) and later disease.

Keep in mind a very important fact: every human being has desires. In fact, this is a world of desires and that is why in India they call it *Kamaloka*, a word made up of "Kama" (desire) and "loka" (world).

When you want something with your heart or mind, you search for a way to make it real; to materialize it on the physical plane. When you get it, you are left satisfied; otherwise, you are left with anxiety or distress.

People feel conflict when there is disagreement between what they feel (in the heart) and what they think (in the mind). They feel something deep and soulful that would make them grow, but the mind blocks them with a thousand different arguments.

The mind in its negative phase is a receptacle full of repressions, fears, ideas, beliefs, false myths, negative thoughts, etc. When your mind malfunctions (in its critical rather than creative aspect) it censors everything you want to express with the heart. Obviously, the mind has a positive side, but imagine someone in the role of censor: this person would find himself at a crossroads not only because there would be a confrontation between what he feels and what he thinks, but also between the will to satisfy a feeling and having doubts, a product of the mind's fear or laziness at the moment of action.

For example: you love someone yet you do not show it; you want to pursue a career but your mind prefers to do otherwise; you feel an emotion but choose to hide it behind the veil of morality; you want to have sex with someone but you do not give into your desire until your mind is made up.

The world is filled with repressed people, and a heart that suppresses what it feels is a spirit that cannot laugh, jump, dance, and celebrate. People have become ill with seriousness when in fact being happy does not equal being irresponsible. And so much seriousness results in numerous diseases and rigid personalities.

Neither mind nor thought should block the spirit, nor should they silence the heart's voice because happy people are those who listen and act from the heart, like a river flowing endlessly or a flute that allows air to pass so that a melody can be heard. But what happens if the mind seals up our communal flute with repressions and fears? Well, then there is no sound, no music, and no joy in our lives.

Through holistic massage you will be attentive to each person. You will know if their heart is closed (rational, unexpressive, delaying their life journey) and you will analyze them individually according to the answers they provide you.

It is fantastic being able to create a bridge between feeling and thinking; between love and intelligence. Love is energy and it comes from the heart, whereas intelligence is also energy but it comes from the mind. Love is not blind, it is energy flowing at all times, but it gets interrupted by the mind. Massage makes the mind take a side step so that the individual is able to recognize himself; so that he is able to feel with his soul, with love, with intelligent energy, without borders or shells.

You will encounter recipients who are mostly led by their minds, who are tied to their preconceived notions, prejudices, traditions, rigid moral concepts, and ideas. Individuals who constantly overanalyze everything, who are very rational, very analytical, and not very unintuitive, are not only unhappy but are also not free. And the physical body will demonstrate this through tension, stress, muscle contractions, energy blockages, etc.

Buddha said, "Be a shining light for yourself," and holistic massage therapy aims precisely to help you quietly tune into your essence and receive energy, a state where the borders of the mind dissolve so you can once again feel the fullness of your existence.

Massage provides you with the momentum to express your feelings and creative desires. In so doing, you can climb to a new state of consciousness beyond feeling and thought: the state of being, existing; becoming aware that you are alive, breathing, mindful of all the wonders that nature gives you moment by moment.

The techniques in this book are aimed at freeing the spirit, polishing the heart, silencing the mind, and transcending all that ties us down. Do not let any myth or social paradigm lock your being. You are made to express yourself, to flourish as an individual, to forge your destination. Holistic massage can help you eliminate repressions by liberating your body and your spirit. With this in mind, at the start of the session the recipient is naked, not just physically but also by letting their soul travel internally and freely toward freedom, pleasure, and growth.

For example:

**FEELING A:** Someone feels love for someone else and wants to show it with a gift (flowers, for example).

**THOUGHT B:** That someone does not return the affection, does not look at him or her, has a different lifestyle, etc. The mind will make up excuses to deny feeling A.

**CONSEQUENCE:** Energy lessens, therefore the action is not carried out (does not give the flowers).

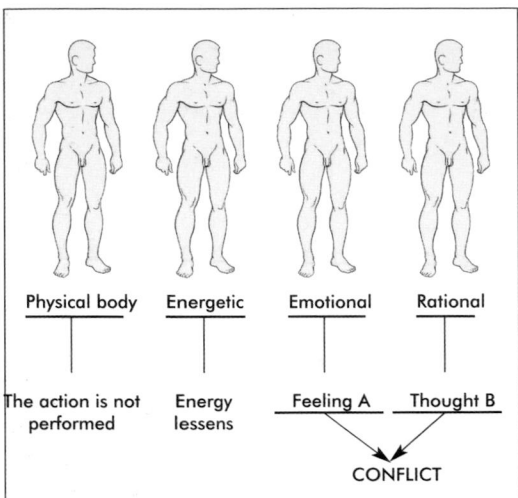

| Physical body | Energetic | Emotional | Rational |
|---|---|---|---|
| The action is not performed | Energy lessens | Feeling A | Thought B |

CONFLICT

spinning on each of the seven points. The chakras are described as lotus flowers with varying numbers of petals (the speed of energy is different in each chakra).

The first five chakras are along the spine, at an astral level, and work through *kundalini* energy. Traditionally, kundalini energy is in the first chakra (in the genital area) or an inch below the navel, in the space between the vertebrae. It is psychosexual energy, generating all movement of life. There is no life in the human body without this energy, which flows through the central passage (*sushumna*) feeding centers of consciousness.

When energy builds in a particular chakra, the individual is characterized by certain behavioral tendencies that are associated with that chakra.

The seven basic chakras generate desires and bring forth positive and negative qualities. However, when the chakras are not functioning properly, the individual is afflicted by energy blockages, negative thoughts and emotions, and poor physical condition.

This is a very simple and superficial case, but it serves to illustrate this mechanism. Furthermore, there are people who repress deeper aspects of themselves by "shutting" their heart, which then results in more problems.

For example, if someone wanted to sing since childhood and he was not allowed to pursue that path, it is likely that in the future he will have trouble with his throat, thyroid gland, and self-expression.

Little by little, you will begin to see examples of people with repressed feelings who end up having low energy, low self-esteem, and little interest in life.

## THE SEVEN CHAKRAS: THE DISKS OF AWARENESS

According to traditional Indian wisdom, chakras are centers of energy and knowledge that make up conscience.

The term chakra in Sanskrit means "wheel" since energy looks like the spokes of a wheel

### *The seven desires*

The seven basic desires that the different chakras generate are as follows:

1. **Muladhara Chakra:** Desire for survival.
2. **Swadisthana Chakra:** Sexual desire.
3. **Manipura Chakra:** Desire for food.
4. **Anahatta Chakra:** Desire for love.
5. **Vishudda Chakra:** Desire to create and express.
6. **Ajna Chakra:** Desire for knowledge.
7. **Sahasrara Chakra:** Spiritual desire.

The first three chakras are part of the animal kingdom, since they are related to survival, sex, and food.

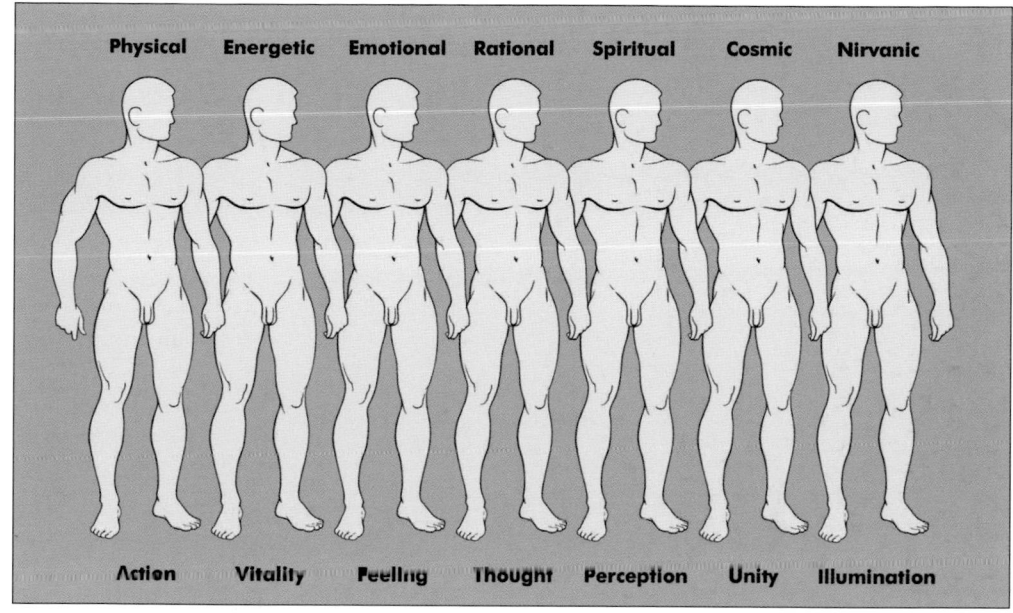

| Physical | Energetic | Emotional | Rational | Spiritual | Cosmic | Nirvanic |
|----------|-----------|-----------|----------|-----------|--------|----------|
| Action | Vitality | Feeling | Thought | Perception | Unity | Illumination |

**NOTE:** *In reality, the bodies are not far apart. Rather, they are interwoven with each other.*

The next two are related to the human realm: here the individual gives love, receives love, and is able to express himself artistically.

The last two belong to the divine realm: the use of intuition, intellect, and imagination as a means of attaining knowledge and spirituality.

From all this, it can be deduced that we are animals that became human beings through love, and that we can become aware of our divine essence.

Consciousness gets affected when a chakra is malfunctioning. For example, if a person feels the desire to love someone but that feeling is not reciprocated, such sense of rejection will lead to anxiety and cause an overload of the food chakra, expressed as an excess or loss of appetite. When we cannot satisfy an immediate desire, we try to fill that void by pushing its energy on to another desire. There is an energetic disorder that starts to affect the energy field, and if we let it go on it can affect the functioning of a particular gland or organ.

Tantric massage works on the chakras, harmonizing the flow of energy, and then enhancing it.

Someone with most of his energy in the first chakra will tend to focus most of his awareness on material things: he will speak a lot about cars, houses, material goods.

If, on the other hand, his energy is mostly in the second chakra, his entire psyche will focus on sex and he will perceive everything in sexual terms.

If his energy is concentrated in the third chakra, he will be the type of person who never stops thinking about food: as he eats lunch, he will start to wonder what he will be having for dinner.

If most of his energy is in the fourth chakra (in the heart), he will be a compassionate, loving, and kind person who cares for others.

If his energy is in the fifth chakra, he will be a creative, expressive, and artistic being with the need to express what is in his soul.

If most of his energy is in the sixth chakra (the third eye), he will have a tendency toward intellectual pursuits, listen to his intuition, or be highly imaginative. With his own insight, he will create a very sensitive field of intuition.

If his energy is concentrated in the seventh chakra (on top of the head), he will be an enlightened being who is consciously connected to the higher power and the universe.

This last chakra means eliminating duality; consciousness expands when this center is awakened, thereby unifying the finite with the infinite.

According to yoga, the soul ascends through a tenth opening toward Nirvana at the time of death. Its gland secretes serotonin, a chemical that opens the mind to other realities or mystical experiences.

Every individual's spiritual destiny is to bring the energy of the lower chakras toward the top of the head, raising awareness through the first three chakras: from the animal to the human to the divine by illuminating consciousness.

However, when the chakras are not in harmony within each of the different bodies, then there are problems: energy level drops, causing pain and disease in the physical body.

In the table below, you will see a description of each chakra so you can better understand them.

---

It is important that the therapist know what the symptoms of imbalance are in any given chakra so that he can determine what type of massage is required for treatment.

---

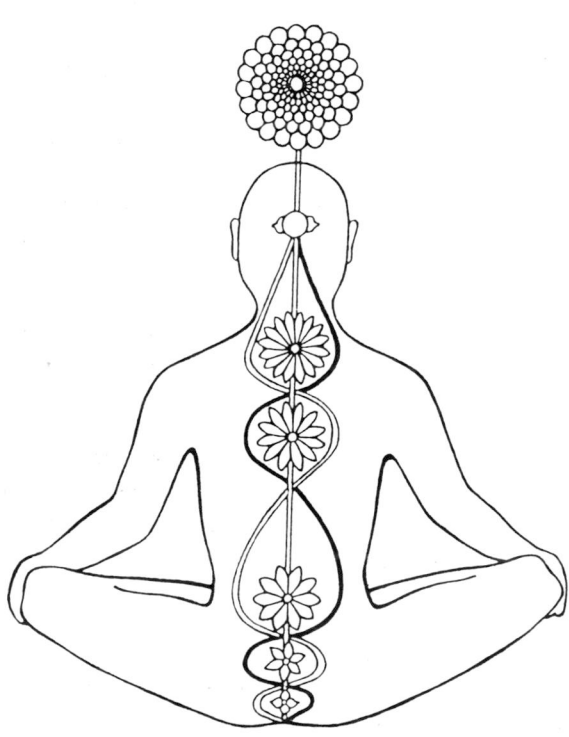

# THE SEVEN CHAKRAS

## FIRST CHAKRA: Root
### *Right to Have*

**NAME:** Muladhara.

**ELEMENT:** Earth.

**INFLUENCED SIGNS:** Taurus, Virgo, and Capricorn.

**PERSONALITY:** Terrestrial.

**PLEXUS:** Coccygeal.

**LOCATION:** Base of the spine, between anus and genitals.

**ENDOCRINE GLAND SYSTEM:** Genitals (testes or ovaries).

**COLOR:** Intense spiritual red.

**GEMSTONES:** Garnet, black tourmaline, red stones.

**DESIRES:** Survival, comfort, economic wellbeing, relationship with the earth.

**PURPOSE:** Prosperity, abundance, comfortable living, economic stability.

*This chakra manifests the right to survival. It involves money, property, and everything related to our earthly needs.*

**PSYCHOLOGICAL SYMPTOMS OF BALANCE:** Self-confidence, mastery of desire.

**SYMPTOMS OF IMBALANCE:** Selfishness, depression, instability, lack of savings, shyness and distractibility.

**SYMPTOMS OF EXCESS:** Fear of change, material obsession, overweight.

**SOMATIC SYMPTOMS:** Hemorrhoids, sciatic, constipation, knee problems, poor circulation in the legs, bone problems.

## SECOND CHAKRA: Sexual
### *Right to Feel*

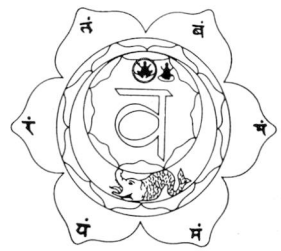

**NAME:** Swadisthana.

**ELEMENT:** Water.

**INFLUENCED SIGNS:** Cancer, Scorpio, and Pisces.

**PERSONALITY:** Aquatic, mobile, fickle.

**PLEXUS:** Spleen.

**LOCATION:** About three inches (eight centimeters) below the navel.

**ENDOCRINE GLAND SYSTEM:** Suprarenal.

**COLOR:** Vital orange.

**GEMSTONES:** Coral, orange stone.

**DESIRE:** Sexual, unity of opposites: yin and yang, Shiva and Shakti, female and male.

**PURPOSE:** Pleasure, conquest, handling and opening sexual energy.

*It is free expression of sensitivity, sensuality, and sexuality. This chakra operates the most important energy: sexual energy.*

**PSYCHOLOGICAL SYMPTOMS OF BALANCE:** Endurance, patience, confidence, knowledge of sexual desire.

**SYMPTOMS OF IMBALANCE:** Anxiety, fear, rigidity, frigidity, impotence, instability, bottling up emotions, rejection of pleasure, insensitivity, talking nonsense (the tongue is connected to the sexual center).

**SYMPTOMS OF EXCESS:** Sexual Addiction, anxiety over pleasure.

**SOMATIC SYMPTOMS:** Kidneys, bladder, prostate, sexual organs.

## SEVEN CHAKRAS

### THIRD CHAKRA: Meals
*Right to Work*

**NAME:** Manipura.

**ELEMENT:** Fire.

**INFLUENCED SIGNS:** Aries, Leo, and Sagittarius.

**PERSONALITY:** Fiery, energetic.

**PLEXUS:** Solar.

**LOCATION:** In the navel.

**ENDOCRINE GLAND SYSTEM:** Pancreas.

**COLOR:** Sunny yellow.

**GEMSTONES:** Citrine, topaz, amber.

**DESIRE:** Food.

**PURPOSE:** Provide vitality, strong willpower, inner power, motivation to act.

*It is related to willpower, vitality, personal power, self-esteem, and all low unprocessed emotions (fear, anger, rage, anxiety) that get stuck in the organs and alter their functioning.*

**PSYCHOLOGICAL SYMPTOMS OF BALANCE:** Inner strength, determination, fair actions.

**SYMPTOMS OF IMBALANCE:** Doubt, shyness, low energy, fatigue, digestive problems, submission, obesity.

**SYMPTOMS OF EXCESS:** Hastiness, wanting to dominate others, anger and frequent quarrels, ulcers.

**SOMATIC SYMPTOMS:** Stomach ulcers, hepatitis, gallstones, excess weight in the belly area.

### FOURTH CHAKRA: Heart
*Right to Love and be loved*

**NAME:** Anahatta.

**ELEMENT:** Air.

**INFLUENCED SIGNS:** Gemini, Libra, and Aquarius.

**PERSONALITY:** Loving, sensitive, caring.

**PLEXUS:** Heart.

**LOCATION:** In the center of the chest.

**ENDOCRINE GLAND SYSTEM:** Thymus.

**COLOR:** Lively green.

**GEMSTONES:** Green quartz, emerald, and rose quartz.

**DESIRE:** Loving and being loved.

**PURPOSE:** Balance in relationships with others and with self.

*Linked to everything affective. Represents the desire for emotional, loving unity and brotherhood. Manifested through affection, compassion, love, tenderness, and solidarity.*

**PSYCHOLOGICAL SYMPTOMS OF BALANCE:** Compassion, acceptance of reality, and grand openness of emotions.

**SYMPTOMS OF IMBALANCE:** Instability, shutting emotions, loneliness, sadness and melancholy, passivity, low self-acceptance, sunken chest, shallow breathing.

**SYMPTOMS OF EXCESS:** Situations that lead to having to depend on others, excessive attachment or detachment.

**SOMATIC SYMPTOMS:** Cardiac and respiratory problems. Hypertension.

## FIFTH CHAKRA: Throat
*Right to Speak and communicate*

**NAME:** Vishudda.
**ELEMENT:** Ether.
**PERSONALITY:** Mobile.
**PLEXUS:** Laryngeal.
**LOCATION:** In the throat.
**ENDOCRINE GLAND SYSTEM:** Thyroid.
**COLOR:** Lavender blue.
**GEMSTONES:** Aquamarine, turquoise.
**DESIRE:** Communication, expression.
**PURPOSE:** Interact harmoniously with others from within, use energy creatively.

*This center contains communication skills, artistic self-expression, speaking one's self-truth. As long as it is well balanced, it can communicate, express, and create in accordance to the Universal Creation.*

**PSYCHOLOGICAL SYMPTOMS OF BALANCE:** Creative artistic development, spiritual elevation.
**SYMPTOMS OF IMBALANCE:** Stagnation, obsession, repression of what is intended to say, inability to let loose, blocked creativity. Hoarseness, stiff neck, stiff shoulders.
**SYMPTOMS OF EXCESS:** Talk a lot but say very little, screaming.
**SOMATIC SYMPTOMS:** Sore throat, vocal problems, hypo- and hyperthyroidism, flu.

## SIXTH CHAKRA: Third Eye
*Right to See clearly*

**NAME:** Ajna.
**ELEMENT:** Thought.
**PERSONALITY:** Intuitive, imaginative.
**PLEXUS:** Frontal.
**LOCATION:** Between the eyebrows.
**ENDOCRINE GLAND SYSTEM:** Pituitary.
**COLOR:** Bright white.
**GEMSTONES:** Lapis lazuli, white quartz.
**DESIRE:** Strength through inner knowledge.
**PURPOSE:** Provide a clear view of events, intuitive knowledge, awaken the sixth sense.

*It is responsible for developing the individual's ability to see things clearly through intuition. It also uses imagination and intellect. When it is activated, it awakens extrasensory abilities.*

**PSYCHOLOGICAL SYMPTOMS OF BALANCE:** Psychic development, lucid intellect, extrasensory perception.
**SYMPTOMS OF IMBALANCE:** Insensitivity, inability to create new ideas and use intuition, failing to believe in dreams. Inability to visualize, intellectual stagnation.
**SYMPTOMS OF EXCESS:** Paranoid fantasies, nightmares, hallucinations.
**SOMATIC SYMPTOMS:** Headaches, confused thoughts.

## SEVEN CHAKRAS

**SEVENTH CHAKRA: Crown**
*Right to Know*

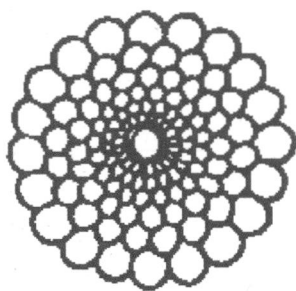

**NAME:** Sahasrara.

**ELEMENT:** Light.

**PERSONALITY:** Transcend the limits of the self by joining the spiritual.

**PLEXUS:** Crown.

**LOCATION:** On top of the head.

**ENDOCRINE GLAND SYSTEM:** Pineal.

**COLOR:** Violet.

**GEMSTONES:** Amethyst, diamond, white quartz.

**DESIRE:** Spirituality, mystical union.

**PURPOSE:** Expand awareness.

*It is the lotus flower on top of the head that receives divine energy and the gift of life. It is a spiritual sun that connects the individual with God. This flower is so beautiful that it has 1,000 petals and it contains all Sanskrit sounds.*

**PSYCHOLOGICAL SYMPTOMS OF BALANCE:** Cosmic consciousness, inspiration, enlightenment.

**SYMPTOMS OF IMBALANCE:** Depression, insanity, psychosis, confusion, slowness of mind. Worry, rigid personal beliefs, little open mindedness.

**SYMPTOMS OF EXCESS:** People who think they know it all or who always want to be right. Spiritual or intellectual elitism. Awakening the most dangerous of personal egos, isolation, dissociation.

**SOMATIC SYMPTOMS:** Tumors; pressure in the skull.

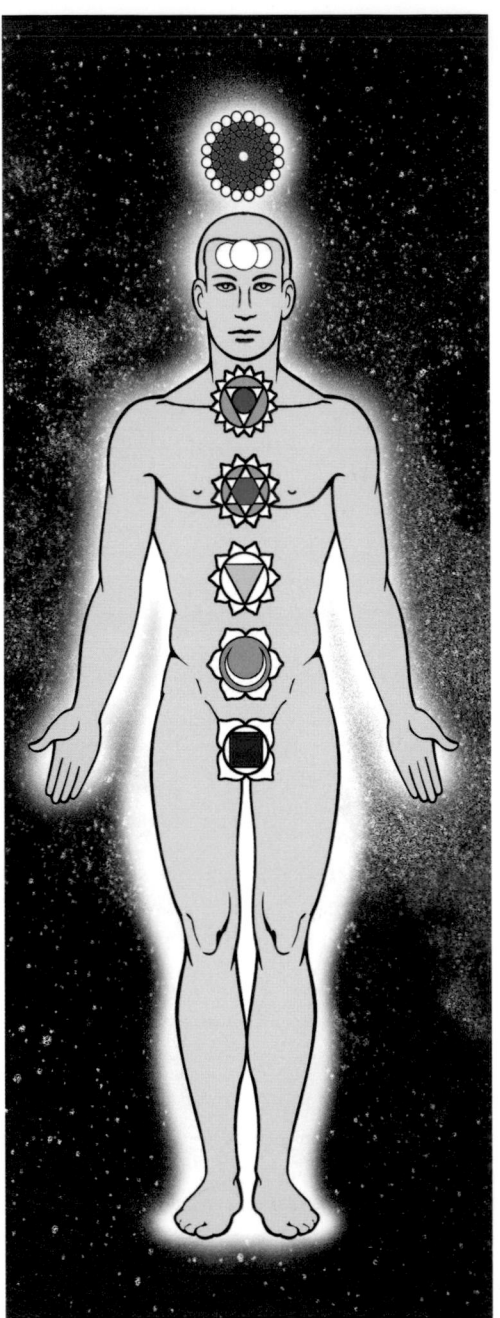

goes. Just as there are dynamic and violent acts made up of misused energy that generate muscle contractions, there is also the more subtle form of energy: thought. A chain of thoughts become a single idea that is then taken as truth and becomes belief. If belief is not natural (for instance, "men do not cry") it can lead to respiratory problems, asthma, heart attack, depression, grief, boredom, submission, etc.

Emotional energy (literally "energy moving outward from within") is completely harmful if it is not expressed. But through the years we have been condemned to suppress our emotions.

Keep in mind that there was a time when magical and wise women were labeled as witches and burned; and Christopher Columbus was laughed at for thinking that the Earth was round. Oftentimes it is easier to adopt a foreign thought than to develop your own.

On the other hand, thoughts are so powerful that monitoring them requires discipline, mental gymnastics, and attentive consciousness. According to the nature of thought, we either attract creative energy or generate diseases and problems.

Knowing that energy is transformed into its opposite offers us the possibility to change tension into relaxation, and stress into rest. For example, a muscle spasm in the trapezius or shoulder blades is repressed energy causing pain; like a stone blocking normal energy flow. If we think of the muscle contraction as if it were a small fist (yang energy) and work on it with great force, yang (tension) will give way to yin (relaxation) as if the fist opened up. And indeed, this is what happens with a muscle contraction: it transforms tension into relaxation.

We can draw out energy through our hands, shoulders (near the collarbone), hair, exhalation, feet, and shoulder blades; just as we can let it in through the solar plexus, head (seventh chakra), inhalation, healthy food, and soles of the feet.

Releasing blocked energy is painful because it is a process of change. So to treat those whose energy has been contracted for a long time, we might need multiple sessions.

## TOUCH

Undoubtedly, the most forgotten of the human senses is touch. And that should be no surprise to us because as children we are repeatedly told "do not touch that!" And we are kept from exploring the world through touch. These are basic years in which, lacking intellect, we try to gain knowledge using our hands. Through our hands, we are able to explore everything, including the body and genitals, and this is the first repression imposed by the mother.

Today we avoid touching, hugs, and even making eye contact; we have been taught to repress feelings. Crying, for example, is considered a sign of weakness rather than sensitivity, and touch is synonymous with "manhandling" instead of internal experience, pleasure, and relaxation of the body. By hugging, cuddling, touching, or gliding the hands gently we can reconnect, reawaken the skin, stir up emotions, and light up the heart.

So-called Western education focuses solely on competitiveness, ignoring sensitivity. A man or woman who is extremely competitive is under stress, suffers hair loss, damages their glands, smokes, gains weight, loses their flexibility, becomes stiff, causes pain to their muscles, gambles with their health . . .

Holistic massage is a return ticket to the internal home; pleasure, joy, sensitivity, harmony, and relaxation of the nervous system. It is a contemporary tool to recover touch and feeling, and to deepen the meditative state. This is achieved by making contact with deeper and richer areas.

Touch is a balm, a beautiful relief. I remember when I was young, I used to come home tired from playing basketball and my grandmother massaged my feet and back. Although she did not know any techniques, her loving hands were able to relieve my pain.

Massages allow us to feel touched, loved, and taken from the cold to the warmth that every body and soul seeks: the warmth of affection.

## THE BODY: THE MAGICAL CREATION

Very few people are aware that their physical body is a loan.

Starting from the premise that the heartbeat is a miracle (nobody consciously makes their heart beat; it is a mystery of living energy), ask yourself how many liters of blood run through your veins; how many vertebrae hold up your body, your Tree of Life; how many muscles or bones you have; how many times you breathe per minute.

The truth is we know nothing about the house we inhabit.

According to tantra, the body is a storage of strength, it is a temple of the soul on earth, which is why all spiritual paths must start by understanding its functions, systems, reactions, capabilities, flexibility, strengths, and, overall, the whole mystery it encapsulates.

Have you ever thought that one day you will leave your body? Or that it will last longer if you care for it and allow it to enjoy pleasure? How long has it been since you last enjoyed a massage, took a warm bath, went out for a jog or a walk, practiced yoga, or went out dancing?

Interestingly enough, we only pay attention to the body when it is in pain or ill; we are not aware of it when we are well and healthy. We should be more loving towards it, and a good way to do that would be by receiving a massage; a beautiful gift that keeps the physical body in harmony with the other bodies and, at its deepest therapeutic power, heals it.

Through massage we aim, first of all, to get to know the body: if the spine is reliable; if the digestive system works well; where is the pain; how are the muscles; how is sleep, etc.

The body is a wonderful creation. It works according to its own wisdom of life: it heals after it is injured, oxygenates the brain, promotes digestive processes, generates hormones, reacts to stimuli, makes the blood flow, etc. As a proverb says, "When you touch the human body, you touch the sky."

During massage, we first read the physical body: knowing when a person is feeling defensive (with crossed legs and arms); feeling admiration (head cocked to the side); feeling pleasure (smiling face); feeling depressed (sinks the chest and takes shallow breaths); and so on.

Reading the body is a gift that the therapist has to cultivate in order to know which type of massage each individual requires.

# THE SKELETAL SYSTEM

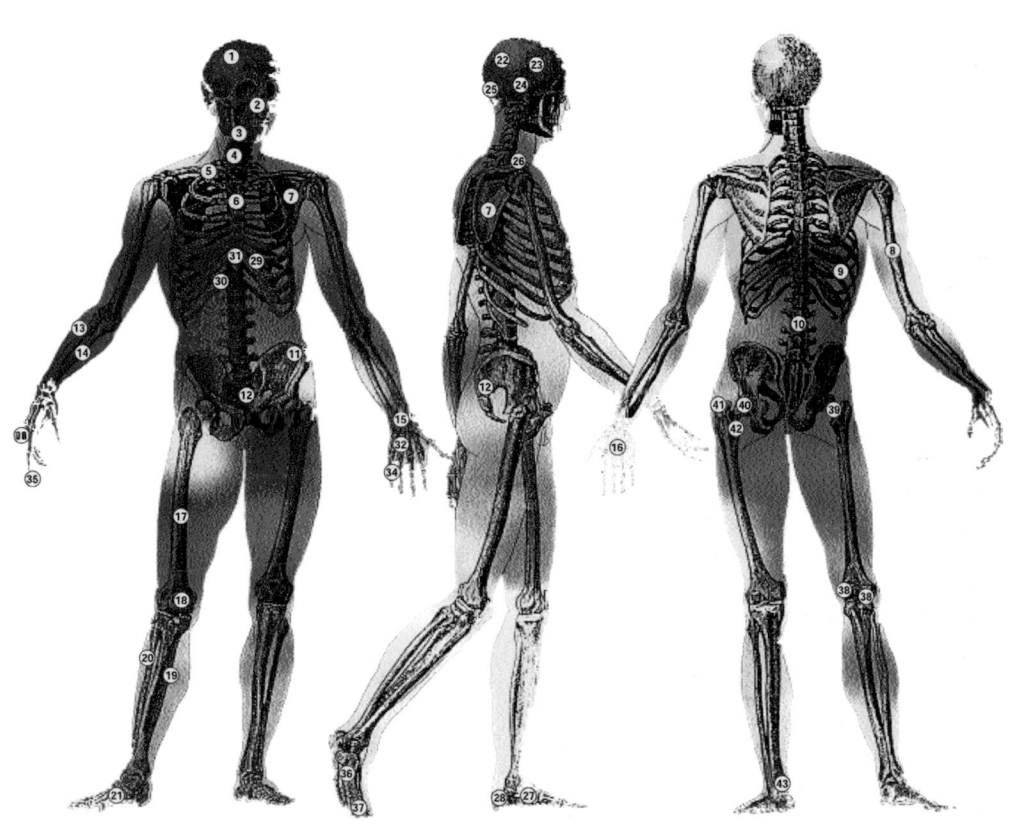

1. *Cranium;* **2.** *maxilla;* **3.** *mandible;* **4.** *cervical vertebrae;* **5.** *clavicle;* **6.** *sternum;* **7.** *scapula;* **8.** *humerus;* **9.** *ribs;* **10.** *lumbar vertebrae;* **11.** *coxal;* **12.** *sacrum;* **13.** *radius;* **14.** *ulna;* **15.** *wrist bones;* **16.** *hand bones;* **17.** *femur;* **18.** *patella;* **19.** *tibia;* **20.** *fibula;* **21.** *foot bones;* **22.** *parietal;* **23.** *frontal bone;* **24.** *temporal bone;* **25.** *occipital bone;* **26.** *clavicle (lateral view);* **27.** *talus;* **28.** *calcaneus;* **29.** *costal cartilages;* **30.** *floating ribs;* **31.** *xiphoid process;* **32.** *metacarpals;* **33.** *proximal phalanges;* **34.** *intermediate phalanges;* **35.** *distal phalanges;* **36.** *metatarsals;* **37.** *phalanges;* **38.** *femoral condyles;* **39.** *femoral neck;* **40.** *femoral head;* **41.** *greater trochanter;* **42.** *lesser trochanter;* **43.** *styloid process.*

## THE CIRCULATORY SYSTEM

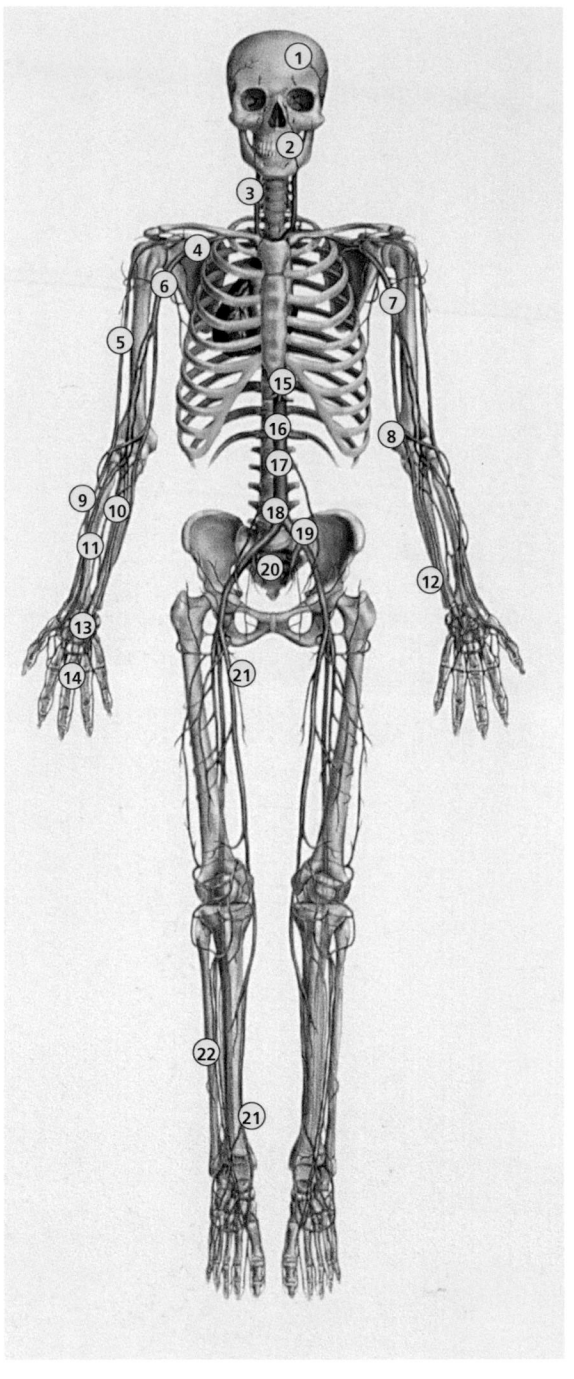

1. *Superficial temporal artery;*
2. *Facial artery (external maxillary);*
3. *External jugular vein;*
4. *Subclavian vein;*
5. *Cephalic vein;*
6. *Axillary vein;*
7. *Humeral vein;*
8. *Basilic vein;*
9. *Cephalic vein;*
10. *Median antebrachial vein;*
11. *Radial artery;* 12. *Ulnar artery;*
13. *Deep palmar arch;*
14. *Superficial palmar arch;*
15. *Hepatic vein;* 16. *Renal vein;*
17. *Aorta;* 18. *Inferior vena cava;*
19. *Iliac artery;*
20. *Internal iliac vein;*
21. *Saphenous vein;*
22. *Anterior tibial artery.*

## THE NERVOUS SYSTEM

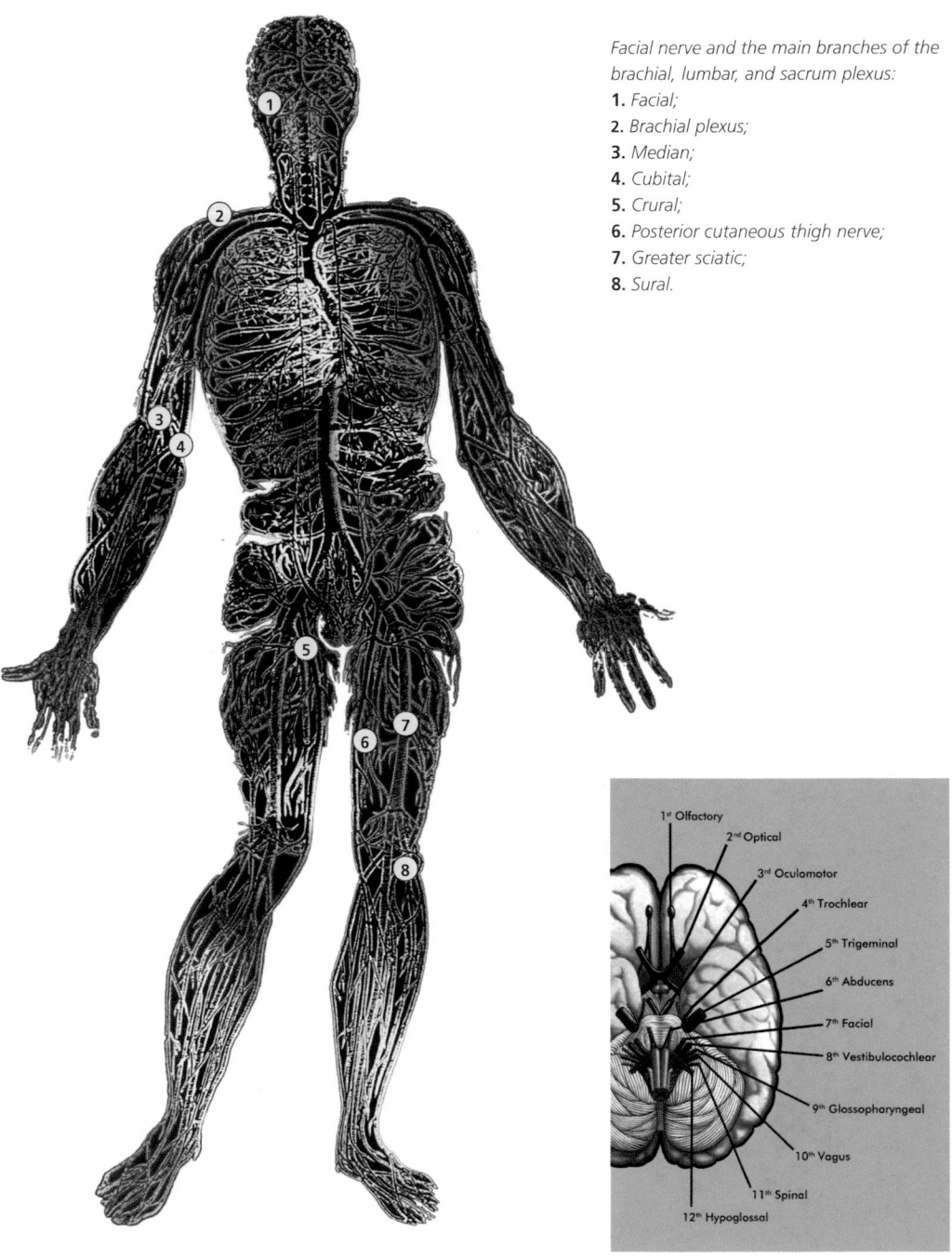

Facial nerve and the main branches of the
brachial, lumbar, and sacrum plexus:
1. Facial;
2. Brachial plexus;
3. Median;
4. Cubital;
5. Crural;
6. Posterior cutaneous thigh nerve;
7. Greater sciatic;
8. Sural.

1st Olfactory
2nd Optical
3rd Oculomotor
4th Trochlear
5th Trigeminal
6th Abducens
7th Facial
8th Vestibulocochlear
9th Glossopharyngeal
10th Vagus
11th Spinal
12th Hypoglossal

## THE MUSCULAR SYSTEM

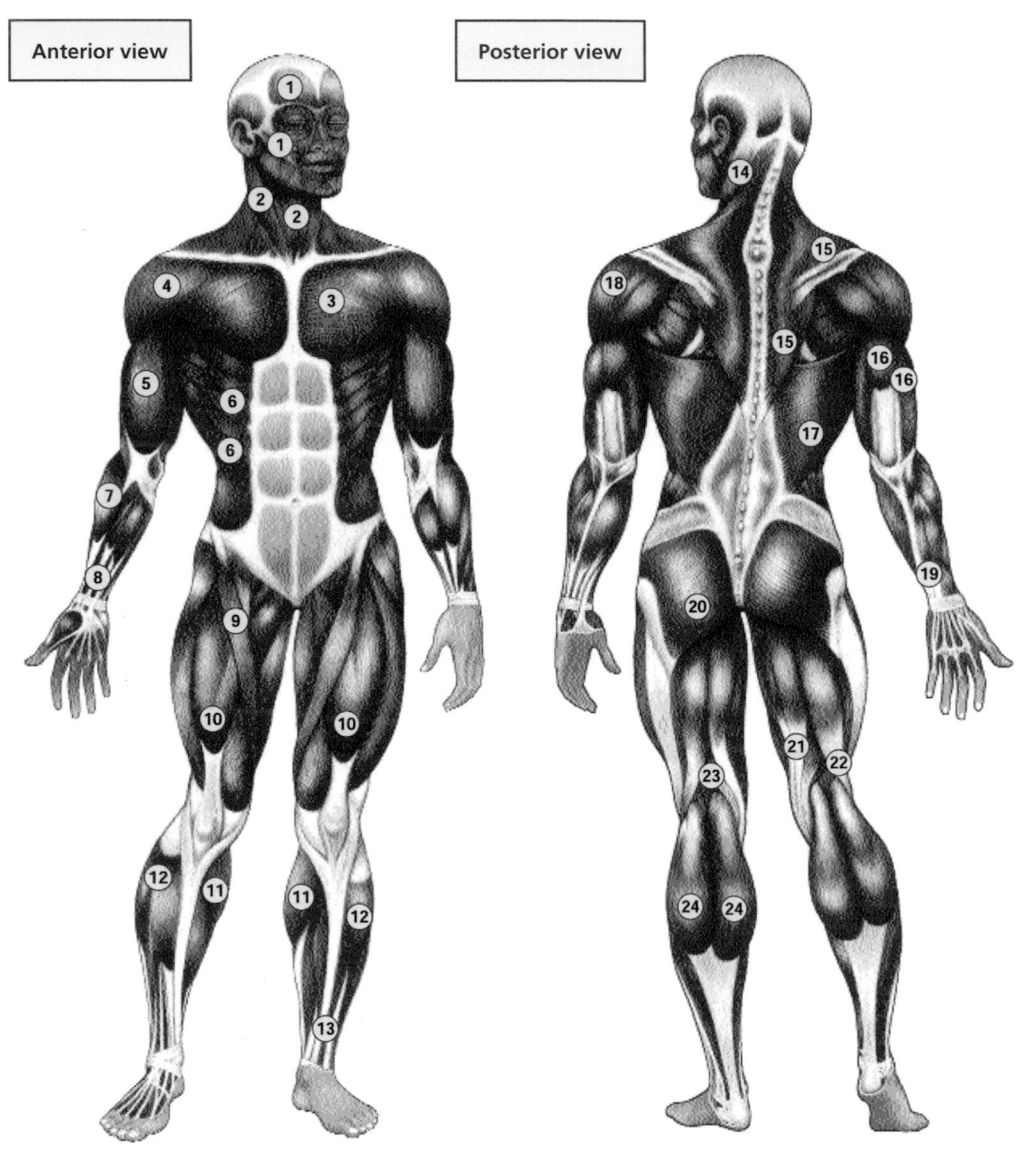

**Anterior view**

**Posterior view**

**Anterior view: 1.** *face muscles;* **2.** *cervical musculature;* **3.** *pectoralis major;* **4.** *deltoid;* **5.** *biceps;* **6.** *oblique;* **7.** *forearm muscles;* **8.** *flexors of the hand;* **9.** *sartorius;* **10.** *quadriceps;* **11.** *gastrocnemius;* **12.** *anterior tibial;* **13.** *extensor digitorum.*
**Posterior view: 14.** *sternocleidomastoid;* **15.** *trapezius;* **16.** *triceps;* **17.** *latissimus dorsi;* **18.** *deltoid;* **19.** *extensors of the hand;* **20.** *gluteus maximus;* **21.** *semimembranosus;* **22.** *biceps femoris;* **23.** *semitendinosus;* **24.** *gastrocnemius.*

# THE INTERNAL ORGANS

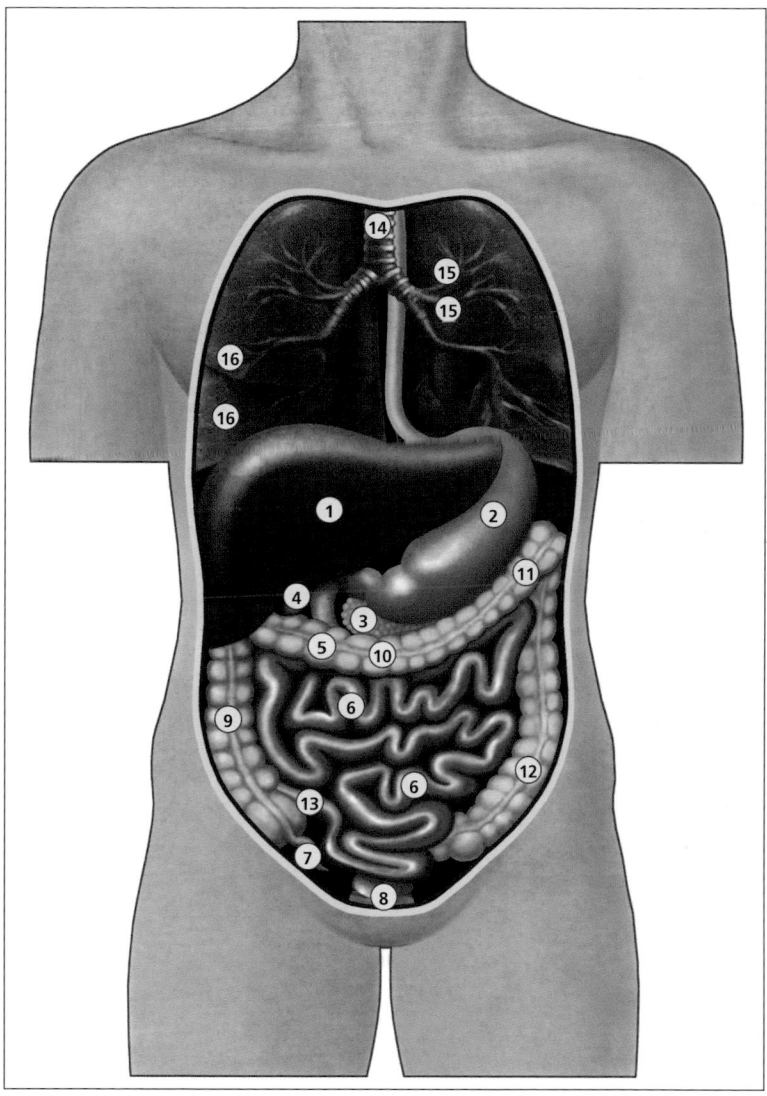

**1.** *Liver;* **2.** *stomach;* **3.** *pancreas;* **4.** *gallbladder;* **5.** *large intestine;* **6.** *small intestine;* **7.** *appendix;* **8.** *rectum;* **9.** *ascending colon;* **10.** *transverse colon;* **11.** *longitudinal tracts;* **12.** *descending colon;* **13.** *ileum;* **14.** *trachea;* **15.** *bronchial tree;* **16.** *pulmonary lobes.*

# PRINCIPLES OF EACH METHOD

## SHIATSU

This Japanese massage method comes from the traditional Chinese massage, acupuncture, Do-In, and ancient oriental medicine.

It is based on the knowledge that the vital *qi* energy brings the body to life. It flows through rivers of energy or meridians (six yin, six yang) inter acting in complete balance.

Shiatsu has its etymology in the word "shia" (thumb) and "tsu" (pressure) and so it requires that you press with your thumbs, use your elbows, hands, as well as apply holds, friction, and rubbing.

The purpose of shiatsu massage is to tone up when there is lack of energy and to sedate when there is an excess of energy (*kyo* and *jitsu*), all done to maintain proper flow of vitality through the meridians. It gives great emphasis to the emotions that can affect health, believing that anger damages the liver; sadness hurts the lungs; apathy affects the heart; fear creates bladder and kidney problems; and worry hurts the spleen.

When an organ is not working properly, the therapist must find the path of its corresponding meridian, and sedate it or strengthen it as needed.

Although its historical and scientific origins prove the existence of shiatsu thousands of years ago, in the box to the right I share with you a beautiful legend.

### Objectives

Reset or balance the flow of energy through the meridians, sedating or stimulating this energy to

> *Legend has it that in Japan there was once a beautiful girl named Shia Tsu. She did not get along with her mother-in-law who was jealous of her and envious of her youth and energy.*
>
> *One day, the young Shia Tsu went to see a wise old man who lived in the forest. She told him her problem and asked him for a poison she could use to kill her mother-in-law. The old sage gave her a poison that took three months to have an effect and told her the following: "Serve her tea every afternoon and place two drops of poison in her cup. So that no one suspects anything, after she drinks the tea give her a massage. She will soon die without anyone realizing that it was you who poisoned her." Shia Tsu went home and the next day, she did just as the old sage told her, she served her tea and then gave her a massage. She did this every day. Meanwhile, her relationship with the mother-in-law started to change: as they chatted more and more, they stopped thinking of each other as rivals, and instead became good friends. She continued the tea and massage ritual until the poison that remained in the bottle was enough for just one day. Shia Tsu felt that her mother-in-law was not so bad after all, and she had shown herself to be a woman who no longer had any bad habits.*
>
> *She went to the wise old man and exclaimed: "I do not know what happened. I did what you told me to do during three months, but instead of feeling ill and dying, she became nice and friendly. Now I do not want her to die! I would miss her so much! Please give me an antidote!" The sage smiled and said: "What happened is completely natural. What I gave you in the bottle was not poison, it was rosewater. Massage brought you two closer together."*
>
> *Shia Tsu was so enchanted with the power of massage that she made sure that her techniques were spread worldwide.*

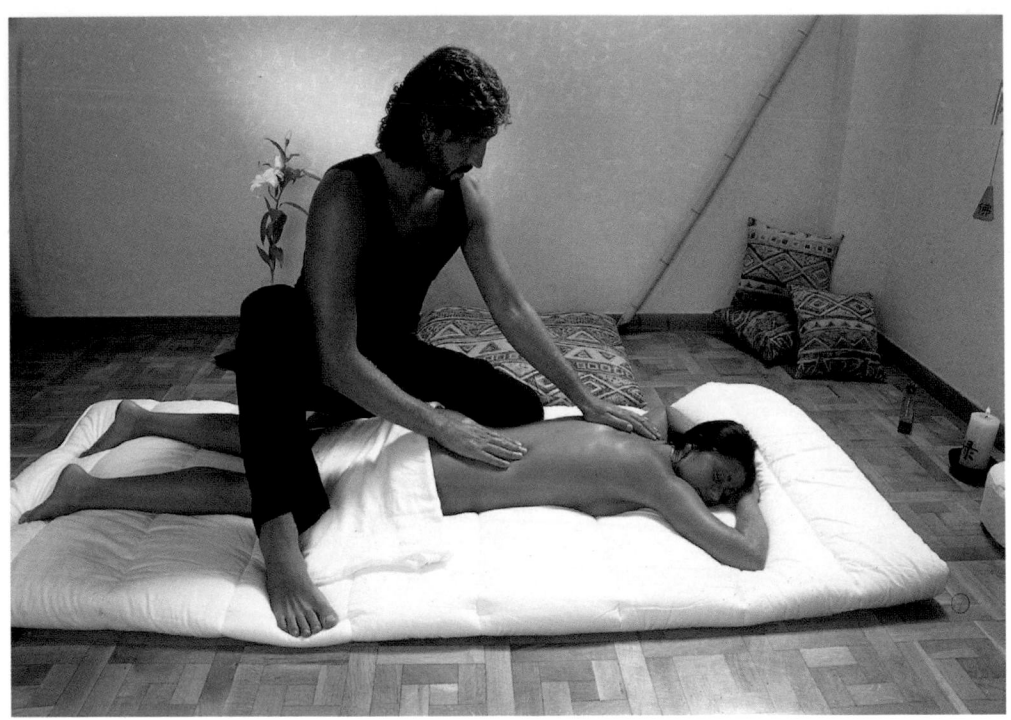

achieve a perfect state of homeostasis. Just as blood flows through our veins, *qi* energy flows through the meridians of our energetic body.

## Benefits
- Releases energies that are blocked by mental or emotional stress.
- Relieves pain.
- Activates blood and energy circulation.
- Gives a feeling of weightlessness.
- Opens the energy channels (meridians) and acupressure points (tubes).
- Provides a feeling of wellbeing and relaxation.
- Eliminates dense energy and restores the entry-way for new energy.

## Contraindications
- Women who are more than six months pregnant.
- After a long journey.
- Hypertensive people.
- Recent heart surgery.
- Women who are menstruating.

## Method
- Apply pressure with your thumbs and sedate or stimulate the points as needed.
- To sedate, go counterclockwise; to tone up a point, go clockwise.
- The points are like the head of a pin.
- Zen shiatsu aims to unlock the whole body through stretching.
- Pressure stimulates blood circulation and energy.
- Kneading helps improve musculature so that contracted points (sometimes very old and deep) come to the surface of the skin.

## TANTRIC MASSAGE

This scientific, spiritual, and artistic system is based on aligning and stimulating the seven chakras of the animal, human, and divine psychology that each person possesses.

Tantric massage comes from the rich experience of tantra and its origin dates back to India's golden age.

Tantra is a natural path that is oriented toward pleasure, joy, awareness, love, intelligence, and creative use of energy. It is not a religion, but rather a free and conscious journey. It focuses on developing an energy system that everyone can use to connect to the universe and inner teacher.

Tantra utilizes massage as a meditation between partners, where both are taken to an inner state of fusion and unity.

It also includes dance, meditation, specific breathing exercises, stimulating the chakras, mantras and mudras, as well as techniques for elevating sexual energy into spirituality through the *maithuna* ritual.

Tantric massage gives the recipient the ability to transcend the boundaries of ordinary consciousness towards a full and deep state of self-awareness.

By focusing energy on the chakras, this delicate massage opens up the luminous fragrance that each being has within. There is deep respect for others because through it we are able to see ourselves, God, and all Creation.

By working on the chakras, we can experience an internal journey of consciousness, from the root of the spine to the top of the head, and our body is spiritualized by vibrating as the essence of light.

Tantra is an experiential current that seeks freedom for the individual in all aspects. Its origin is matriarchal and emphasizes the power of the divine feminine, so it does not condemn women as male-dominated systems typically do. Nor does it condemn pleasure, sex, and food, which instead are used as tools to evolve.

It is a spiritual and mystical science, not a religion claiming that we are not separate from anything. Everything is a unit and therefore we do not need to tie ourselves down; rather, we make ourselves aware that God is in everything and is everything.

Tantra is immersed in life and in harmony with natural laws, without being tied to any holy book (although there are four fundamental tantric texts). It invites us to fully engage in life by concentrating on unity, and not believing in Good and Evil but rather in what is right. Philosophical discourses are unnecessary because it simply tries to encourage the individual to set his personality free.

Etymologically, tantra means "tissue that expands consciousness," and for this purpose multiple techniques are used through art, science, mysticism, yoga, massage, spirituality, and psychology. Its psychology is centered precisely in acting, feeling, and thinking from the inner consciousness in parallel frequency with the sublime, creating the possibility for connection at every moment.

Today it has become a pragmatic and accessible pathway for modern men and women, as it provides everything and it requires adherence to a minimum. As Osho, tantric master said: "You are already perfect, do not strive to become someone. There is no need for conflict."

This practice consists in getting rid of darkness through a process of internal transformations that take you from depression to celebration; from rigidity to flexibility; from criticism to creativity; from impulse to consciousness. Through daily practice, you will change and evolve because perfection is neither limited nor static. For more information, you can read my book *The Art of Tantra*, published by this same publisher.

Tantra does not ask you to be perfect, but rather gets you to use your inner spiritual skills (which are already perfect) to make contact with God. It pushes you toward full self-consciousness and it does not want you to reject the world, but accept it as the school of life.

Tantric massage guides us to restore our energy balance, align our chakras, emotions and psyche, and give the body pleasure and deep relaxation. In tantra, you accept desire without suppressing it; you fulfill it and transcend it as a conscientious witness that you are the master of your life.

---

### PRINCIPLES OF TANTRA

- Do not create conflicts.
- Live spontaneously.
- Be flexible.
- Do not divide—unite.
- Do not stagnate—flow.
- Freedom from control.
- Be focused.
- Feel perfection in everything.
- Be aware, alert.
- Accept reality.
- Do not be moralistic or critical.
- Do not seek security.
- Be receptive, be open.
- Be simple and natural.

- No attachment.
- Surrender to life.
- Accept unidentified desire.
- Do not hold back.
- Focus on the present.
- Love all living creations.
- Be creative.
- Lift up energy from the sacrum to the crown.
- Celebrate existence.
- Do not create internal stress.
- Use sexual energy as fuel.
- Eliminate possession and jealousy.
- Harmonize with silence.
- Dance and celebrate the music.

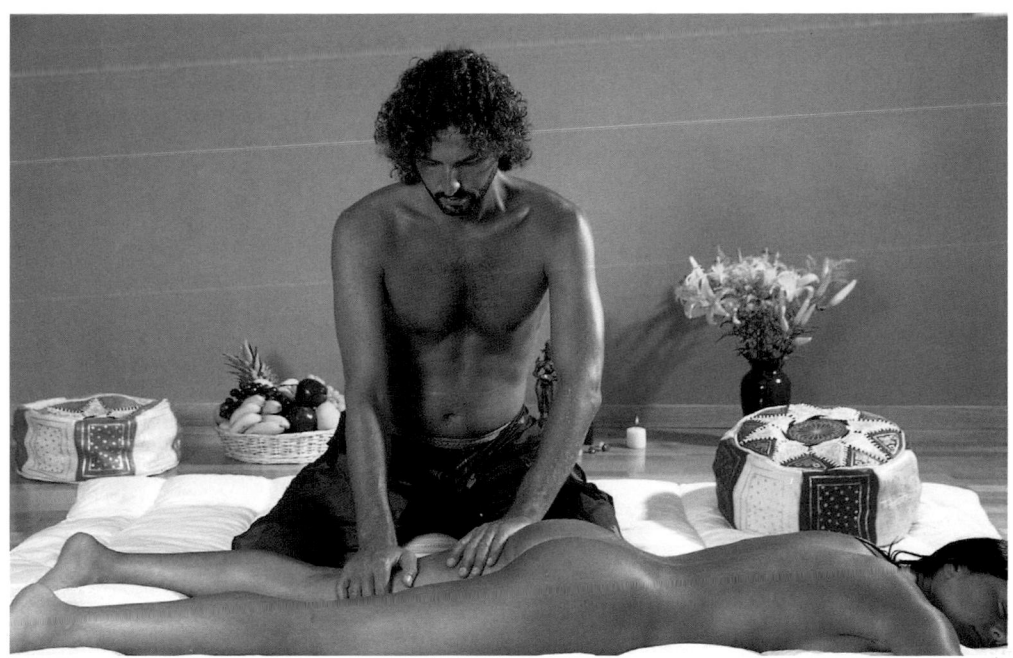

Similarly, it also allows you to enjoy every aspect of your energy.

The formula consists in uniting consciousness with energy; sex with meditation; love with intelligence; creativity with sensitivity; insight with celebration; massage with activity.

## Objectives

- Develop energy flow through ducts in the spine.
- Cleanse, activate, and balance the chakras.
- Deepen your level of consciousness.

## Benefits

- Eliminates the feeling of division or separation.
- Eliminates fear.
- Activates individual creative potential.
- Creates a connection between the body and the spirit.
- Quiets the mind.
- Provides the experience of feeling an oceanic joy.
- Counteracts taboos and body shame.

- Allows feeling the movement of energy and emotions.
- Creates inner peace.
- Transmutes dense energy.
- Eliminates emotional, mental, and sexual repression.
- Increases awareness levels.
- Develops wisdom and intelligent use of vital energy.

## Contraindications

- Pregnant or menstruating women.
- People with mental health problems.
- People recovering from a recent heart surgery.

## Method

- Directly on the chakras, starting from the spine, the frontal area, and the soles of the feet.
- Conscious breathing: cleansing breath and circular breathing.
- Visualization of the chakras.
- Use color.

- Use special oils for each chakra.
- Sounds for each chakra.
- Affirmations and meditations to activate inner potential.
- Stimulation through aromas and scents.
- Use gemstones.

## REFLEXOLOGY

Over the last thirty-five years, reflexology has become popular in the West, but the Egyptians were the first to see the benefits and pleasure it provides. Numerous reliefs and papyri that have been found lead us to believe that there were expert foot massage therapists.

This effective and ancient technique treats the soles of the feet to stimulate or sedate nerve endings that relate to the functioning of the entire human body.

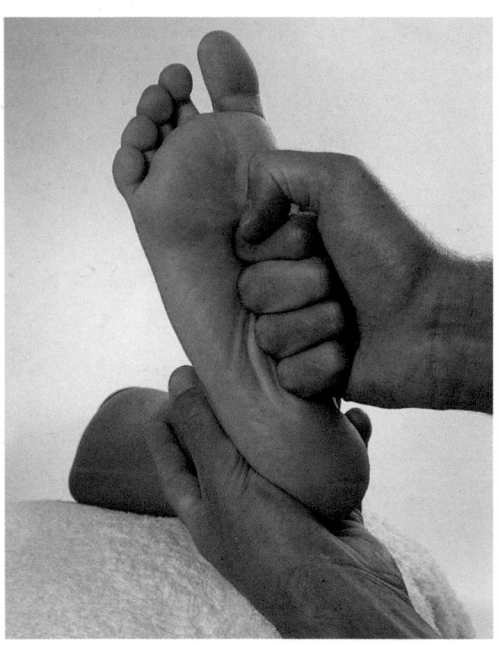

This practice is very beneficial and it can be used to treat anything from gastrointestinal problems or breathing difficulties to headaches, back aches, and sciatic nerve pain; as well as all organs, from the kidney to the liver, etc.

By stimulating the reflex points we are able to detect "crystals" where there is a malfunction; these are akin to tiny balls and they are formed by uric acid. These toxins accumulate and become painful. These crystals are very noticeable when we massage down the foot with our thumbs.

These organisms are eliminated through urine, but the recipient has to begin a massage treatment to solve and harmonize their particular problem.

The feet and spine are two areas of the body that get the least amount of attention, even though they exert most of the effort. They continuously support the body's weight, but unlike the spine, our feet often must do so with poor quality footwear.

Healthy feet are crucial for us to be in good condition elsewhere in the body, both physically and psychologically.

It is interesting to note how people walk in yoga workshops: some step down hard on the whole foot, while others do so timidly with the tip of the toes. There are those who walk mechanically by clicking their heels as they pass by, etc. By getting to know the students, we can be sure that their gait matches their lifestyle: those who walk in a hurry are active; those who tip-toe are shy, etc. Feet give us a real map to a person and let us know what type of therapy to provide.

It is also important, from the reflexology point of view, to carefully observe the condition of the feet and toes. Calluses, blisters, or moles will determine the condition of the glands and organs of the recipient. For example, if someone has bunions or calluses that correspond to the throat area, they probably have difficulty expressing themselves.

On the other hand, scars or deformities will affect other aspects of the functioning of the body.

Feet are also important because we receive two energies: the *prana* or *qi* (the vital energy of the Sun) and *apana* (the vital energy of the Earth), that serve as antenna from below and from above. The Earth is yin energy and the Sun is yang. Nature does not leave anything to chance but always obeys the law of balance.

I recommend that you walk barefoot every day for some time to receive this energy. Many people have their feet bound for long hours not knowing that this amounts to imprisoning their whole body.

In a reflexology session (ideal for stressed or very tired people) the recipient may experience deep relaxation as well as a mixture of pain and pleasure, tickling, crying, laughing, needing to urinate, and many other sensations. Sometimes even emotions and muscle contractions that accumulated over months or years are unlocked.

The feet serve the therapist as a computer, as each specific point will be like a key that displays the contents of the entire organism.

### Objectives

- Release uric acid and toxins, provide a thorough cleansing.
- Balance the body's functions.
- Switch old structures and bad habits.
- Eliminate waste.
- Stimulate and correct the body's functions and systems.
- Eliminate pain in the feet and in other areas.
- Unlock both muscular and energy problems.

### Contraindications

- Pregnant or menstruating women.
- Hypertensive people.

## Method

- Press each point for one to three minutes using the five following techniques:
  — Using your thumb, press into and pull out of the point or zone.
  — Raising and lowering both thumbs alternatively, as a ladder.
  — Rotating your thumb clockwise to tone, or counterclockwise to sedate.
  — Slide your knuckle on the sole of the foot, to-and-fro.
  — Pinching and kneading.
- The number of sessions are determined by the recipient's needs and reactions.

## SENSITIVE MASSAGE

Sensitive or "Californian" massage places emphasis on developing sensitivity, the healing power of touch, and the unity between body and soul.

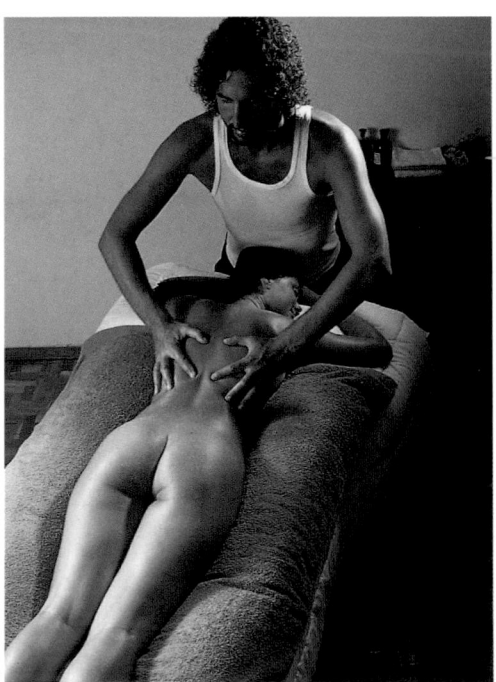

It gently stimulates the body so that the recipient enters into a deep state of relaxation from the skin to the muscles.

In addressing the entire body (naked, as is often the case) there is the possibility of the recipient feeling "natural" again, because unless it is in the shower or at a nudist beach, the body cannot fully perceive the air, sun, water, or land surrounding it. And if we bind the body constantly with uncomfortable clothes, tight shoes, or ties, we move further away from our primitive freedom.

Through sensitive massage, we give back our body a sense of connection and physical and energetic unit. This hands-on therapy first places value on the sacred home, our body. Through touch, it takes both the recipient and the giver to a world of sensation and pleasure.

The beneficial effect of caresses and hugs between people are well known. For example, research has been done comparing infants who were loved and touched, and others who were not. It has been determined not only that the former are more sociable and cheerful, but that those who were not touched tend to cry and remain unhappy.

However, we do not need any statistics to tell us how pleasant and sweet it is to experience sensitive massage; we simply need to feel affection through the loving touch of another.

### Objectives

- Reset the deep contact between body and soul.
- Achieve a state of mental silence to open up to pleasure and joy.
- Focus on the individual so that he is in harmony with his deepest self.
- Release emotional blockages.
- Bring ease and flexibility to certain personality traits.

## *Benefits*
- Deep relaxation of the physical body, especially the muscles.
- Balances vital energy flows.
- Calms the nervous system.
- Clarifies and stops uncontrolled mental processes.
- Encourages a meditative state.
- Activates blood circulation.
- Unifies all body "parts."
- Frees accumulated energies.
- Activates touch and human contact.

## *Contraindications*
- None, as this is truly a gentle and relaxing massage.

## *Method*
- Focus on basic human personalities.

## WHAT DOES EACH ONE DO AND HOW DO THEY DIFFER?

Although the four methods use different techniques, they all aim to holistically integrate the individual. They work on the body, vital energy, mind, emotions, and personal openness toward freeing the spirit.

**Shiatsu** places greater emphasis on balancing *qi* energy, using pressure, stretching, and rubbing particular points on the meridians to restore order in the whole body. According to shiatsu, health is the harmonic cycle of entry and exit of yin and yang energy; starting at the nostrils, this energy travels to the right and left sides of the body.

**Tantric massage**, on the other hand, considers it essential to work on the seven major chakras in order to cleanse, balance, and activate them.

To do so, we use different hand motions, rely on breathing techniques, use gemstones and essential oils, and practice specific visualizations and meditations.

Tantric massage tries to penetrate deep into the subconscious and bring a ray of light to each specific function by analyzing the concerns and desires of the individual, and eliminating conflict, unrest, and dissatisfaction in his personal life.

**Reflexology**, meanwhile, focuses on stimulating the reflex points of the feet to heal and balance the physical body.

And finally, **sensitive massage** provides a wealth of techniques to enhance sensitivity in each individual, and thereby positively influence his personal characteristics.

Each of the four methods is sufficient on its own; however, combining all four increases their power and allows us to work effectively on something as simple as physical discomfort, up to organ dysfunction or something as severe as an imbalance in the chakra system. There is no problem that cannot be treated by joining these four methods, so their application only depends on how long each individual takes to restore their energy; on how open they are to experiencing pleasure; on their level of sensitivity; and on their interest in deepening their spirituality.

### *Suggestions*

- Do a comprehensive reading of your recipient to know which technique is best to use.
- Treat every recipient as you would yourself.
- Pay attention to their reactions to a particular technique: if they show signs of pain, change it. There are hundreds of ways for them to get what they need.
- Always protect your vital energy. Before each session, visualize a blue circle of protection around yourself, as well as therapeutic fire in your hands.
- Guide your breathing and your recipient's breathing.

- Mind your posture (especially the spine) by evenly distributing the weight of your body.
- Never stop touching the other person during the session.
- Prepare a quiet environment where you both can feel comfortable.
- Do not talk too much during the session and avoid all trivial topics. Only ask questions related to the massage session.
- Always allow a few last minutes to enjoy the effects of the session.
- Make massage an art, as though in every session you were to paint a different picture.
- Connect with the vital energy that enters your head and goes out your hands, and always maintain a higher level of consciousness through breathing.
- Stay healthy through a purification program that addresses all aspects of your being.

Do not smoke, do not eat tamasic or heavy foods, and do not waste energy on things that are not worthwhile. (In the next chapter you will find a holistic purification program for therapists).

## PRACTICING HOLISTIC MASSAGE

We must get a thorough first impression of the recipient: their body posture, whether they walk straight, if they have nervous tics, if they look away, if they cross their arms, if they are talkative, etc.

Similarly, we have to find their dominant personality trait: if they are cerebral, submissive, dominant, aggressive, tense, etc. By doing so, we can determine which massage to apply and at which rhythm.

Since we cannot always use every method in each session due to time limitations, we will apply therapeutic holds to treat specific problems.

We will refer to the general treatment practices of sensitive and Zen shiatsu techniques as "basic massage," and the treatment for each particular problem will be called "special massage."

We can do a thirty-minute session of basic massage, and another thirty minutes for special massage. We can also vary according to the recipient's needs, taking into account that the basic massage techniques are the same, and the only thing that varies is the pace (which may be *yin* or *yang*).

**Yin rhythm:** Slow and deep for yang (stressed and tense) people.

**Yang rhythm:** Dynamic, superficial, and deep for yin (anemic, depressed or low energy) people.

Deciding on where on the body to initiate the massage is important. Although we usually start on the back, if the person is very cerebral, we will start with the head so that the energy that is accumulated in this area begins to move outwardly through the rest of the body.

If the person has low energy, we can start with the feet and work our way up. If they are feeling disoriented or confused, we do an overall massage that integrates all body parts, and makes them feel physically and spiritually complete.

---

### FACTORS TO CONSIDER WHEN MAKING A DIAGNOSIS

1. Physical cause.
2. Psychiatric cause.
3. Energy level.
4. Worries.
5. Left or right side of the body (yin or yang) where there is pain.
6. Psychological association to the malfunction of one or more chakras.
7. Lifestyle (healthy or bad habits).
8. Personality.
9. Physical appearance.
10. Blocked shiatsu points.
11. Relationship with own body.
12. Relationship with life.
13. Eating habits.

---

Everyone is different: not only are our bodies different, but we harbor our own unique thoughts and feelings. As therapists, we must keep this in mind so we can determine which treatment to give each person. On page 66 you will see a list of main disorders, their causes, and possible treatments.

This manual provides an effective, thorough, and accurate system to find the energy and psycho-emotional causes of the recipient's problems through their physical symptoms.

**Example 1:**
*An individual with sciatic pain, insomnia, financial problems, and concern for his brother.*

First, we will ask if he has an injury on the sole of the foot, if he sleeps on a sagging mattress, or if there could be any other physical cause for his pain.

If neither of these is the case, we begin to relate his ailment to his psychological identity and his chakras; in this case, the first chakra and the area from the back of the leg to the heel. The first chakra is material and economic survival, so the first cause of his problems might be located right there.

The recipient says that he is concerned about his brother's health (yang aspect, right side of the body), so we deduce that he suffers insomnia because his mental energy is too cluttered with this worry. We will do a sedating yin massage on the leg area (zen shiatsu massage) beginning at the back, then on the sacrum to strengthen and energize from the first chakra up throughout the spine (tantric massage). Then we will work on the foot with reflexology to make contact with the material, and finally the head, arms, and face to silence the mind.

**Example 2:**
*A depressed individual who lacks energy, feels chest pain, and is having problems with her daughter because she left to go study abroad.*

This person has an excess of yin energy, which is causing her to feel low energy; her chest is blocked by repressed emotions and weariness on the left side (yin, feminine) because her daughter left.

We need to balance her left and right sides. So we start with her left foot (reflexology) and go up on that same side while applying tantric massage. Then we go down her right side while applying a tantric massage, and finish on her right foot using reflexology.

Subsequently, through breathing techniques and tantric massage, we will work on opening and releasing the heart chakra (blocked emotions) and cleansing her system.

# The Therapist's training and wisdom

When a student decides to set off on an energy path through a particular discipline such as massage, he must be careful with his body and his energy level.

Through the Sun, food, air, water, and land, nature provides us with a quota of daily energy to live by. If you are training to become a therapist (or already are one) and you work providing energy, you should not give away some of your quota to others; rather, you must become a receptive channel where energy flows from you onto your recipient. For this to happen, you have to purify yourself.

The purification or catharsis should cover all aspects of your being; from the physical (flexibility, strengthening, or elimination of toxins), to the energetic, by receiving vital energy (*qi*) through breathing exercises. We work on our astral or emotional body through meditations corresponding to each chakra; and we work on our being through different kinds of yoga poses.

1. **Purification of the physical body:** Food, good rest, and yoga exercises.
2. **Purification of the energetic body:** Breathing techniques (*pranayama*).
3. **Purification of the emotional body:** Chakra meditation.
4. **Purification of the rational body:** Yoga practice and a positive mental attitude.

This program can be modified and made more flexible so that it does not become an enforced discipline, but a conscious act that gives you pleasure and energy.

## PURIFICATION PROGRAM FOR HOLISTIC THERAPISTS

### 1. *Physical cleanse*

**SUGGESTED FOODS:** Cereals, fresh and dried fruit, honey, whole pasta, legumes, vegetables, fish, purifying tea, garlic, and milk.

**AVOID:** Meat, fried foods, spices, cigarettes, sugar, white flour, and sausages.

**IMPORTANT:** Eat every three hours.

**FASTING:** It is advisable that you fast whenever you feel that your body needs it. How often you do it is up to you. Fasting cleanses your body of toxins, and also helps clear your mind. And it has to be conscious, not forced.

While fasting, you will not feel anxious or hungry because you will do breathing exercises that allow you to feed on qi. During the twenty-four to thirty-six hours of fasting, drink three to four liters of water daily.

**SUGGESTED ACTIVITIES:** Immersion baths with mineral salts, self-massage, walking outdoors (barefoot to make contact with the ground, whenever possible), yoga, tai chi, and dance.

## 2. *Energy cleanse*

**PRANAYAMAS, BREATHING TECHNIQUES:** "Prana" means energy and "yama" means absorption. They are, therefore, breathing exercises to absorb energy. This science can nourish and benefit us by providing enormous vitality potential.

The same state of feeling inspired and creative has to do with the "inspiration" of vital energy. That is because when you have energy and you harmonize it, you become creative.

This works specifically on bodily energy, so it is important to practice it every day.

**BREATHS:**

- **Polarized (seven cycles):** Consists in breathing alternately through one nostril while covering the other.

  First, cover the right nostril with your right thumb and inhale through the left nostril; then cover the left nostril with the left index finger and exhale through the right nostril. Inhale with the right nostril while covering the left nostril and lastly exhale through the left nostril while covering the right nostril.

  Repeat this cycle seven times.

- **Bellows (three cycles of fifty):** This breathing is very energizing and enlivens your spiritual fire in the same way that air kindles a real fire. It is done by breathing rapidly through the nostrils, imitating a pair of bellows. Thus, air flows in and out vigorously.

  Do fifty sets of one inhalation and one exhalation. You may get dizzy by increasing the amount of oxygen that flows to your brain; but do not worry, this sensation goes away. Stop and do it again after a few minutes, or lessen the number of repetitions to thirty.

  This technique should not be done by those suffering from hypertension nor those who recently had heart surgery.

- **Complete (twenty-one cycles):** Inhale gently through your nose, holding in the air for five to ten seconds while concentrating on the chakras. Exhale from the bottom to the top of the head to restart the process.

  As you inhale, be aware that fresh and renewed energy is entering your body. When you hold it in, it gets stored inside you and when you exhale, it gets distributed upward through your chakras, quieting your nervous system and allowing *kundalini* energy to feed your cells, organs, and chakras.

---

When you are done with the breathing, lie down on the floor and breathe freely to distribute energy throughout your entire body. Remember that an important energy rule states that "energy follows your thoughts."

---

## 3. *Chakra cleansing*

The emotional body is purified through meditation and dance.

As I stated in the previous chapter, each chakra has good and bad aspects. Tantric practice aims to emphasize and enhance the positive qualities that benefit us, while weakening anything that prevents our evolution. So we will not focus on eliminating fear, but rather in increasing love; we will not try to do away with anger, but rather cultivate serenity.

**MEDITATION:**

- **Meditative dance:** With your body relaxed and naked, close your meditation room and burn your favorite incense.

  Play rhythmic music (drums), let your body synch up to the beat, and dance freely.

*To the left is the sitting meditation position. The polarized breathing steps are shown above.*

Tantric dance has three key pillars: conscious breathing, relaxed body, and eyes closed to the world by disconnecting the mind. It removes blockages or pain you are experiencing in any body part (especially on the hips, head, shoulders, neck, and pelvis) and activates energy with the help of a deep cleansing breath, consisting of serenely inhaling through the nose and exhaling through the mouth.

*Kundalini* energy will open up the first chakra and energize your entire system. Let out everything you feel; the cornerstone is free movement, breathing, and perception. Meditation should last fifteen to forty-five minutes.

| CHAKRA CHARACTERISTICS | | |
|---|---|---|
| CHAKRA | WHAT IT STIMULATES | EMOTIONS IT ELIMINATES |
| Muladhara | Abundance | Attachment |
| Swadisthana | Sexual energy | Repression, rigidity |
| Manipura | Personal power, health | Anger, rage |
| Anahatta | Love and devotion | Fear, insensitivity, harshness |
| Vishudda | Creativity | Criticism, guilt |
| Ajna | Intuition, positive imagination | Depression, confusion |
| Sahasrara | Spiritual freedom | Selfishness |

- **Sitting quietly as a buddha:** After dancing, sit up straight and feel as though you are a buddha, a magnet of light. Notice abundance in your first chakra; sexual energy in the second; inner strength in the third; love and compassion in the center of the chest; creativity in the fifth; inner clarity on the third eye; and your freedom and connection to the universe at the top of your head.

Spend a few minutes on each and see yourself unite with the divine until gradually the boundaries between individual consciousness and universal consciousness disappear. As you do so, you will feel that your field of perception expands.

## 4. *Mental cleanse*

We will work on purifying the mind by doing yoga asanas, which stimulate the seven chakras and benefit your mental state.

Different yoga practices will enrich you in several ways:

- **Hatha yoga:** improves body and mind through *asanas* and *pranayamas*.
- **Tantra yoga:** improves sexuality through conscious sexual act (*maithuna*), dance, and meditation with your partner.
- **Karma yoga:** improves action through conscious life activities.

- **Bakthi yoga:** awakens affection and compassion by cultivating internal love.
- **Mantra yoga:** increases creativity by chanting mantras or a favorite song.
- **Jnana yoga:** provides clear insight and intuition through knowledge of the soul.
- **Raja yoga:** connects you with the cosmos through deep meditation.

As you do each pose, breathe slowly and gently through your nose. Do not force your body because it does not have to "get" anywhere; do not worry if you have little flexibility. In the same way that a tree takes years to grow and bear fruit, your body needs time, practice, and patience to increase its flexibility.

## *Sequence of yoga asanas*

You will perform each asana while concentrating on the body part you want to stimulate, on the chakras that activate, and on smooth and conscious breathing. Remember to do each pose with pleasure, without competing or feeling pain.

Respect the order of the asanas if you are just starting, since they are arranged so as to not injure your body and to perfectly balance the spinal function. Hold each asana pose for thirty seconds to three minutes. Before doing the sequence it is very important to do fifteen minutes of free dance to warm up and let energy flow.

## SEQUENCE OF YOGA ASANAS

**1. Clamp:** *Benefits the kidneys and adrenal glands. The spine becomes very elastic. Massages the stomach and internal organs. Stretches the legs, eliminating fatigue; the meridians, improving the flow of qi; and relaxes the neck. Stimulates the first, second, and third chakras. Improves blood circulation.*

**2. Inclined plane:** *It is an intermediate pose. Stretches the arms. Strengthens the waist and lower back. Prepares the body to bend backwards after having bent forward in the previous pose.*

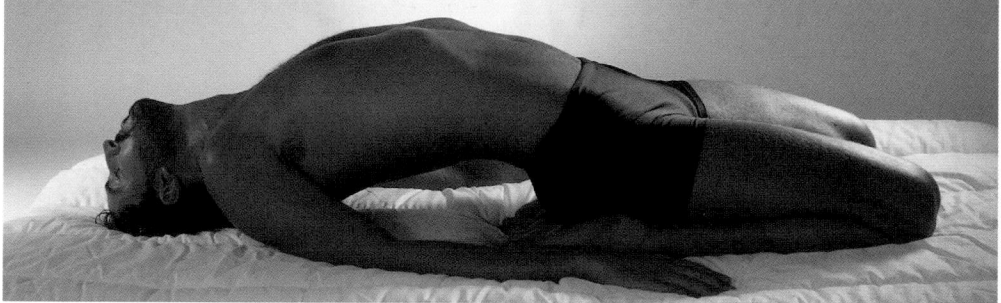

**3. Diamond fish:** *It is a cold expansion pose. Opens the chest and improves breathing by stretching it. Activates the fourth, fifth, and sixth chakras. The spine takes on an important angle. Stretches the quadriceps. Opens the hara. Relaxes the cervical vertebrae, jaw, and facial muscles.*

**4. Tent:** *This asana stretches the legs, eases tension in the neck, and supplies blood to the brain. Strengthens the arms. Relaxes the heart. Gives flexibility to the spine. Stretches the calves by removing lactic acid and other toxins that cause fatigue.*

**5. Cobra:** *Opens the chest. Strengthens the arms. Stimulates kundalini energy in the first chakra. Stretches and relaxes the legs. In particular, it stimulates the fifth chakra. Stretches the abdominal area. Relaxes the pelvis.*

**6. Stretched cat:** *An intermediate resting pose that can be used several times between poses. Greatly eases tension in the back. Stretches the arms. Relaxes the body. Produces a sense of protection and surrender.*

**7. Lobster:** *Gives an intense massage to the lower part of the spine, sacrum, and pelvis. Supplies blood to the adrenal glands and stimulates the kidneys. Awakens and directs energy to the solar plexus. Stretches the legs and considerably increases their flexibility. Works on the first two chakras. Enables transmutation of sexual energy.*

**8. Boat:** *Benefits balance in the body. Strengthens the abdominals. Stretches the legs. Develops equanimity. Another variation of this asana is the "floating caliper" (as shown in the box).*

**9. Ship:** *Powerfully stimulates the lower area, activating the first two chakras. Enhances blood flow to the kidneys and strengthens the lower back, thereby increasing energy in the body. Strength and balance develops at the same time.*

**10. Cradle:** *Massages the back and relaxes it after the previous poses. Rock smoothly from side to side to intensify the stimulus. Relax the neck.*

**11. Plow:** *Irrigates blood to the heart, throat, thyroid, brain and upper chakras, third eye, and to the top of the head. Deeply relaxes the back muscles. Stretches the vertebrae. Takes vital energy or prana in reverse, so that it rejuvenates. Improves skin and tissues. Develops concentration. Generates heat in the body. Increases flexibility in the legs, improves circulation, and eliminates fatigue. Revitalizes.*

**12. Camel:** *Opens the chest. Stimulates the third, fourth, and fifth chakras. Broadens and deepens breathing. Fully stretches the back from the sacrum to the cervical area.*

**13. Spinal twist:** *Rejuvenates the vertebrae. Gives full flexibility of movement to the spine. Stretches muscle contractions of the trapezius. Massages the stomach, which helps digestion.*

**14. Beetle:** *Bends the back and spine forward. Stretches the neck. Offsets the previous pose, allows spinal discs to align.*

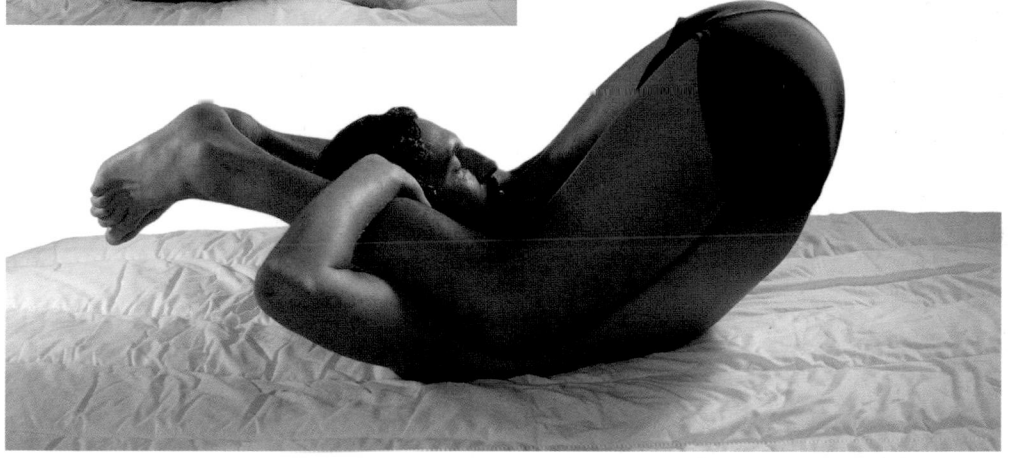

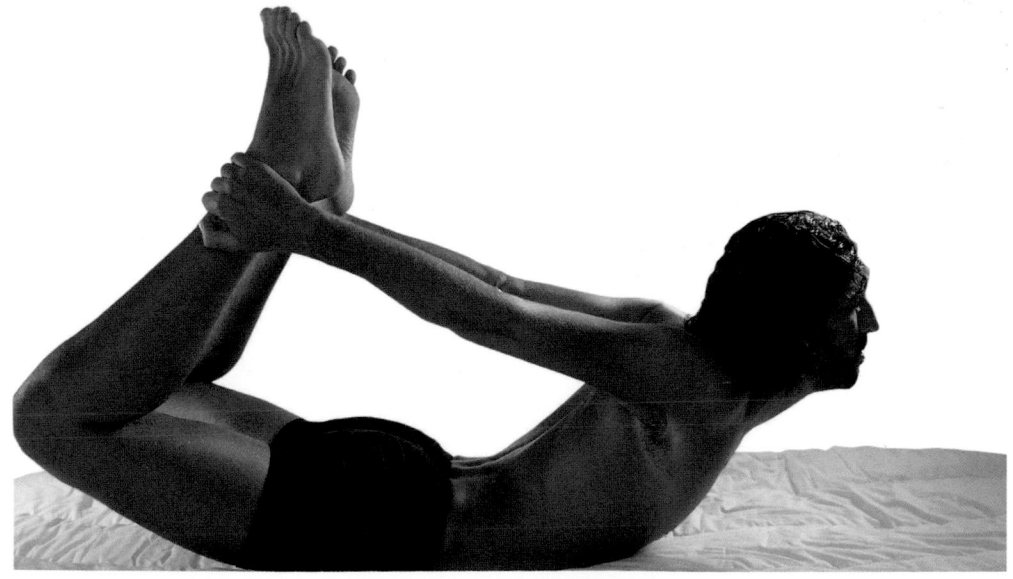

**16. The Mongoose:** *An intermediate restful position. Relaxes the body. Stretches the legs and relaxes the spine. Stretch your neck with your head facing forward and your chin to the chest.*

**17. Cascabel or scorpion:** *Strengthens the lower body and kidneys, and makes blood and energy flow upward. Transmutes energy.*

**18. Knee on the forehead:** *Massages the stomach area. Stretches the legs. Relaxes the back. Benefits seven cervical vertebrae.*

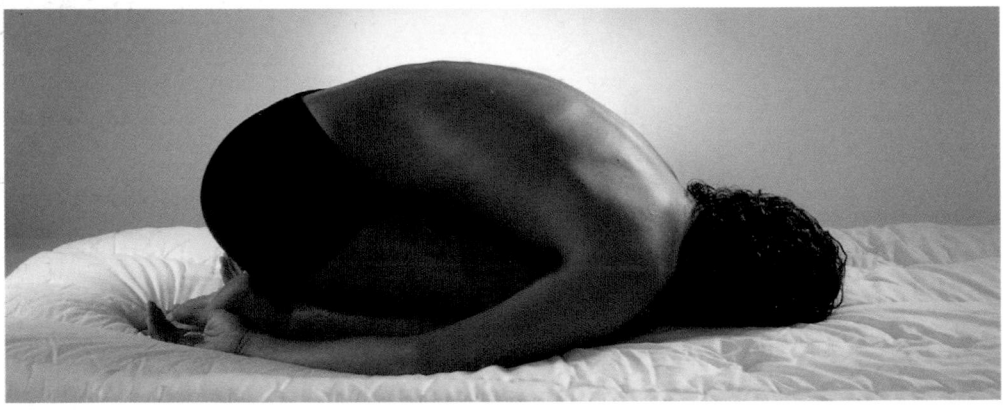

**19. Folded leaf:** *Relaxes the whole body and produces a deep inner bliss. Absorbs the benefits of all the poses done. It is a position of rest and relaxation.*

**20. Half clamp:** *It has the same benefits as the clamp, except that it allows greater flexibility in both legs and the spine.*

**21. Bridge:** *Releases tension in the entire lumbar area.*

**22. Head stand:** *Reversed pose by which we receive terrestrial and cosmic radiation in reverse, thereby rejuvenating ourselves. Beneficial to the thyroid, parathyroid, pineal, and pituitary, bringing blood to the heart and relaxing it. Provides security and emotional self-control. Stimulates the brain and relaxes the nervous system. Removes and prevents varicose veins. Improves energy circulation. Benefits intestines and thymus gland, which regulates growth. Transmutes sexual energy into spiritual power.*

**23. Cervical cleanse:** *Make semicircles from shoulder to shoulder; never complete circles because it damages the neck.*

**24. Triceps stretching:** *Behind the back, join both hands; one above and one below.*

**25. Stretch arms up:** *Stretch your arms up as much as possible.*

**26. Stretch your arms back:** *Let your hands acquire elasticity and flexibility.*

**Final relaxation:** *Now enjoy the entire yoga sequence and its effects. Breathe smoothly and peacefully. Relax all body muscles one at a time until you no longer feel them. Enjoy fifteen minutes of maximum pleasure.*

## THE SIX QUALITIES OF A GOOD THERAPIST

The therapist needs to consider the following guidelines.

**1.** Breathing.
**2.** Correct posture.
**3.** Techniques.
**4.** Awareness through touch.
**5.** Strength and sensitivity.
**6.** Notice the recipient's reactions.

### 1. *Breathing*

It is a cornerstone for success in your practice as a therapist. Through breathing you can absorb the energy of the cosmos and transmit it to the recipient. If you are not breathing, you are not renewing yourself and you will get tired, giving away the energy you have.

Breathing is a bridge between the source of the universe, you, and the recipient. Therefore, breathe with a conscious rhythm in a deep and circular manner, without gaps between inhalation and exhalation.

### 2. *Correct posture*

It is crucial that your body be comfortable for the massage. The back must always be right; vertical in order to be aligned and parallel to the Earth's axis. A bent spine leads to poor breathing, and it will get locked at the solar plexus or the heart.

Vary the position of your legs so they do not become fatigued, especially if you work on the floor, or switch sides if you use a massage table.

### 3. *Techniques*

The vast number of techniques offered by this book lets you work from all angles and solve different problems.

The best way to retain the techniques presented to you in the practical part of the book is to first understand them and then put them to practice by looking at the pictures. Only then will you be able to do them with your eyes closed.

Remember, I offer technical guidance using four methods. Except in tantric massage and reflexology, you can vary the order of exercises without altering the massage.

### 4. *Awareness through touch*

Using your fingers to feel the different blockages, muscle contractions, or uric acid crystals will be like transmitting to your inner antenna information that will help determine where to focus your work. Through your hands you will perceive more than what your intellect can understand, so that gradually, with practice, you will develop your own intuitive wisdom.

### 5. *Strength and sensitivity*

You will know to apply the correct amount of pressure suitable to each body. On weak backs you can apply about 6.6 pounds (3 kg) of weight with your hands, but on strong backs, especially in men, the pressure you apply can be around 12 to 15 pounds (5.6 to 7 kg).

When there are muscle contractions, especially in the trapezius and upper back, you should exert more force and pressure on the blocked energy (yang) so that your strength and pressure (yang) lessens it, and the contraction will relax (yin).

Work while paying attention to your own sensitivity, using your skin to communicate with the soul.

### 6. *Notice the recipient's reactions*

It is also important that you sensitively perceive the inner state of your recipient as it changes, gives in, loosens up, releases fears, etc.

There are those who, during the massage, release emotional stress, conflict, repression, and all kinds of emotions that they are unable to express in wakefulness.

In a meditative and serene state, they become vulnerable, giving themselves permission to mourn, laugh, be carefree, and connect with themselves.

Let them express their own emotions without speaking: holistic massage is geared towards existential expression, consciousness, the language of the heart; not the intellect and mind. Guide the recipient toward releasing emotions through sustained, deep cleansing breathing (inhaling deeply through the nose and out the mouth, emptying the lungs). Remember that it is a sacred moment of silence and overall wellbeing.

## COUPLES' MEDITATION

Massage helps two individual beings feel as if they are one. Massage causes alchemical phenomena and energetic unity. But you can also feel the complete opposite—rejection—since energy has two paths: attraction or repulsion.

Let yourself flow with pure life energy and do not see your body as your identity but rather view the divinity that dwells within. Envision life full of pleasure, abundance, and beauty. From the moment a heart begins to beat, there is beauty because there is life.

A massage turns into meditation when you communicate using energy and silence, and you and your partner will surely enjoy it.

## BEGINNERS AND PROFESSIONALS

The difference between a beginner and a professional is just a matter of practice. It is very important to understand that massage is learned by practicing massage. The experience gives you wisdom.

When you start working with your hands on different people you will come to your own understanding and conclusions about its therapeutic effects.

You will notice that in some individuals the effect is faster; in others it takes longer due to how long they have had a particular muscle contraction or problem. If a muscle contraction or pain in the upper back area has been there for months, obviously a single session will not be enough to reset energetic balance. You will need to do more sessions.

The way you treat the recipient and the service that you offer will be vital for you to regularly see clients. The ambience that you offer, your energy, your wise words, and advice on the quality of life will also help you capture their commitment and openness to you.

In short, time, experience, practice, and constant learning will give you the necessary skills for you to become a successful therapist. Finally, guide your lifestyle according to your teaching.

## SPIRITUAL OPENING

It is very common that when you begin on a journey of energy, it will open up new sensations and spiritual perceptions to you.

The massage that you learn here, combined with breathing techniques, meditation, practicing with energy, sattvic food, positive mental attitude, and enjoying life, will enrich you in multiple ways.

The energy path is a path to love. So massage is a loving path, and at the same time it is therapeutic, scientific, and sensitive. You will notice that starting a healthy and conscious lifestyle will allow your spirit to develop other characteristics and potential that, until now, were asleep and of which you were unaware. So if you are already an advanced practitioner, I hope to strengthen your enthusiasm and knowledge; and if you are just getting to know the art of massage . . .

Happy initiation!

## DO-IN: THE SELF-MASSAGE

These techniques are very useful and are recommended for therapists as well as for anyone wanting to stay healthy. They relax, help improve circulation, eliminate fatigue, bring back love and sensation to the body, as well as increase the electrical *qi* level. Despite its many benefits, I recommend that therapists get at least one or two massages per week from other professionals, obviously the more the better.

### *Sit comfortably*
Slather your favorite oil over your whole body. All techniques are to be repeated ten to twelve times.

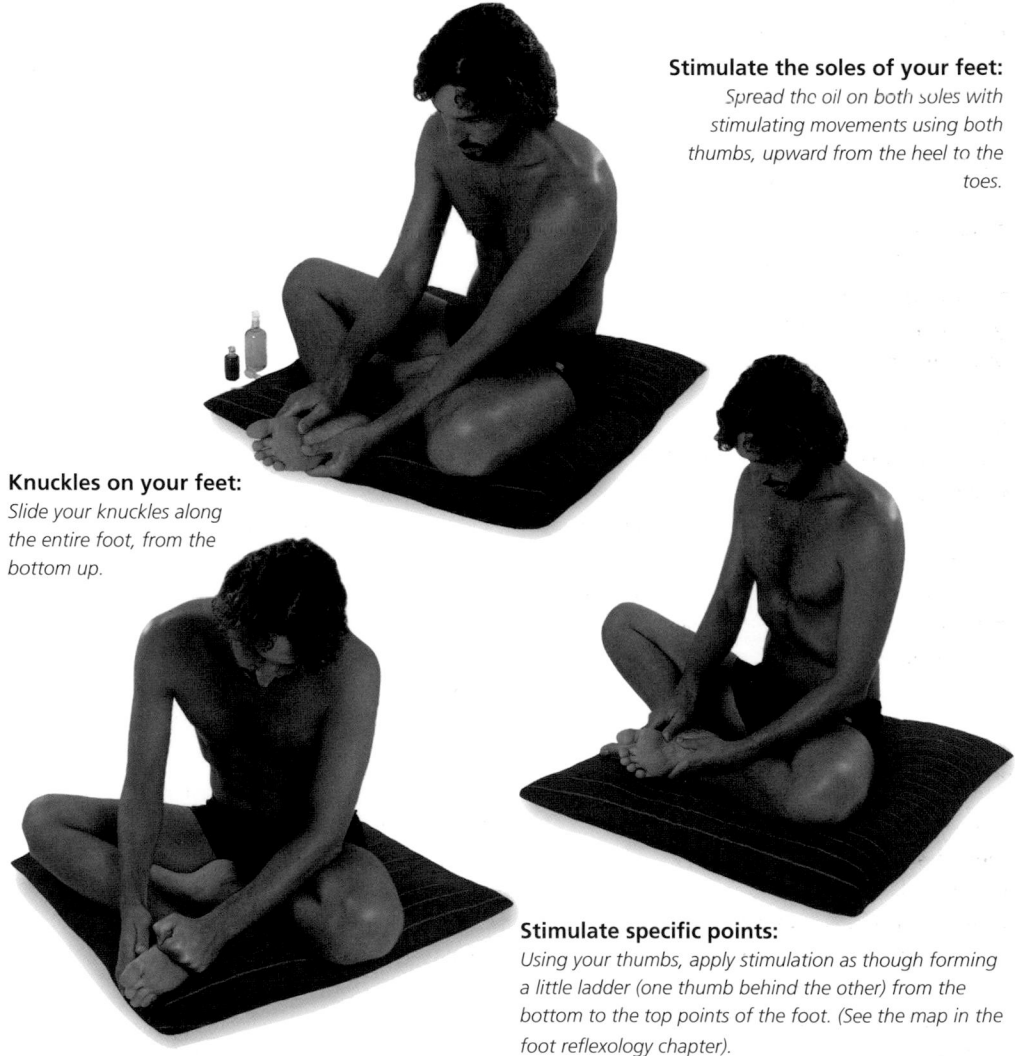

**Stimulate the soles of your feet:**
*Spread the oil on both soles with stimulating movements using both thumbs, upward from the heel to the toes.*

**Knuckles on your feet:**
*Slide your knuckles along the entire foot, from the bottom up.*

**Stimulate specific points:**
*Using your thumbs, apply stimulation as though forming a little ladder (one thumb behind the other) from the bottom to the top points of the foot. (See the map in the foot reflexology chapter).*

## DO-IN: THE SELF-MASSAGE

**Hand on your calf:**
*With both hands, slide your thumbs from your ankle to below the knee pit, while applying deep pressure to the calf muscle. This eliminates fatigue by renewing blood flow and cleaning the cells.*

**Pressure:** *With both hands, press the entire surface of the calf.*

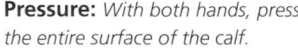

**Rub the kidneys:**
*With both hands, vigorously rub the kidney area like an iron that rises and falls generating heat. These are linked to vitality. Do it for one to two minutes.*

**Kneading:**
*Use the whole hand to stimulate your quadriceps and hamstrings through intensive kneading.*

**Pressure with thumbs on the sacrum:** *With your thumbs, apply pressure along the entire surface of the sacrum. You will find two rows of four holes. Press and loosen them several times.*

**Pressing along the arm:** *With one hand, press all along the opposite arm (from shoulder to wrist), which will be left completely relaxed.*

**Knead the trapezius:** *First with the four fingers of one hand and then the other, knead the whole surface of the trapezius, from the neck to the shoulder well.*

## DO-IN: THE SELF-MASSAGE

### *Lie on your back*

**Opening the forehead:**

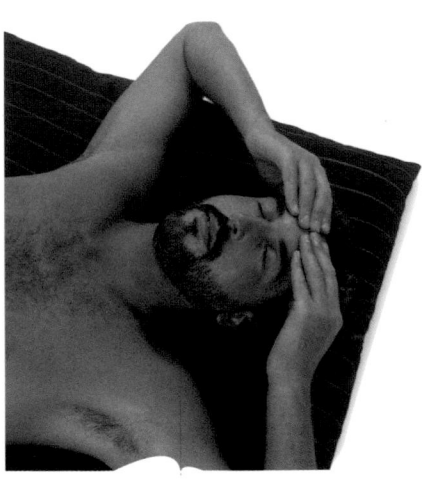

**Circles on the solar plexus:**
*With one hand over the other, make circles from the stomach (third chakra) to three inches (eight centimeters) below the navel (second chakra). The movement should be done clockwise when the energy is low, but counterclockwise to ease tension.*

**Kneading the scalp:**
*With open palms, massage the surface of the head from the temples to the neck. At the end, lie still and enjoy a sense of deep relaxation for ten to fifteen minutes.*

**Opening the chest:**
*From the solar plexus upward, slide both hands down as you open the chest toward the shoulders. Breathe deeply through your nose.*

# ELEMENTS OF A MASSAGE

## PHYSICAL COMFORT

Performing a full session of holistic massage requires, first, that the recipient be comfortable because then it will be much easier for the body to relax. Comfort means a soft bed, preferably with an opening or hole for the face to breathe; those without this opening clog the nostrils and hurt the neck.

If you work on the floor (especially with Zen shiatsu and tantric massage), you must make sure that there is ample room for movement and comfort. Finally, make sure that the person's head is toward the north in order to better receive the telluric energies of the Earth.

## THE ENVIRONMENT: SIMULATION OF THE SIX SENSES

The room temperature must be around 73° and 78°F (23° and 26°C), since the body tends to cool when relaxed.

Be sure that there are no air currents which could cause health problems for the recipient.

In general, it is important that you pay attention to the six senses and their stimuli.

Use light colored clothing, walls, and objects that encourage relaxation. Place flowers, a wooden meditating buddha, candles, nature scenes, a source of water that flows smoothly, gemstones and crystals, a wind chime, and tantric or Zen objects as they help create a meditative aura in your office.

Use fêng shui to decorate the room, remembering to keep a balance between empty and full. Do not fill up the space with too many visual stimuli.

Keep in mind the auditory aspect and play soft background music.

Stimulate the sense of smell with incense, oil, or air fresheners. Make sure that they are of good quality and preferably have the scent of sandalwood, jasmine, rose, or wood.

Stimulate taste gently with candy before the massage, as you converse with your recipient.

Touch will obviously be enhanced during the massage because it will affect the entire body.

Finally, the internal sense will open up as you provide confidence, pleasure, and safety to your recipient. Their inner eye will open as their mind is silenced.

## SPECIFIC OILS

Use a neutral oil or almond essence that is suitable for every type of person. You can purchase excellent brands and products that perfectly penetrate the skin without causing irritation or itching.

Below, I offer a list of basic scents that you can use for massaging, along with their particular aromatic features and application. I also show you the elements and effects of the most suitable mixtures for massage.

## Scents

- **Lemon:** Stimulant, for people who are depressed or whose energy is low.
- **Sandalwood:** Meditative and aphrodisiac, for balancing life energy.
- **Lavender:** Relaxant, for people who are stressed out.
- **Rosemary:** Muscle relaxant for people who feel very tired.
- **Rose:** Antidepressant, for people with emotional problems.
- **Eucalyptus:** Antidepressant, for respiratory and emotional openings.

## Special mixtures (200 ml)

- **Tantric circle:** Thirty sandalwood drops, twenty of musk, and fifteen of patchouli. Aphrodisiac.

- **Forest dream:** Thirty peppermint oil drops, twenty of lemon oil, and twenty of almond oil. Helps to open and energize.
- **Magical evenings:** Thirty orange oil drops and thirty almond oil drops. Stimulant and antidepressant.
- **Ocean breeze:** Thirty peppermint oil drops and thirty eucalyptus oil drops. Refreshing, purifying, unlocks the airways and emotions.
- **Eternal flowers:** Forty jasmine oil drops and thirty rose oil drops. Antidepressant and aphrodisiac.
- **Summer storm:** Thirty cinnamon drops, twenty of orange oil, and twenty of lemon oil. Mobilizing and energetic.
- **Angel flight:** Forty lavender drops, twenty of ylang-ylang, and twenty of chamomile. Sedative.
- **Mountain breeze:** Thirty rosemary drop, and thirty of lemon verbena. Muscle relaxant.

---

### DO THIS BEFORE AND AFTER EACH SESSION

**Before the session**

First, be in a meditative state. Close your eyes, bring your palms together in the center of the chest to unify your own yin and yang energy, imagine a purple circle at the top of your head, and connect with the universal energy. Then breathe gently for one or two minutes.

WINDMILL EXERCISE: Spin back both arms five times then spin them forward five times while inhaling and exhaling deeply. This will give strength to your hands.

**After the session**

LUMBERJACK EXERCISE: Stand with both feet at hip-width distance, take a deep breath, and lower your energy as you exhale forcefully with a loud "aahh." This will clean your solar plexus of any heavy or negative energy that you may have picked up.

Finally, at the end of the session remember to take a shower or wash your hands with cold water.

## COMPREHENSIVE QUESTIONNAIRE

It is important for you to be interested in the inner world, practices, habits, and physical and emotional condition of the person being massaged. Do not meddle in their private life (which you should regard as sacred), but do follow a series of questions that will provide answers to guide you toward the root cause of their problems. The questionnaire also aims for you to get to know each other and gain mutual trust without letting them overwhelm you with every particular problem they have faced in life. If the recipient is able to trust you openly, then they will share their concerns and feelings with you, and tell you what they need from you.

### QUESTIONS

**1.** What kind of job do you have?

**2.** How is the mattress where you sleep?

**3.** How is your energy level? (Tired, stressed and nervous, balanced.)

**4.** Do you have any physical problems or pain? (In the organs, performance issues, muscle aches, etc.)

**5.** How do you feel intellectually and emotionally?

**6.** Ask women if they are pregnant or menstruating.

**7.** Do you feel any pain along the spine?

**8.** How are you as far as material possessions, sexuality, nutrition, emotions, creativity, and intellectual and spiritual level?

### ANSWERS

**The first question** refers to the hours that a person spends at his job. It is important to determine whether they love their job or do it reluctantly. Spending many hours a day at a place where we are unhappy is harmful to our health. Also find out if they work at a computer, as this will surely lead to problems due to poor posture. They may also do hard work where the body is exposed to constant pressure and noise. Before drawing a conclusion, remember that you have to find out if the cause is physical before going into a deeper level.

**The second question** refers to people who do not sleep well because they have a sagging mattress, a very firm pillow, electronics in the room, or because their bed is not positioned to face north. Poor sleep and not enough rest are the main causes of pain in the waist, back, and neck.

**The third question** asks about their energy level. You need to know this so that you are able to determine whether to apply a yin massage (relaxing and slow) if they are stressed and nervous; or a yang massage (dynamic and energetic) if their energy is rather low.

**The fourth question** addresses the physical in order to identify muscular symptoms; for example, pain in the sacrum or shoulder, stomach inflammation, headache, etc.

**The fifth question** addresses the mental and emotional state; for example, if their mind is confused, or if they are feeling chest pain due to repressed emotions.

**The sixth question** is specific to women, as they may be menstruating or pregnant. We cannot do any specific type of massage in either of these cases. (See also the list of suggestions in chapter 2.)

**The seventh and eighth questions** are related, since both indicate the condition of the spine and if there is pain related to the chakras and their function.

These questions, each recipient's body language, as well as your own intuition and experience, will help you discover how to work with each person.

## DISORDERS AND THEIR TREATMENTS

Below, I provide a little guidance on how to work on the most common problems and disorders. However, do not think of it as a strict guide because there can be multiple root causes. It is not a medical diagnosis either but a map that can be used in each case so you can determine what is the most appropriate massage to apply.

Observe your recipient and remember that there can be basic techniques that you practice with all your recipients and others for specific individuals. Base your course of action on the questionnaire as well as on any other factors that may merit consideration so you can best decide which techniques to use for each case.

### Asthma
- **Cause:** Emotional shock.
- **Treatment:** Opening emotional areas: chest and hara. Breathing exercises. Harmonization through tantric massage.

### Low energy
See "Depression."

### Constant headaches
- **Cause:** Negative ideas. Excessive muscle contractions in the neck and trapezius. Emotional stress.
- **Treatment:** Work on the head and neck to unlock them. Specific shiatsu points. Cleansing breaths. Harmonization of higher chakras through tantric massage.

### Sciatica
- **Cause:** Negative overexertion. Stepping incorrectly. Nerves. Sexual energy problems. Malfunction of the first two chakras.
- **Treatment:** Sacral massage with the thumbs going counterclockwise. Zen shiatsu to the sacrum and sciatic nerve. Tantric massage for the first two chakras. Reflexology in the heel area.

### Sore waist
- **Cause:** Physical foot problems (for instance, due to standing for long periods or wearing the wrong shoes). Tension in the two lower chakras. Financial or sexual problems.
- **Treatment:** Kneading, rubbing, Zen shiatsu holds. Calm the two lower chakras through a tantric massage.

### Muscle contraction of the trapezius
- **Cause:** Bad back posture. Everyday life stresses. Cervical problems. Unresolved mental problems.
- **Treatment:** Zen shiatsu holds. Unblock stress points in the upper back. Basic shiatsu techniques. Hot stone massage. Shoulder cleansing. Counterclockwise movements.

### Depression
- **Cause:** Emotional problems. An unfulfilled desire. Exhaustion.
- **Treatment:** Working in the emotional area of the fourth chakra, opening the chest. Rub the kidneys and inner wrists (meridians of the heart, sexual circulation, and lungs). Harmonization of chakras through a tantric massage.

### Headache
- **Cause:** Visual problems. Noise. Liver problems. Contractions in the neck. Stress.
- **Treatment:** Reflexology. Unlock the upper body, and shiatsu on the neck. Pull the hair. Meridian points. Deep breaths to oxygenate the brain. Sensitive massage for cerebral people. Work with Zen shiatsu massage on the face and head.

## Pain in the upper back area

See "Muscle Contraction of the Trapezius."

## Pain along the backbone

- **Cause:** Bone malformations: lordosis, kyphosis, or scoliosis. Physical exertion. Poor sleep.
- **Treatment:** Zen shiatsu techniques. Harmonization through tantric massage. Shiatsu to release blockages in specific muscle contractions.

## Premenstrual pain

- **Cause:** Possible emotional problems.
- **Treatment:** Achilles heel. Shiatsu and tantric massage to the sacral area and waist. Reflexology in the affected area.

## Blocked stomach

- **Cause:** Poor digestion. Unprocessed strong emotions. Undigested personal situation.
- **Treatment:** Ampuku: work on the hara. Circular movements to mobilize energy. Tantric massage to the third chakra. Specific shiatsu points for the stomach.

## Stress

- **Cause:** Nerve disorders. Heavy workload. Uncontrollable thoughts.
- **Treatment:** Working with yin massage: sedate the body. Slow and deep rhythm. Start at the head and end at the feet. Unlock the upper part of the back with Shiatsu. Also apply a sensitive massage (for brainy people) and reflexology. Working with cleansing breaths.

## Poor circulation

- **Cause:** Muscle contractions that obstruct the free flow of blood. Tension and lactic acid in the calves. Insufficient physical exercise.
- **Treatment:** Zen shiatsu to unlock the upper back area. Intense basic massage throughout the body in active yang rhythm. Comprehensive reflexology. Shiatsu and tantric massage to the legs.

# PRACTICE

# ZEN SHIATSU

This healing technique, meaning "finger pressure," is based on traditional Chinese medicine, acupuncture, judo and Do-In, and it is known for its effectiveness, pragmatism, and scientific and spiritual approach.

Although it came to be known a thousand years ago, the first texts on this type of massage date back to 2300 BC in a Chinese treatise on internal medicine called *Huangdi Neijing* ("The Emperor's Inner Canon").

Shiatsu principles are as follows:

- The human body is nourished by *qi* energy flowing through twelve meridians or energy rivers connected to the organs and internal organs with specific functions.

- The meridians have points called *tsubos* that are pressed, soothed, or stimulated in order to balance energy flow.

- The *tsubos* may be empty or filled (*kyo* or *jitsu*), so we need to tone them when they are empty (clockwise) and sedate them when they are full (counterclockwise).

- Strong emotions (extreme joy, depression, fear, anger, worry, boredom, criticism, anger, etc.) have a negative impact on the meridians, which in turn negatively affect the organs and cause disease.

- Shiatsu is based on sustaining perfect health through the constant balance of yin energy (female) and yang energy (male). When energy balance is altered, disease occurs. So, shiatsu

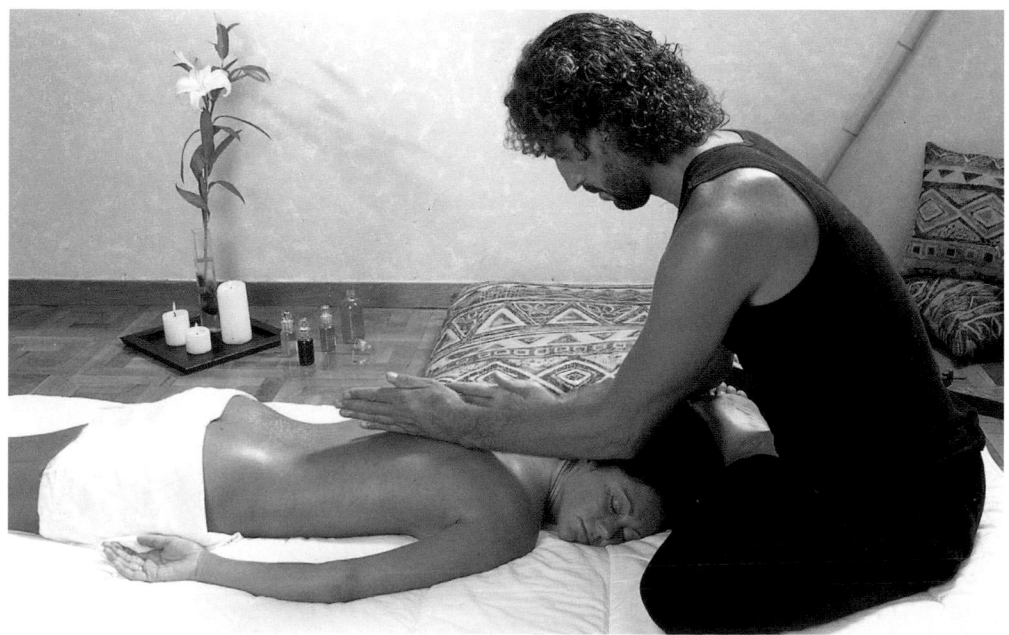

helps to restore harmony the body through pressure, holds, decompression, kneading, and friction.

- The meridians are located on all sides of the body (behind, in front, inside, and outside). They are on the second body (life energy), not on the physical body itself.
- In the twenty-four hours that make up each day, the twelve meridians feed on *qi* for two hours every day.
- Meridians work in pairs. Since energy is never lost but simply transformed, when we soothe a meridian we are also toning its corresponding meridian.
- *Qi* energy is related to five elements (wood, fire, earth, metal, and water).

## *QI* ENERGY

According to Oriental medicine, *qi* energy is a fundamental concept that governs the universe (macrocosm) as well as human life (microcosm). It is the basis of our physical health and it is essential for mental and emotional balance.

*Qi* (see its symbol on page 72) is made up of small energy particles that are found in the air, it is neither oxygen nor nitrogen, and it consists of two complementary poles: yin and yang. Yin is the energy of the Earth and yang is the energy of the sky, the Sun.

Everything in life is governed by balancing both energies. For example, an electric plug has a male part, yang, and a female part, yin; and when it is plugged to a power source, an electric current moves through the wire, producing light. Similarly, in the human body, electricity flows through the meridians producing the light of life.

Scientifically, it has been found that the essence of each atom is light. Therefore, we are moving light. When that light, *qi* energy, does not flow normally through the meridians, blockages occur.

*Qi* circulates throughout the twelve meridians, twenty four hours a day, following a set cycle of two hours each. So energy comes from the lung meridian. This is the first meridian that begins working when we are born, given that our first act out of the womb is to breathe.

- **3 a.m. to 5 a.m.:** Lung meridian.
- **5 a.m. to 7 a.m.:** Large intestine meridian.
- **7 a.m. to 9 a.m.:** Stomach meridian.
- **9 a.m. to 11 a.m.:** Spleen–pancreas meridian.
- **11 a.m. to 1 p.m.:** Heart meridian.
- **1 p.m. to 3 p.m.:** Small intestine meridian.
- **3 p.m. to 5 p.m.:** Bladder meridian.
- **5 p.m. to 7 p.m.:** Kidney meridian.
- **7 p.m. to 9 p.m.:** Circulatory and sexual meridian (also called the pericardium).
- **9 p.m. to 11 p.m.:** Triple heater meridian (or triple burner).
- **11 p.m. to 1 a.m.:** Gallbladder meridian.
- **1 a.m. to 3 a.m.:** Liver meridian.

Twelve meridians form a continuous power supply for everyone's life energy. There are also two extraordinary meridians that make up a microcosmic orbit:

- The governing vessel, a yang energy reserve circulating inside the spine, starting at the head and ending under the nose
- The conception vessel, which starts from a point on the lips, runs down the front and reaches the sexual organs where it joins the governing vessel.

## *KYO* AND *JITSU*: DEFICIENCY OR EXCESS OF *QI*

The lack and excess of *qi* determines whether there is *kyo* (empty, deficient) or *jitsu* (fullness, excess). When *qi* is well distributed throughout the body, it is in perfect health. But *qi* blockages undo this balance and produce *kyo* or *jitsu* in some body parts, and we can become ill because of it.

Overall, in a strong body, *jitsu* shows up as high blood pressure and diseases related to overwork.

Meanwhile, in a weak body, diseases, exhaustion, helplessness, and depression are *kyo*.

To restore energy balance you will have to tone *kyo* to make up for lacking energy and also disperse *jitsu* to remove excessive energy.

General rules you should never forget:

- To sedate a point, do counterclockwise rotations on it with your thumb.
- To tone up a point, do clockwise rotations on it with your thumb.

### *KYO* AND *JITSU* ON THE MERIDIANS

| MERIDIAN | KYO (DEFICIENCY) | JITSU (EXCESS) |
|---|---|---|
| Lung | Cough; chills. | Congestion and bad breath. Strong and painful cough; catarrh. |
| Large intestine | Pain in the shoulders and arms; heaviness; bloating. | Dry and chapped lips; noisy digestive tract. |
| Stomach | Lack of appetite; weak legs. | Gluttony; fever; pain on the outer legs. |
| Spleen | Craving for sweets; drowsiness. Gastritis; numbness in the legs. | Fickle appetite; heavy body. Desire to rest. |
| Heart | Depression; anxiety; inability to make decisions. | Chest pain. |
| Small intestine | Pain in the temples, neck, shoulder and arms. | Earache; ringing in the ears. |
| Bladder | Frequent urination. Back pain. | Pain in the legs and waist. |
| Kidney | Lack of sex drive. Impatience. Neck tension and cold feet. | Ringing in the ears. Dark urine. |
| Circulatory and sexual | Restless sleep or nightmares. Vertigo. Diarrhea. | Headache and stomach ache. Light sleep; fever. |
| Triple heater | Cold and weakness. | Hearing difficulty. Pain on the shoulders and ears. |
| Gallbladder | Low energy; heaviness when walking; chills. Bad breath. | Feeling of a full stomach. Heavy head. |
| Liver | Insecurity; slippage in the legs. Aggressiveness. | Wanting to cry, irritability, and workaholism. |

## WAYS TO APPLY PRESSURE

There are two ways in which we can work on the meridians by using our thumbs: sedating and stimulating, or pushing and pulling.

The amount of pressure you should apply varies between 6 and 19 pounds (3 and 9 kilos). In a physically strong person, we may exert more pressure, while with others we have to be gentler.

Obviously, in many cases the recipient may feel pain as a result of releasing blocked energy.

Apply pressure for three to five seconds, exhaling as you press and inhaling as you release.

In shiatsu massage, you will also work using your elbows, manually kneading, creating friction, and using your knuckles. You will practice them using various techniques.

## THE FIVE ELEMENTS

According to Chinese medicine, five primordial elements play an important role in the human body and its functions. The five elements rule indicates that *qi* is manifested in the universe through water, earth, fire, wood, and metal. Any imbalance in these elements will be manifested as a symptom of illness on the organs and meridians. For example, *qi* imbalance in the wood element can affect the liver and its meridian, or the gallbladder and its meridian, or both. Anger affects not just the liver; muscles will also tend to tighten into fists, causing eye problems through tears. Similarly, these negative reactions can occur to the various elements.

### FIVE ELEMENTS IN THE BODY

| ELEMENTS | WOOD | FIRE | EARTH | METAL | WATER |
|---|---|---|---|---|---|
| Cardinal directions | East | South | Center | West | North |
| Seasons | Spring | Summer | Heatwave | Autumn | Winter |
| Climates | Wind | Heat | Humidity | Dryness | Cold |
| Organs<br>Internal organs | Liver<br>Gallbladder | Heart<br>Small<br>intestine | Spleen<br>Stomach | Lung<br>Large<br>intestine | Kidney<br>Bladder |
| Colors<br>Flavors<br>Feelings | Blue<br>Sour<br>Anger | Red<br>Bitter<br>Joy | Yellow<br>Sweet<br>Meditation | White<br>Spicy<br>Restlessness | Black<br>Salty<br>Fear |
| Fabrics<br>Sensory organs<br>Liquids | Muscles<br>Eyes<br>Tears | Vessels<br>Tongue<br>Sweat | Flesh<br>Mouth<br>Drool | Skin and hair<br>Nose<br>Mucus | Bones<br>Ears<br>Saliva |
| Voice<br>Expressions | Shouting<br>Fists | Speak<br>Chat | Singing<br>Hiccup | Crying<br>Coughing | Moaning<br>Shaking |

## BASIC SHIATSU TECHNIQUES

Below are a set of techniques we call "basic" because they help everyone and they cover a comprehensive practice for the entire body. Later we will see "special massage" techniques for specific problems. Each technique is to be repeated ten to twelve times.

### *Back and facing down*

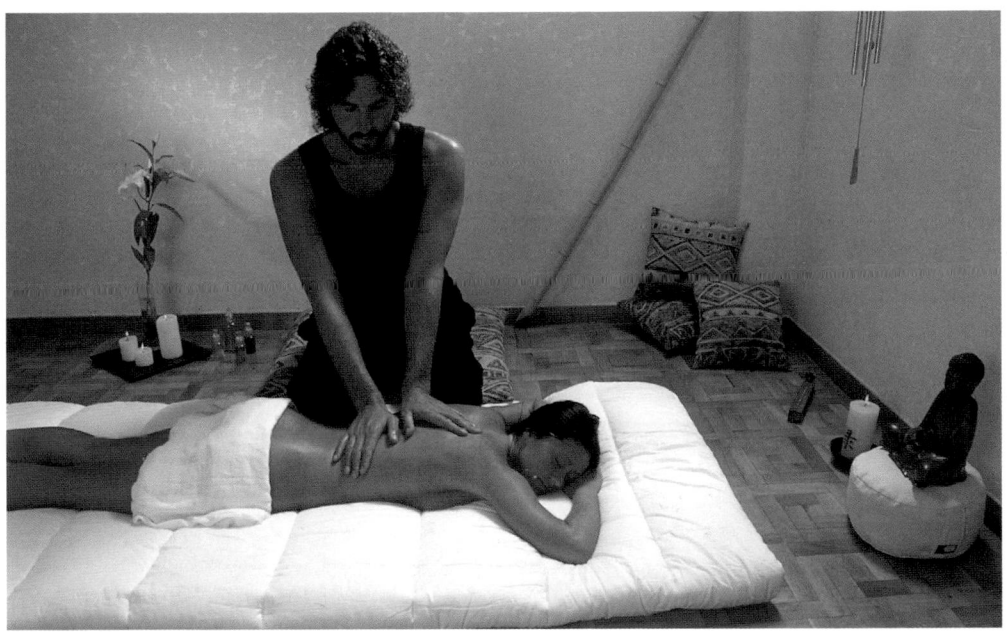

**1. Figure "X":** *Warm up the oil in your hands and place them both on the middle of the back. Slide one hand down to the buttock and slide the other up to the opposite shoulder, so that your hand movement forms an "X." Then switch to the other shoulder and buttock.*

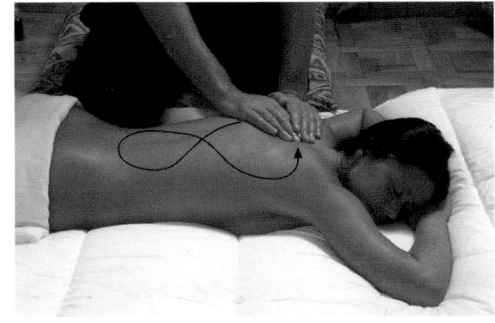

**2. Figure "8":**
*Slide both hands (one over the other) forming a large number "8" across the back. This movement symbolizes eternity, past and future, meeting at this point in the present and generating heat in the back that allows energy to begin to mobilize.*

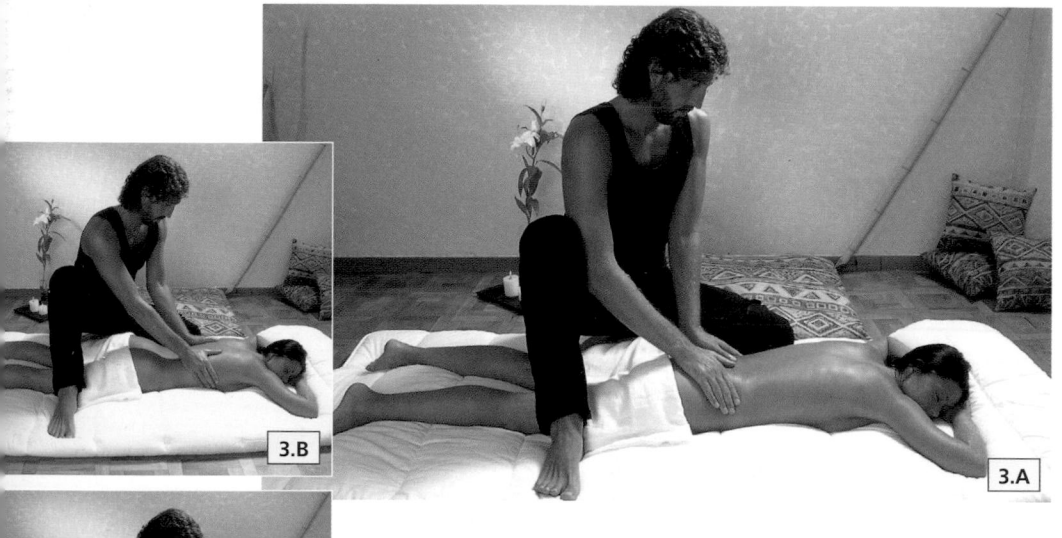

**3. Back openings:** *Eliminates tension in the back by "opening" it in three parts. With both hands forming the wings of a dove, make three movements: first, from the sacrum outward; then from the sacrum to the dorsal area; and lastly, from the sacrum to the shoulders.*

**4. Back massage:** *Place both hands on the sacrum and place your fingers toward the neck. Slide one hand up and then the other along the vertebrae, but not over them. In doing so, create energy in a portion of the bladder meridian and warm up the chakras.*

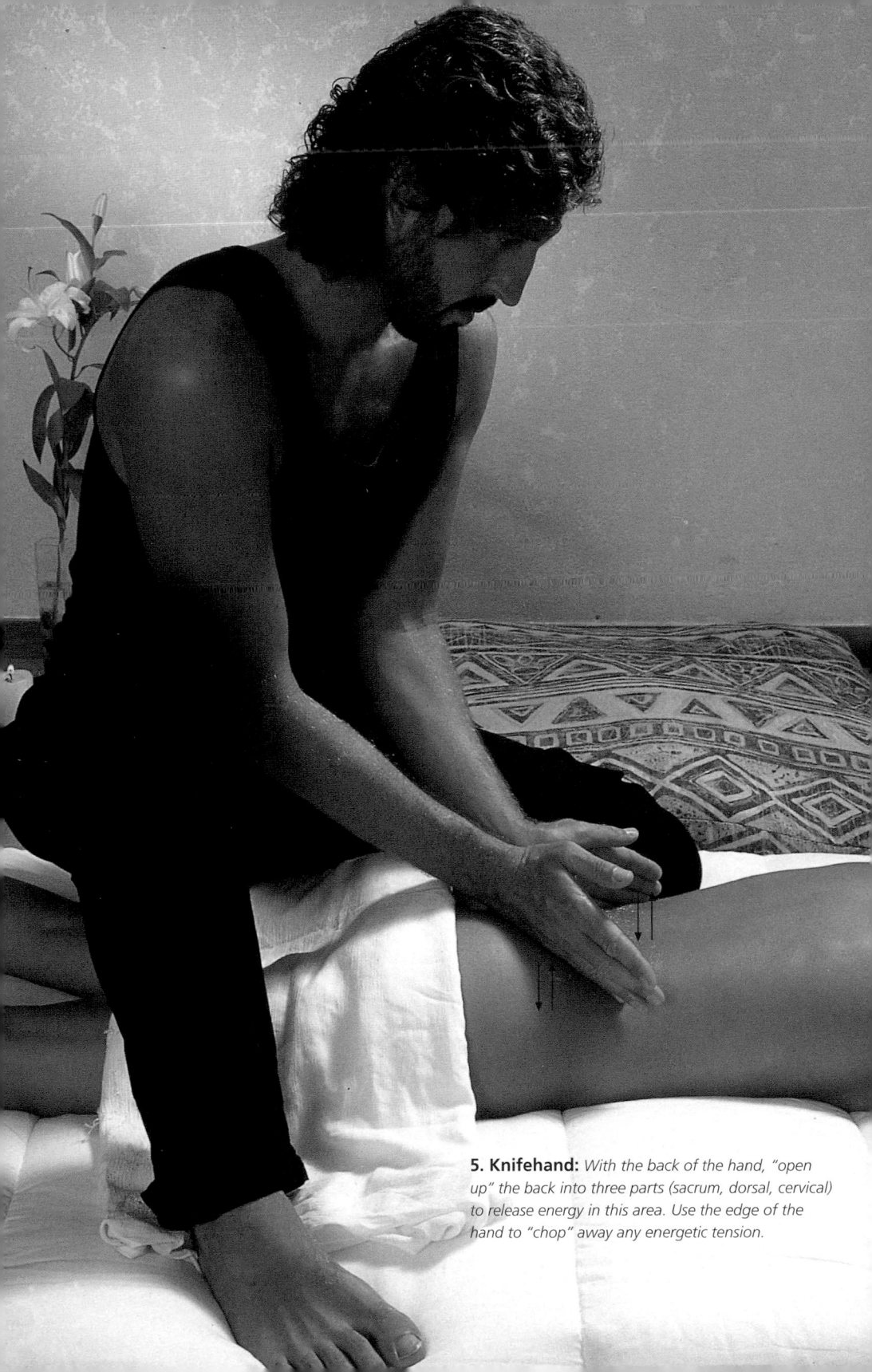

**5. Knifehand:** *With the back of the hand, "open up" the back into three parts (sacrum, dorsal, cervical) to release energy in this area. Use the edge of the hand to "chop" away any energetic tension.*

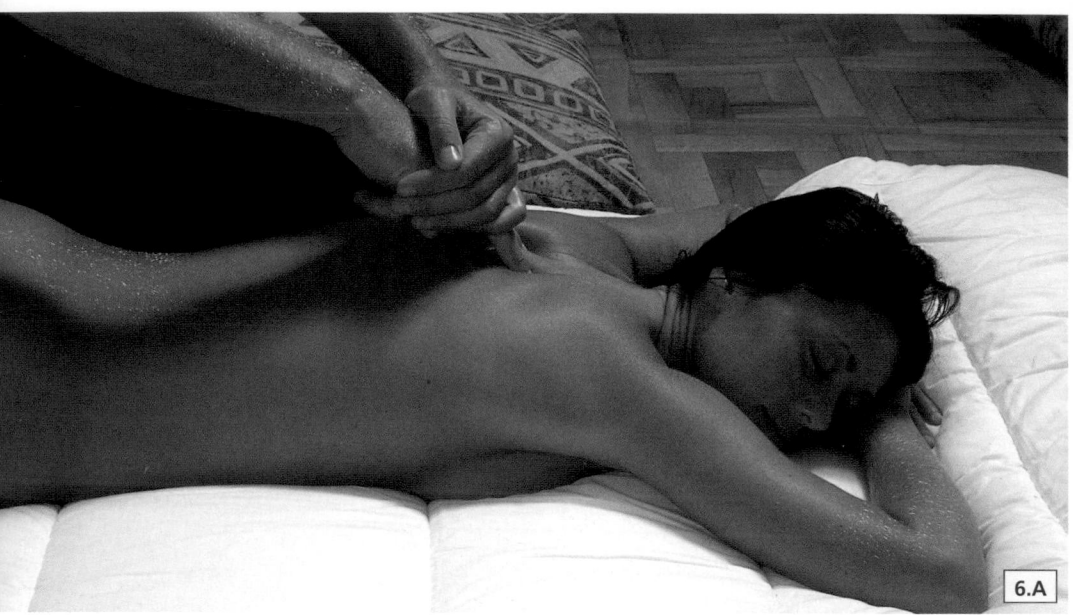

6.A

**6. Fork:** *Place the index and middle fingers of one hand on the cervical area and place the other hand over it to increase the pressure. Slide your finger down the spinal region (but not over the vertebra) toward the sacrum. This technique stimulates the bladder meridian so that the recipient can then eliminate toxins through urination and begin a purification process.*

6.B

**7. Spoons:**
*With a cupped hand, gently hit the side of the spine, moving upwards. This creates air that eases tension through suction.*

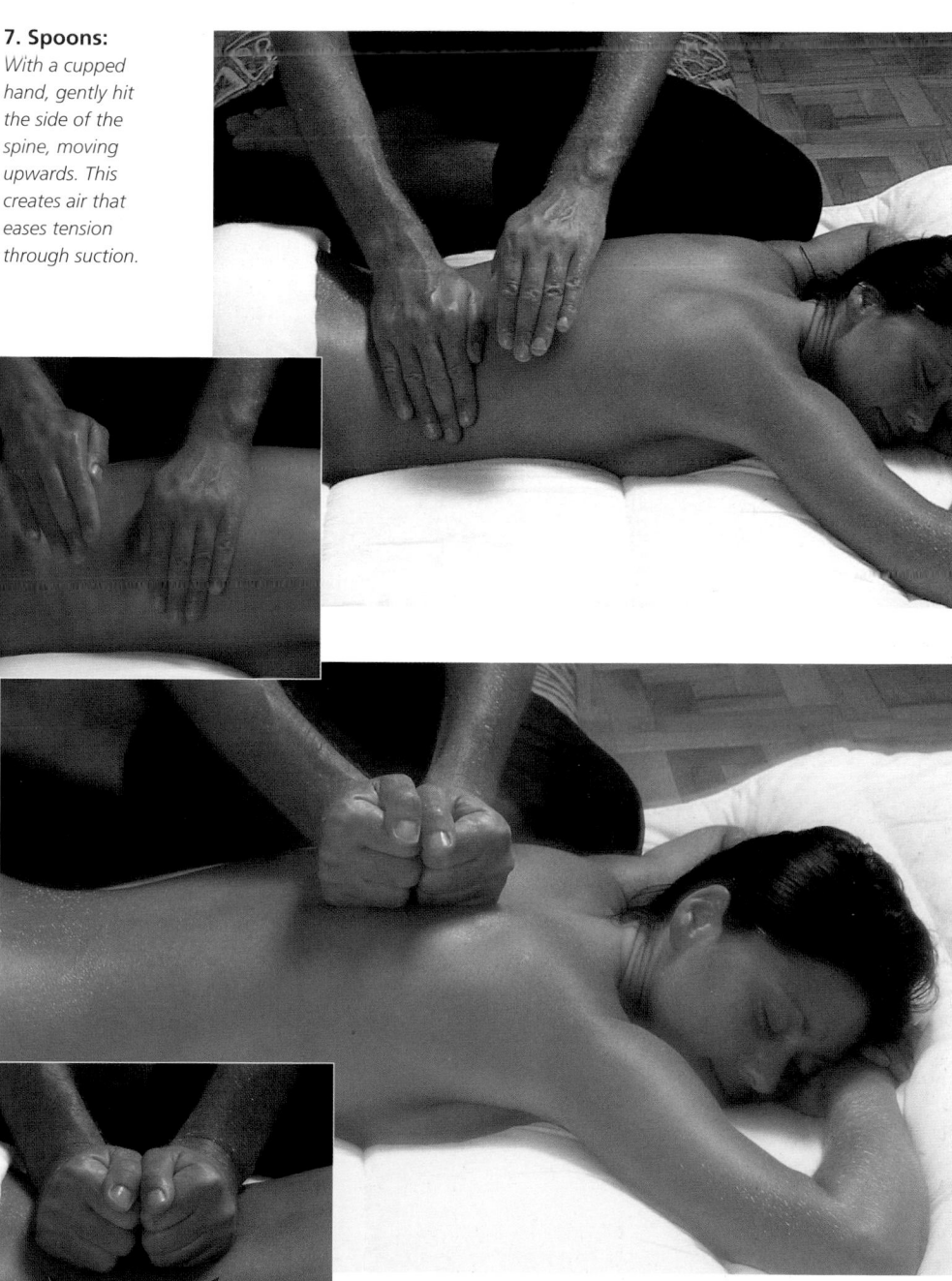

**8. Stamping:** *With clenched fists placed on the spine, press down with one first and then the other, starting at the sacrum. Rotate you one fist up and the other down while moving the hands up along the spine to the neck area. Be sure to always keep your hands together.*

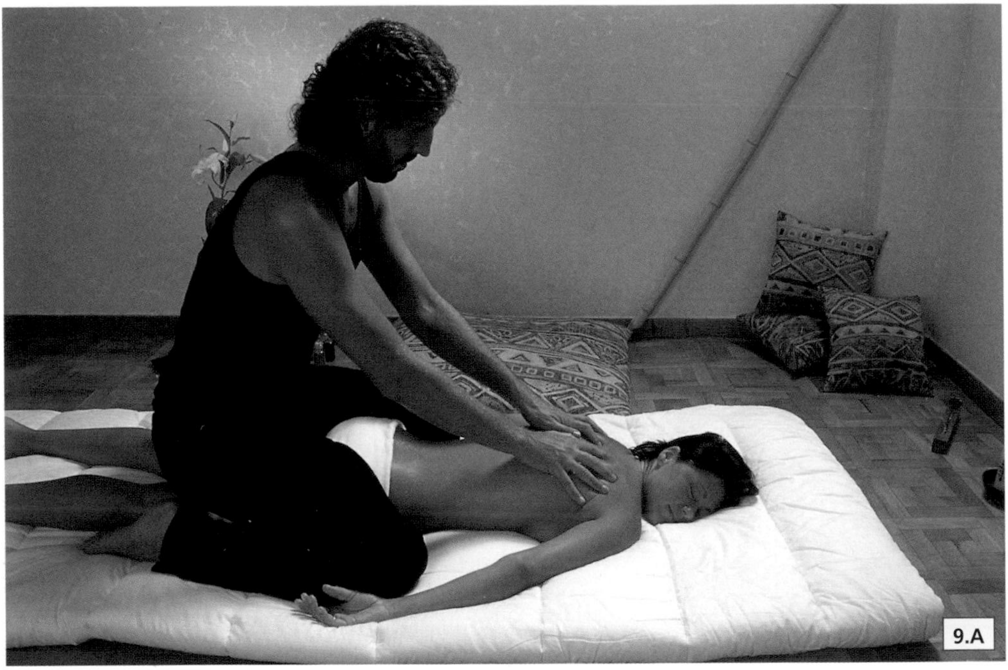

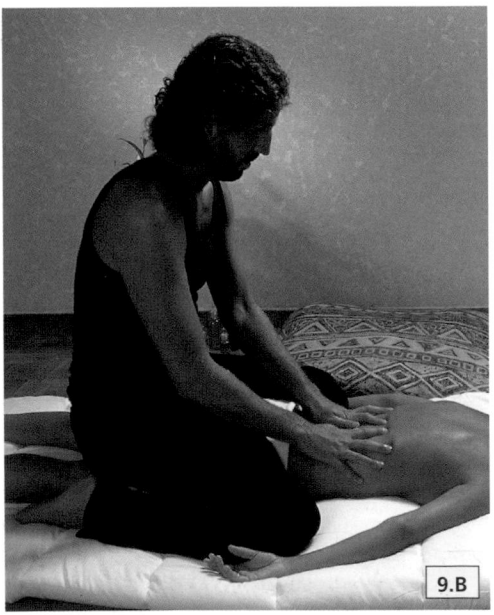

**9. Rake:** *Place both open hands flat on the lower back area and move them up along its entire length until you get to the shoulders; then work your way back down, making zigzag movements. This technique allows you to explore the back and increase blood flow and energy.*

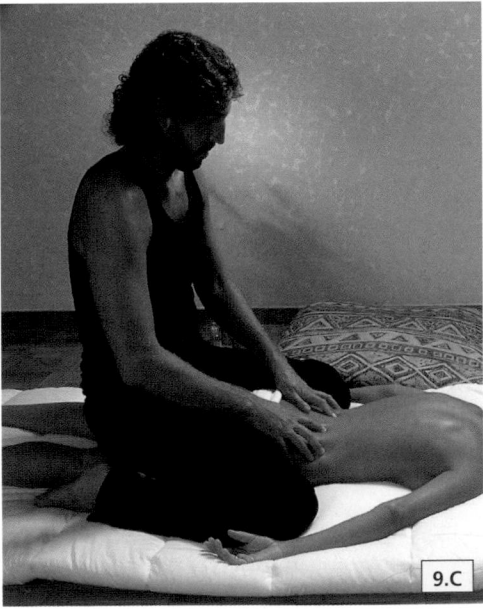

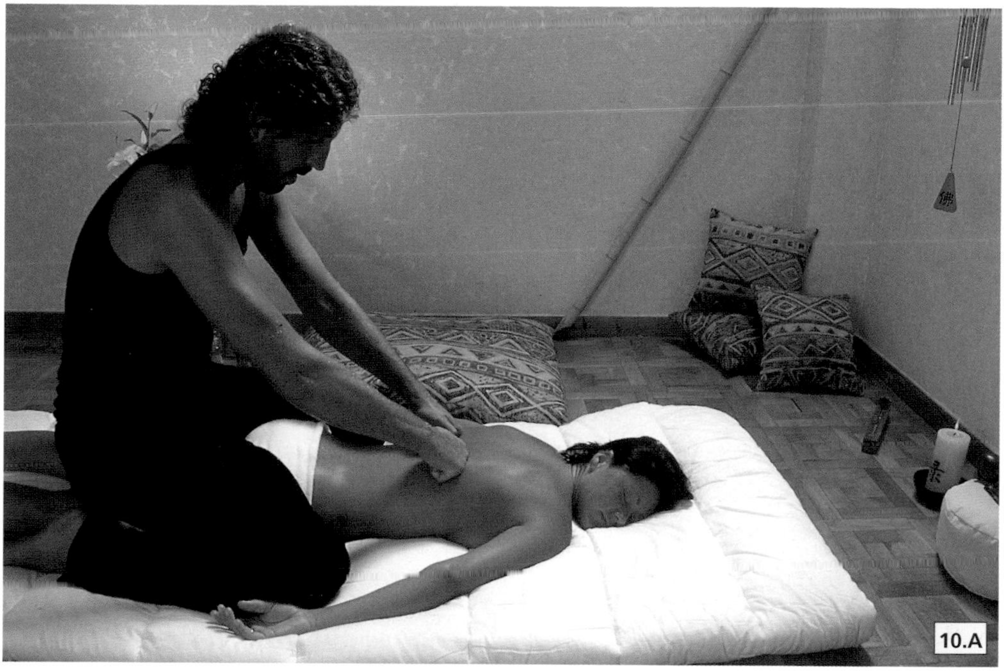

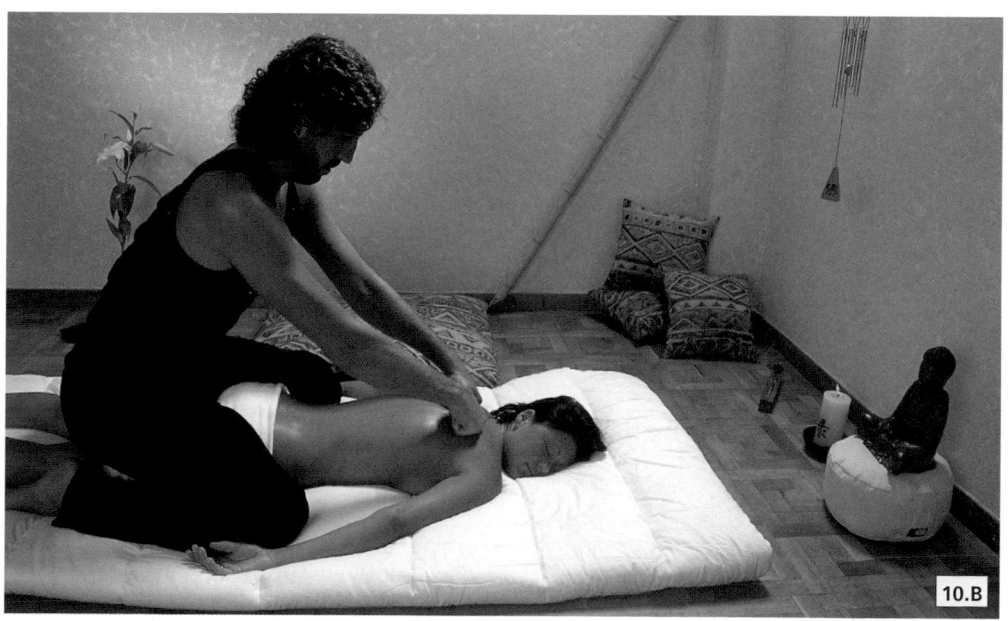

**10. Knuckles:** *Slide the knuckles along the spine (never directly over the vertebrae), in a straight line using your fists.*

### 11. Figure "U":
*With one hand over the other, make a big "U" across the back, without touching the vertebrae.*

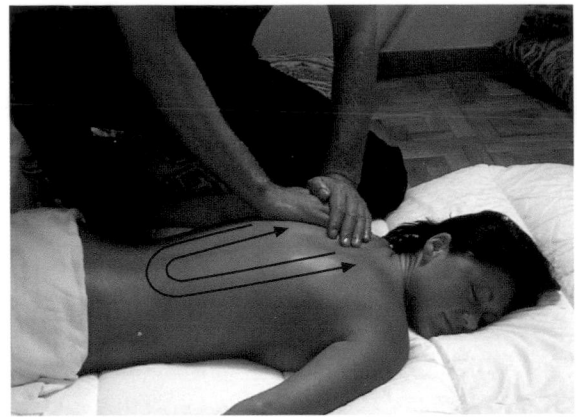

### 12. Slide along the trapezius:
*Move up and down, sliding the three middle fingers from the trapezius to the shoulder to start decompressing the upper area.*

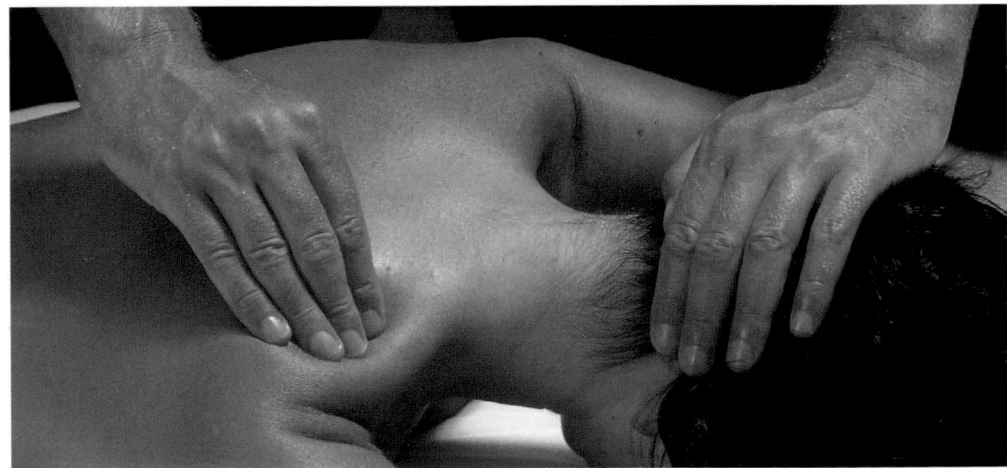

**13. Move along the trapezius:** *Using four fingers, form counterclockwise circles around the trapezius.*

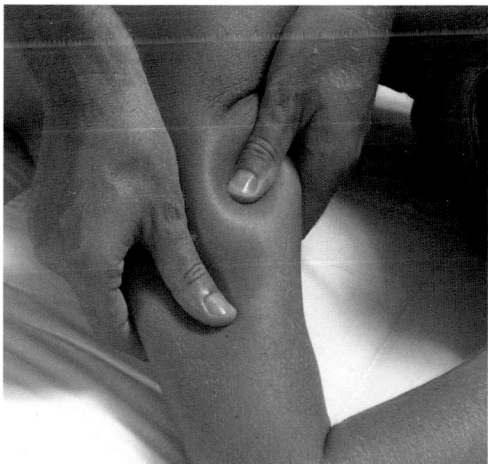

**14. Knead the shoulder:** *With the base of the hands, knead the whole deltoid area, which is where tension builds.*

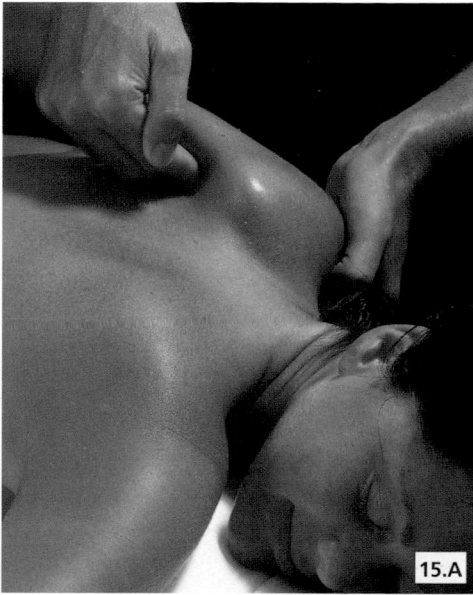

**15. Shoulder blade cleansing:** *Place a hand on one shoulder and lift the shoulder blade. Then, with the four fingers of the other hand, sink into and move the shoulder blade. Pressing only with the thumb, massage any knots and muscle contractions in a counterclockwise motion. If this area is very tense, apply this technique for longer since it is retaining repressed emotions and unresolved situations.*

15.A

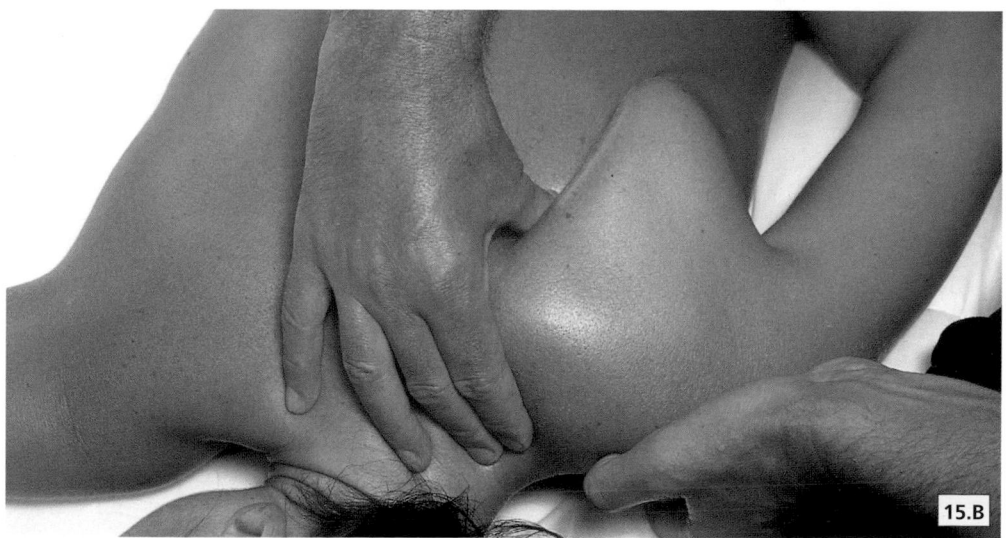

15.B

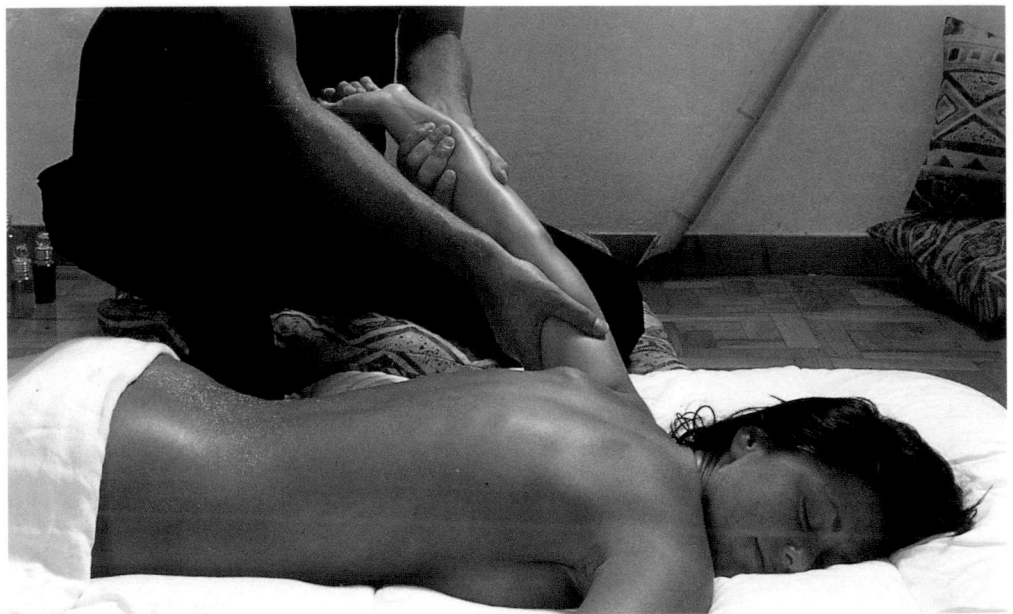

**16. Knead the arms:** *Knead the entire arm by starting at the top (biceps and triceps) and then the forearm. Do it as though you were taking off one of their gloves. This technique eliminates stress.*

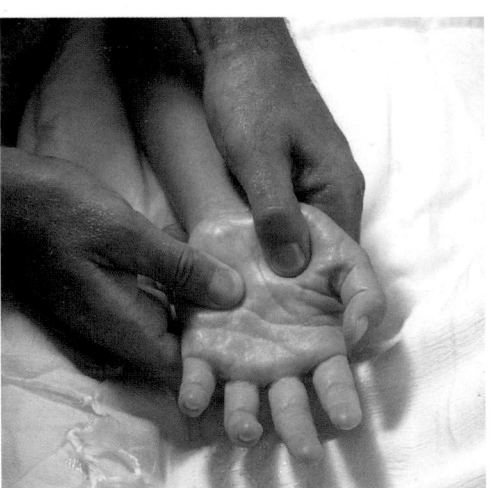

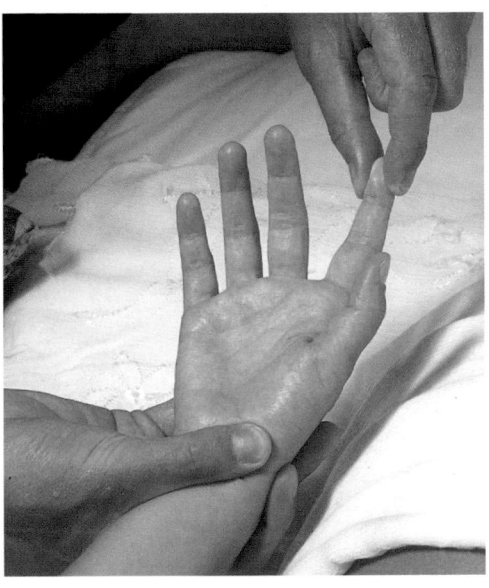

**17. Opening of the hand:** *Open their hand with your thumbs, starting at the center and moving outward.*

**18. Stimulate the fingers:** *Using your thumb and index finger, stimulate each of their fingers. There are meridian beginning and ending points at the tip of each finger.*

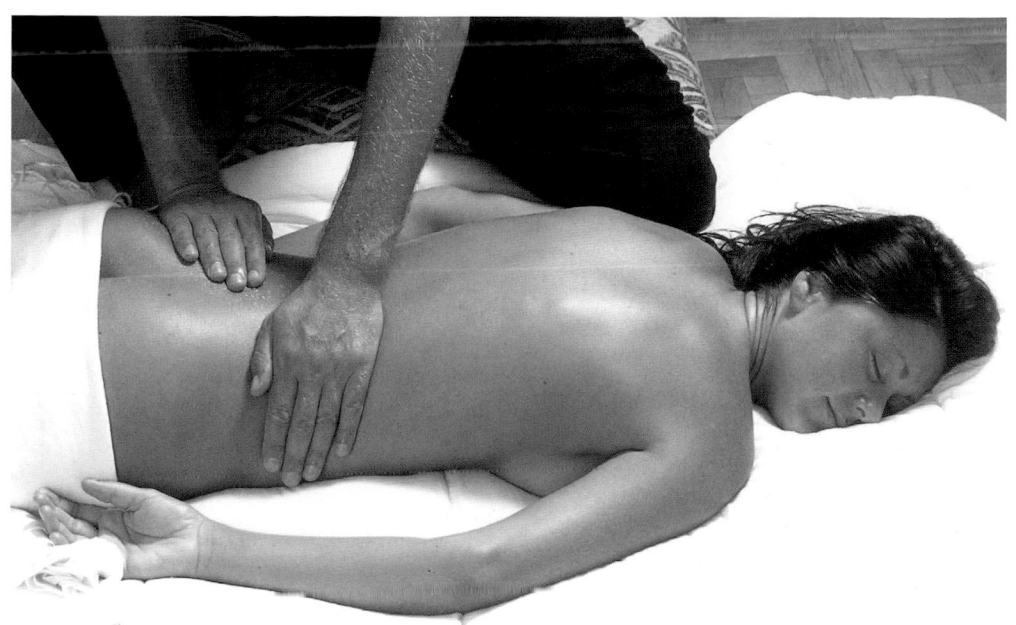

**19. Wave on the back:** *With both hands well supported, move up and down from the sacrum to the neck while making rocking motions across the back.*

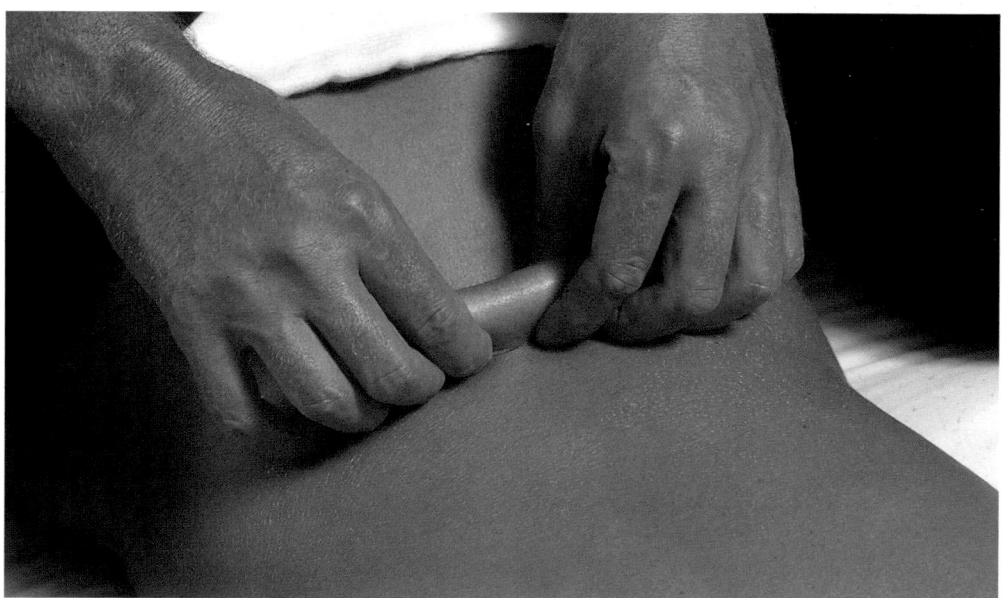

**20. Wave on the spine (kembiki technique):** *Using your thumbs and all of your fingers, grab the skin along the spine and go up along the entire back until you reach the neck. It is as if you were walking on the vertebrae.*

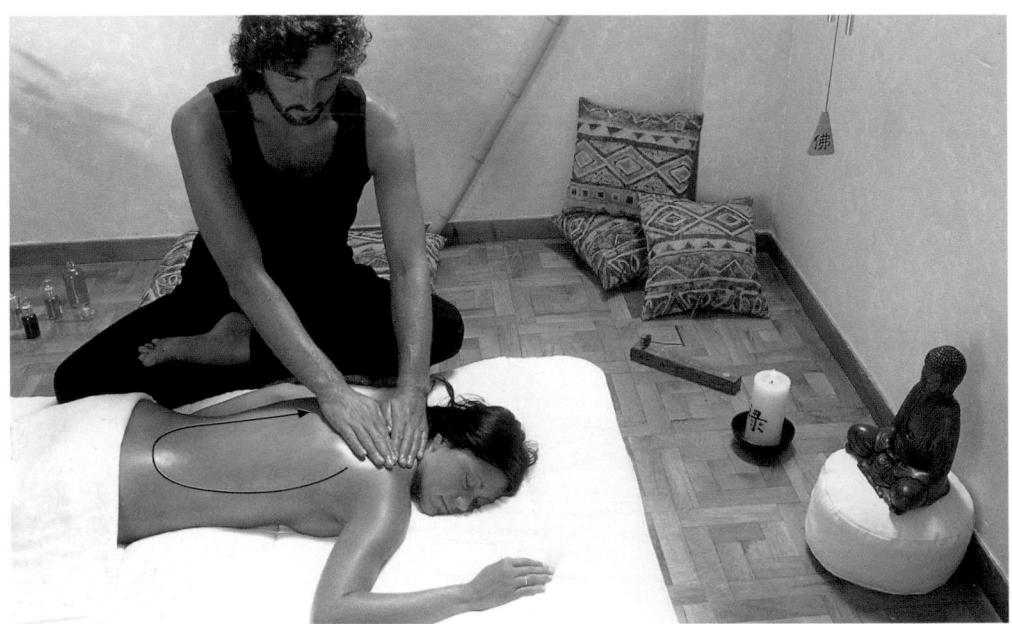

**21. Circular movements:** *Draw a large imaginary circle on the entire back from the sacrum to the neck.*

**22. On eagle wings:** *Place your hands like eagle wings in flight and move down along the spine with your thumbs. Press down slowly to stimulate with your thumbs to release any muscle tension.*

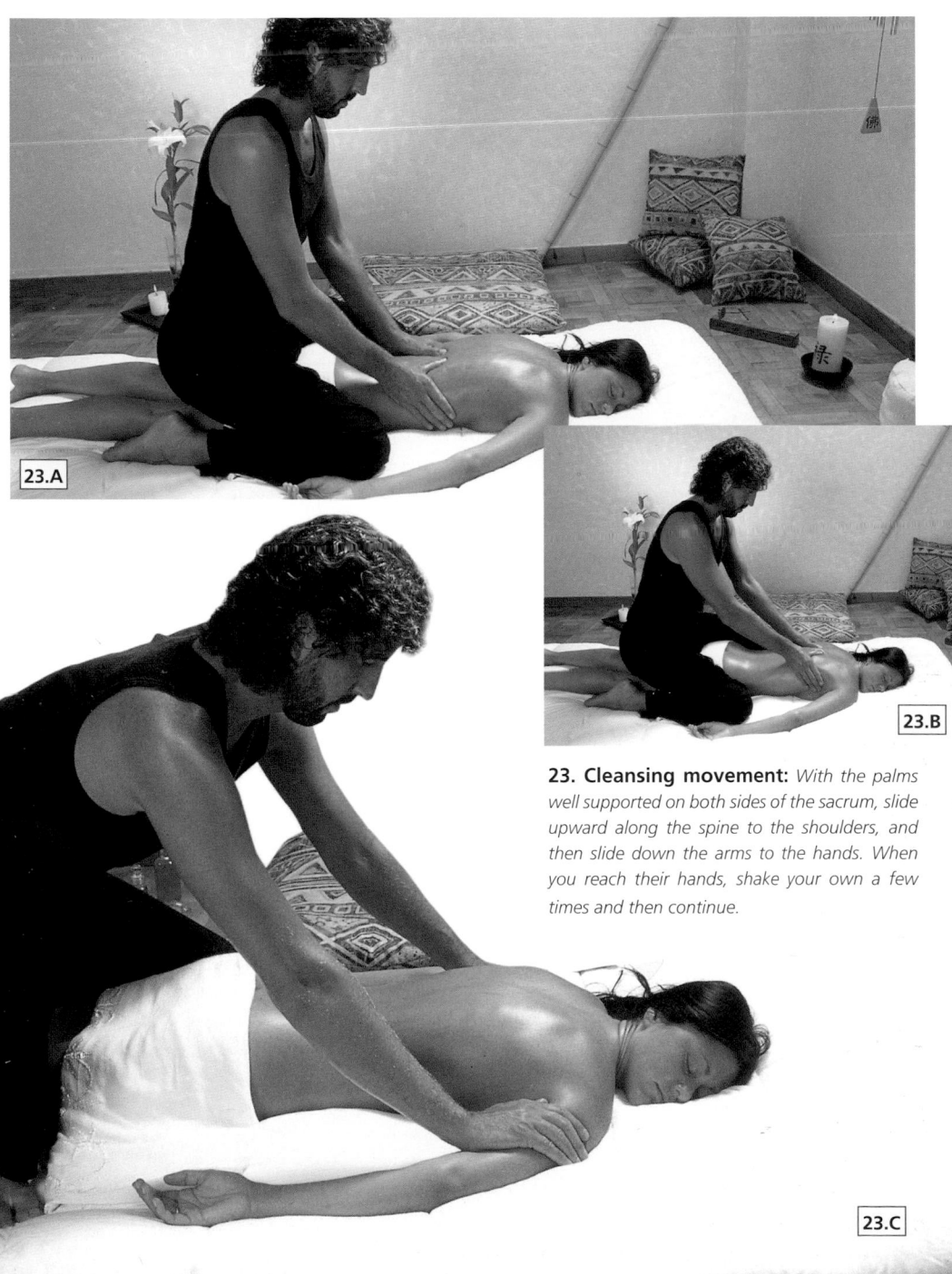

**23. Cleansing movement:** *With the palms well supported on both sides of the sacrum, slide upward along the spine to the shoulders, and then slide down the arms to the hands. When you reach their hands, shake your own a few times and then continue.*

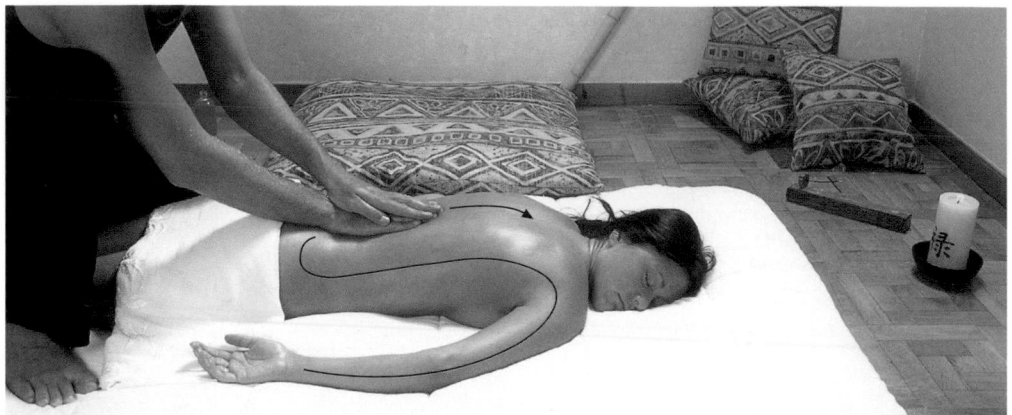

**24. Figure "S":** *With just one hand, move up from the palm of the hand to the shoulder, then down the spine to the sacrum, and then up from the sacrum to the neck. Through the hands, this technique lets in new energy that moves to the spine.*

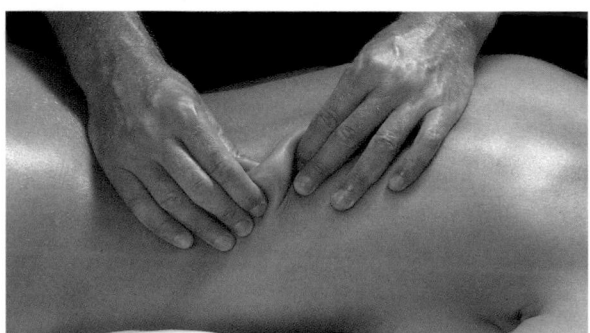

**25. Pinching:** *Using both hands, pinch down the entire back, except on the area of the vertebrae. This technique increases and moves blood supply.*

**26. The great "V":** *Place your thumbs in the middle of the back, on both sides of the spine, make a V-shape up to the shoulder: stagnant energy will be recycled, and there will be a significant increase in blood circulation.*

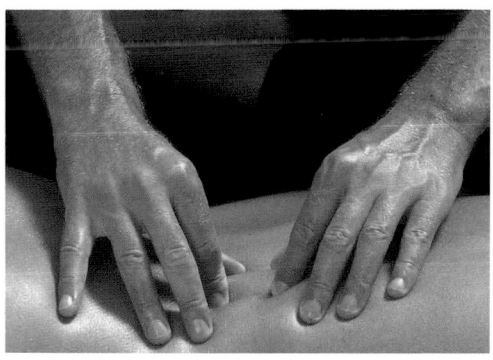

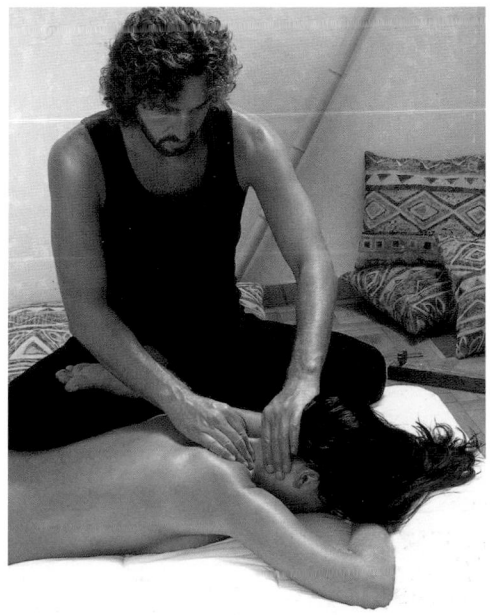

**27. Separate the vertebrae one at a time:** *With the thumb and forefinger, separate each of the vertebrae as though you were stretching them. Initiate the movement from the sacrum (fixed vertebrae) to the neck (moving vertebrae).*

**28. Mobilize the neck:**
*Using both hands at the same time, or first with one hand and then the other, make two circular movements.*

**29. Elbow sliding:**
*Bend the elbow and move down along both sides of the back without touching the vertebrae. Start at the trapezius and stop at the buttocks. You will notice that the muscles gradually soften and relax.*

## *Sitting in front of the recipient's head*

30.A

30.B

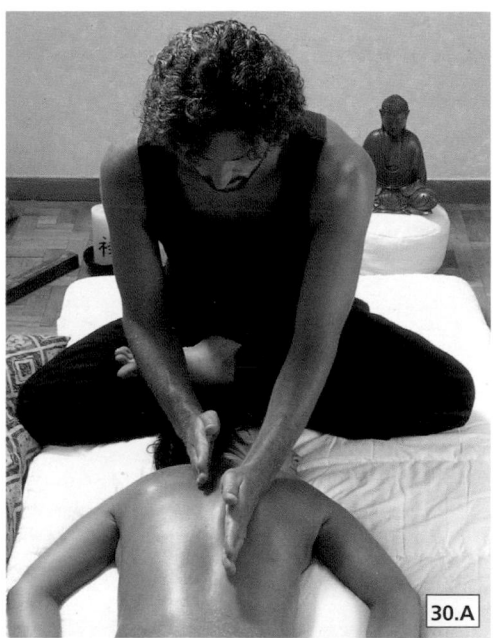

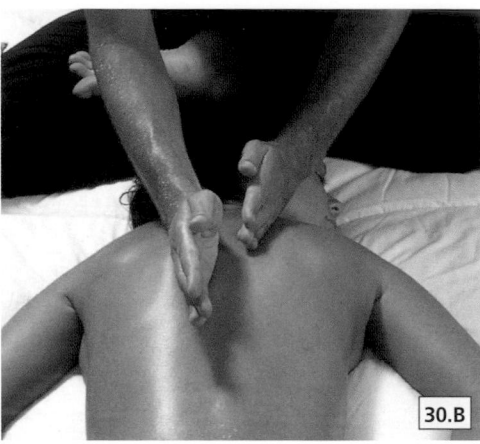

**30. Chopping between the vertebrae:** *With the edge of the hand, strongly rub from the neck area to the middle of the back. This movement produces tremendous pain relief, and it activates the circulation of blood and vital energy.*

31.A

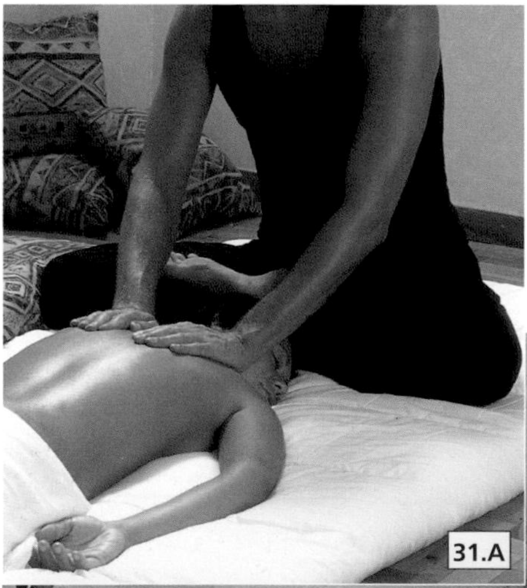

**31. Slide along the entire back:** *Slide both open hands from the center of the back to the sacrum, and then upward to the neck along both sides. Repeat this move again.*

31.B

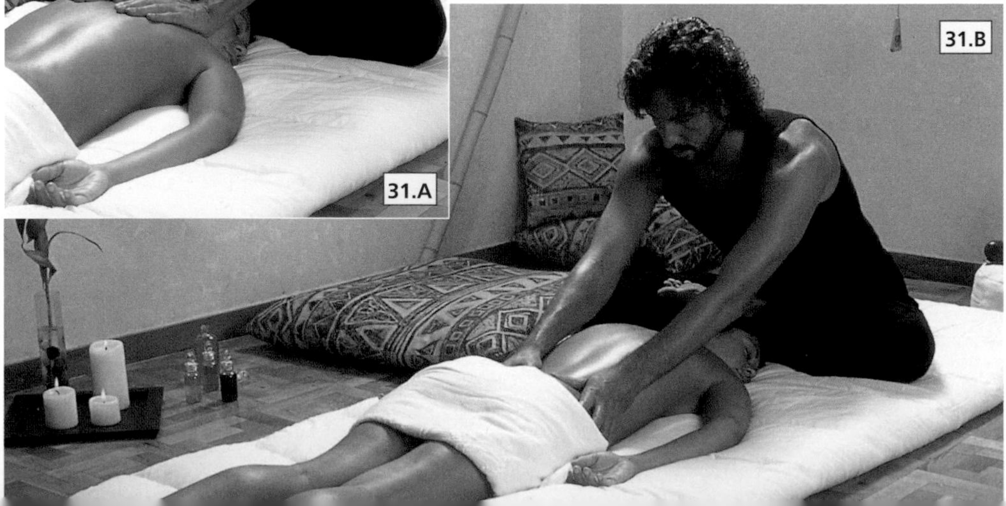

**32. Hammering:** *With clenched fists, gently tap the entire upper back area, except over the vertebrae.*

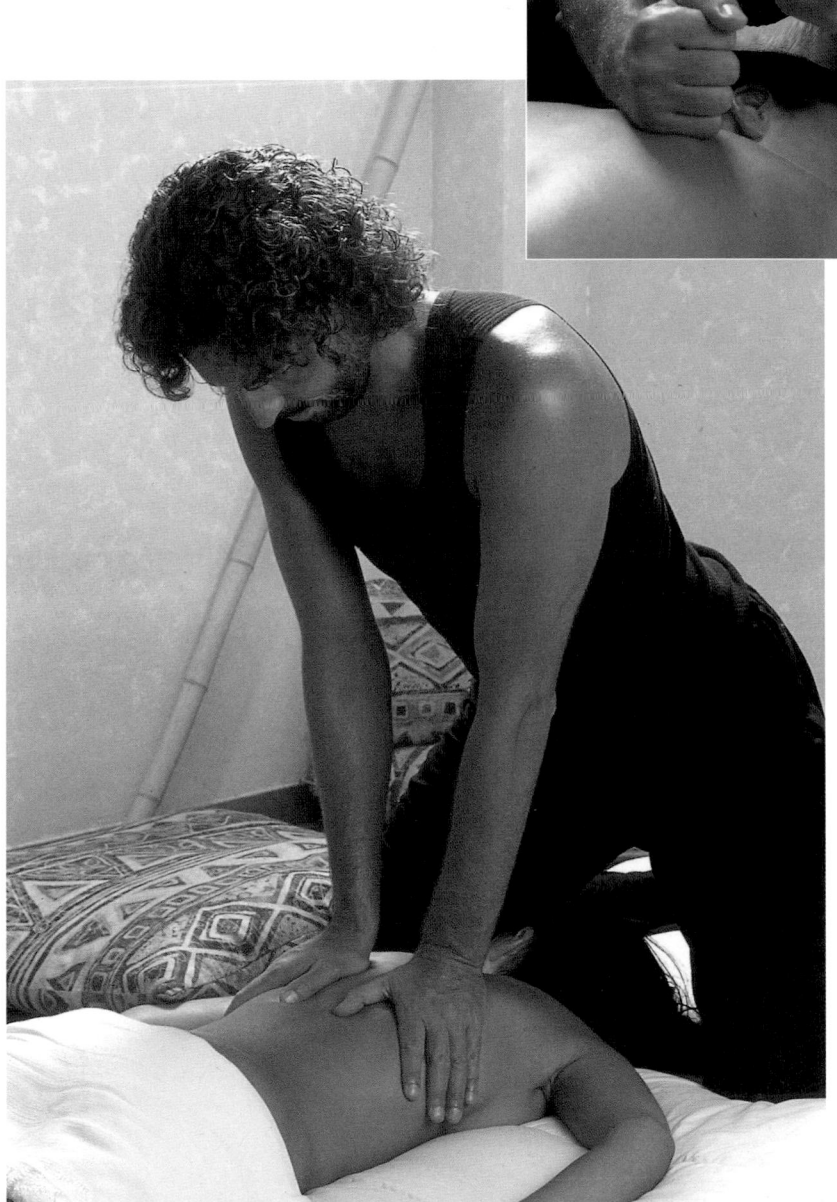

**33. Sustained pressure:** *Press with both thumbs along the entire back (five seconds on each point), from the neck to the sacrum. This technique activates a portion of the path between the meridian and the bladder.*

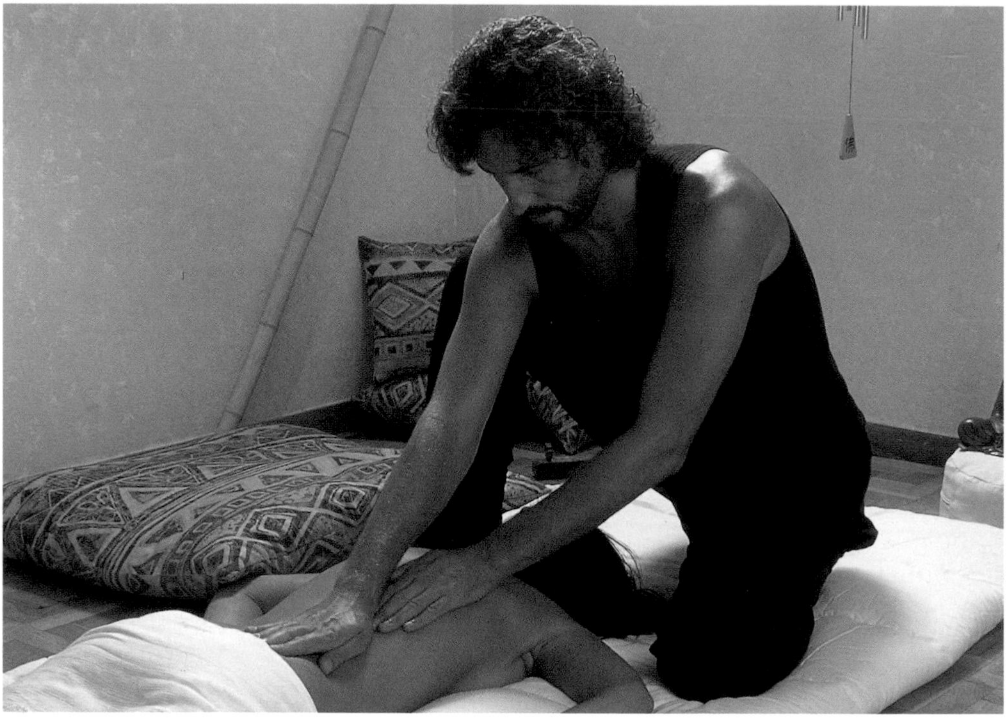

**34. Lateral slide to the arms:** *Slide both hands from the sacrum to the neck; first one side and then the other. Work on the entire sides of the back, up to the shoulder, and go down the arms until you reach the hands.*

**35. Hot stone massage:** *Have on hand a couple of stones and heat them in a saucepan over low heat (two minutes is enough to bring them up to a soothing temperature). Cover them in oil and glide them along the back, buttocks, and legs. You can switch between two sets of stones so that when one set cools off, there is another heated pair ready to be used. Work with a stone in each hand, making slow circular and undulating movements. This technique is very pleasant because it has a dual effect of pressure and enveloping warmth.*

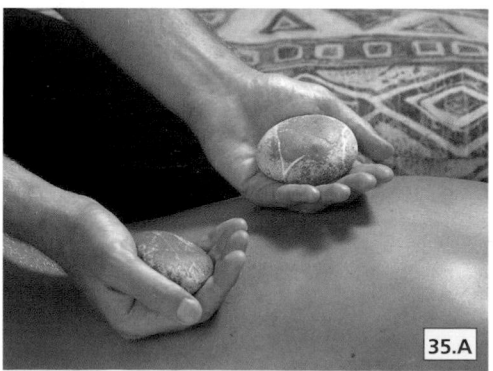
35.A

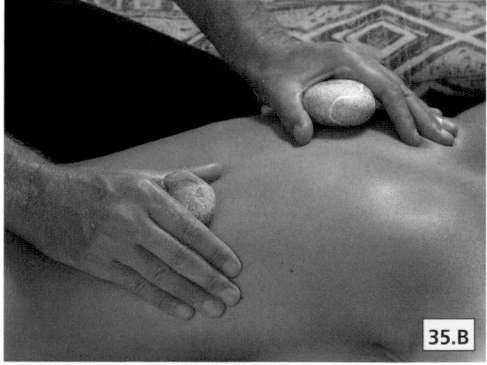
35.B

## TECHNIQUES FOR THE SACRUM AND SCIATIC NERVE

This is one of the most difficult problems to treat because the sciatic nerve is an essential part of our being, and when it does not function properly it causes pain that runs down the leg from the sacrum to the heel.

Below are several shiatsu techniques that are very effective in treating this ailment.

Each technique is to be repeated ten to twelve times.

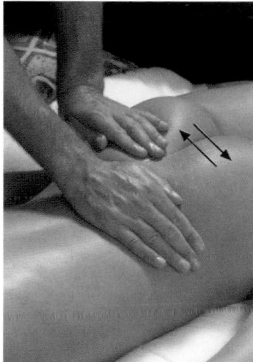

**1. Warm up:** *Alternating both hands, rub the sacrum area with horizontal movements.*

**2. Knead the buttocks:** *We mobilize this important muscle group because it is often a great source of stress. Knead the buttocks with both hands, or stamp down on them with clenched fists, by pressing then sliding your knuckles repeatedly over the entire muscle area, making a half circle motion.*

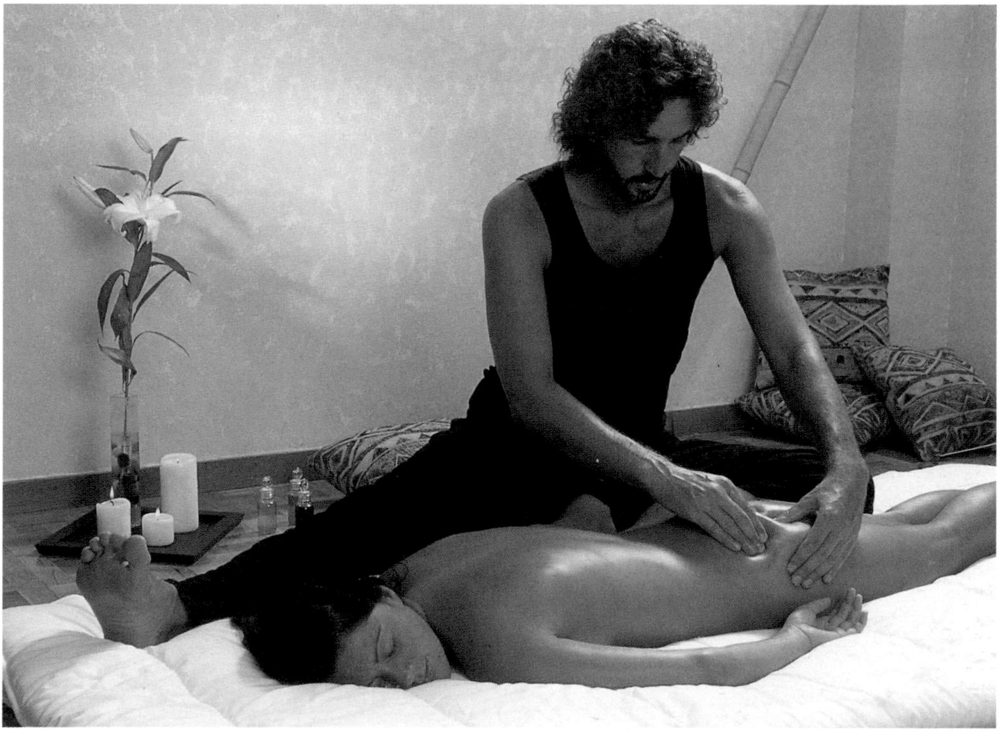

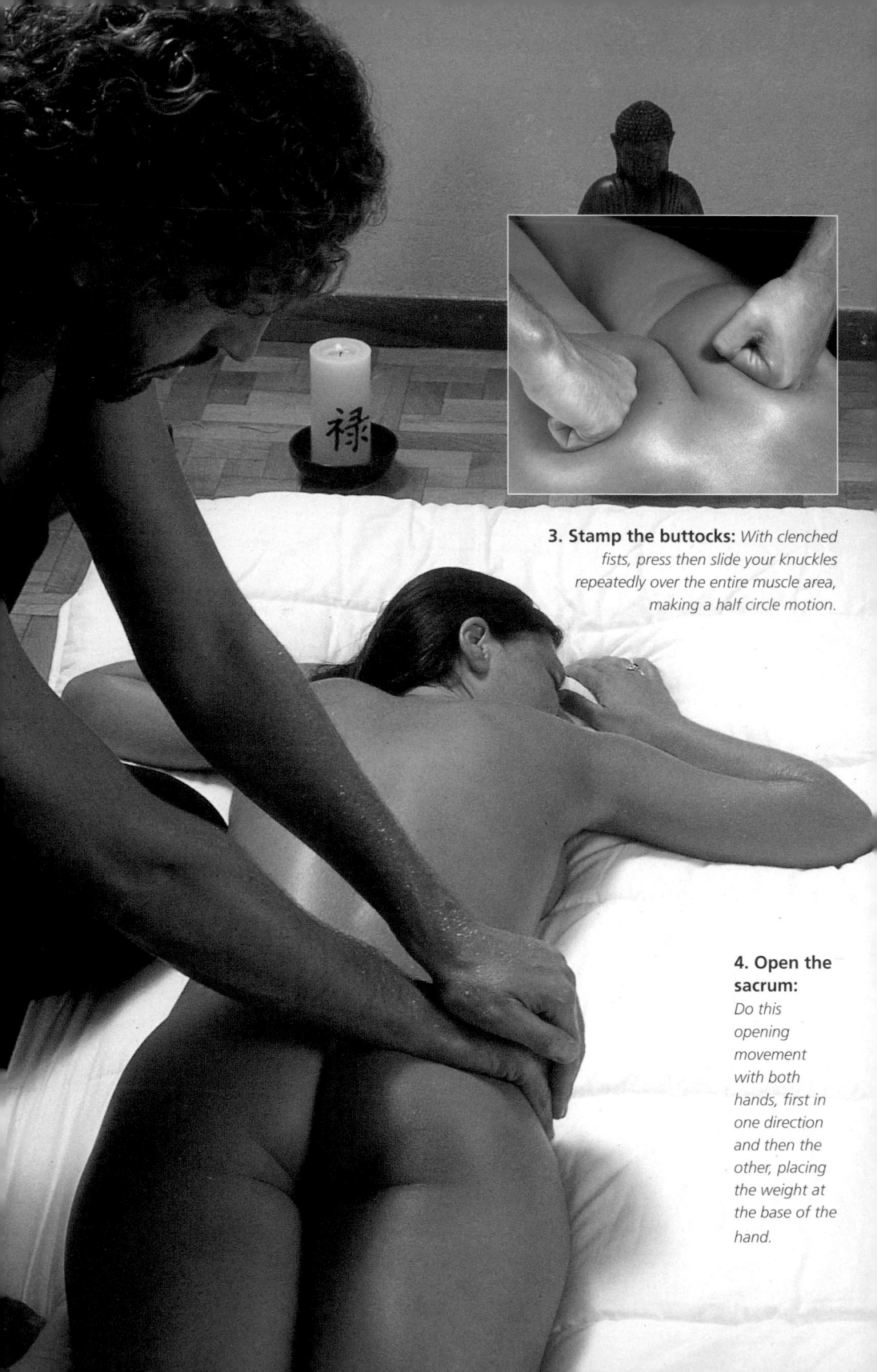

**3. Stamp the buttocks:** *With clenched fists, press then slide your knuckles repeatedly over the entire muscle area, making a half circle motion.*

**4. Open the sacrum:** *Do this opening movement with both hands, first in one direction and then the other, placing the weight at the base of the hand.*

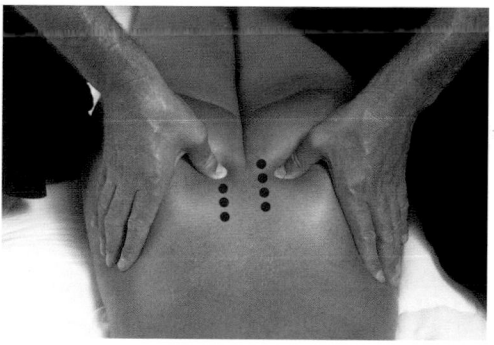 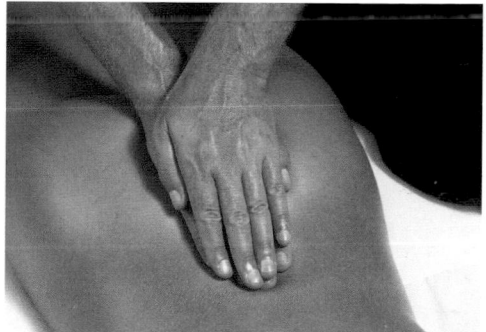

**5. Sacral foramina:** *The sacrum is the strongest bone in the body. It has four foramina on each side. Press down with your thumbs on each foramen to relieve tension. Remember to either push and pull or rotate in a particular direction.*

**6. Press the sacrum:** *Make circular movements over the sacrum with the base of the hand. If there is pain and tension, the movement should be counterclockwise, but if the recipient's energy is low, go clockwise.*

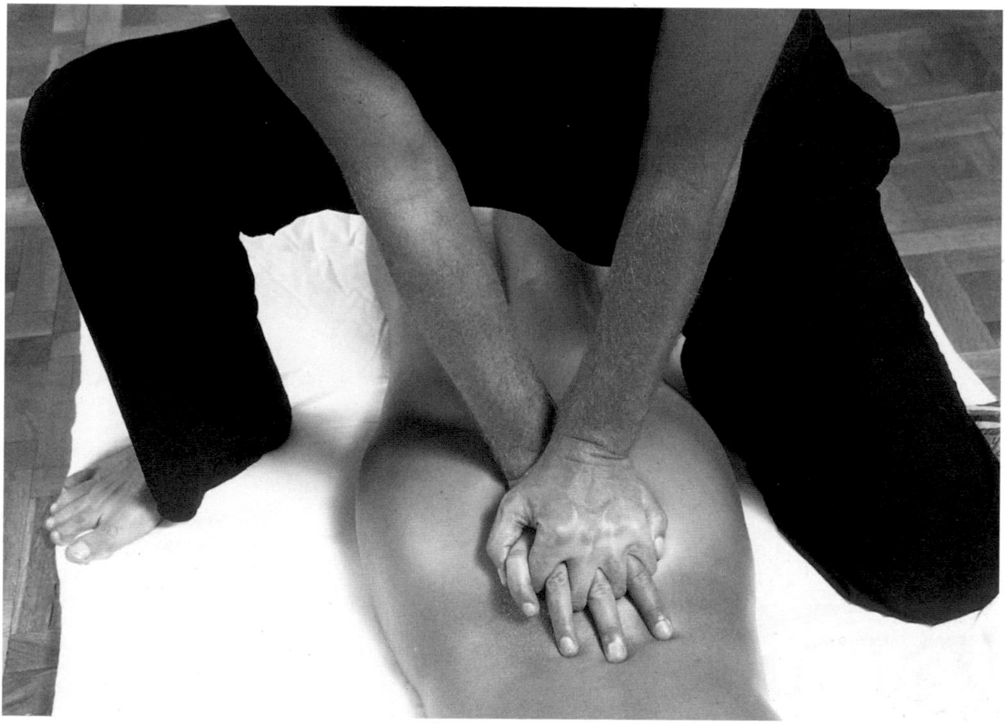

**7. Flatiron:** *With one hand over the other, quickly create stimulating friction that feels nurturing, warm, and energizing to the sacral area. The flatiron can also be used on other areas of the body, specially the back and chest.*

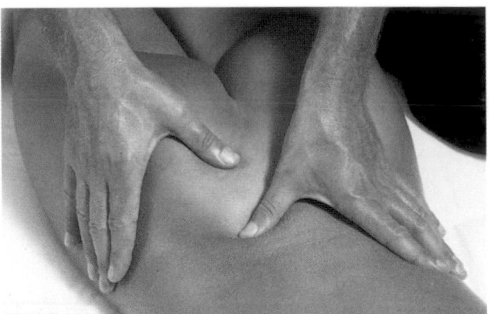

**8. Thumbs:** *With both thumbs, go up and down from the sacrum to the lower back. Go along the sides of the spine, not on the vertebrae.*

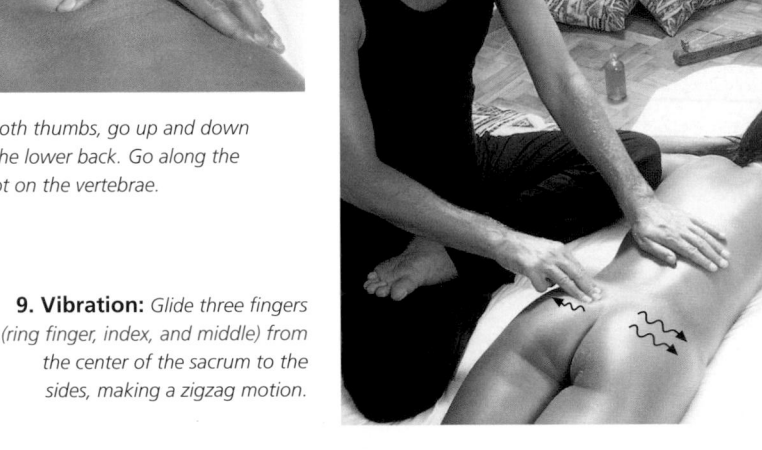

**9. Vibration:** *Glide three fingers (ring finger, index, and middle) from the center of the sacrum to the sides, making a zigzag motion.*

**10. Figure "V":** *With both hands, make a V-shape starting at the sacrum and ending at the dorsal area so as to ease pain.*

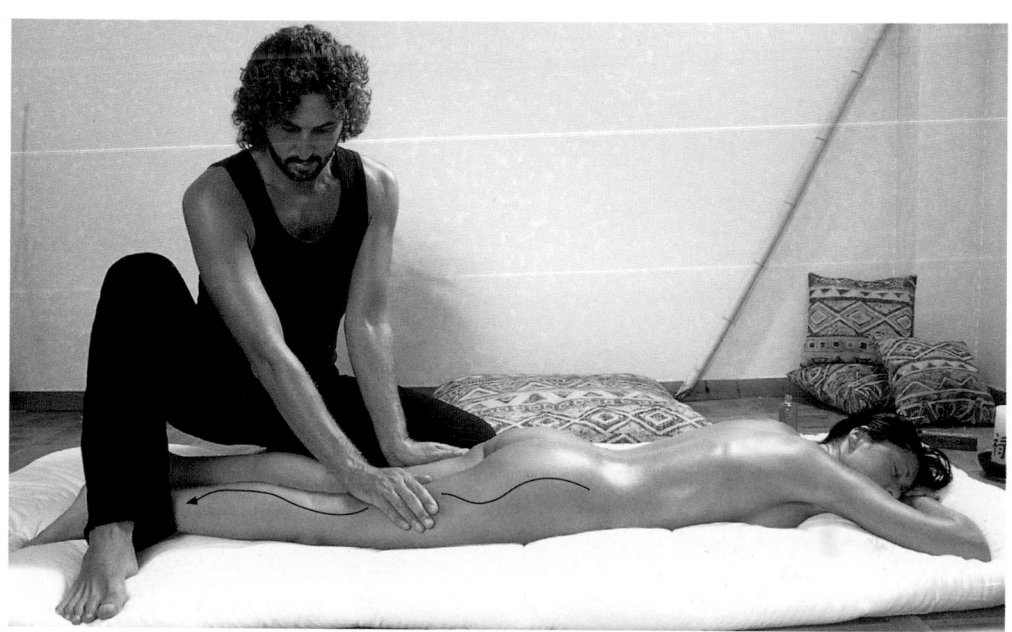

**11. Ocean waves:** *While doing a rolling motion, slide your hand from the sacrum, down the leg until you reach the heel.*

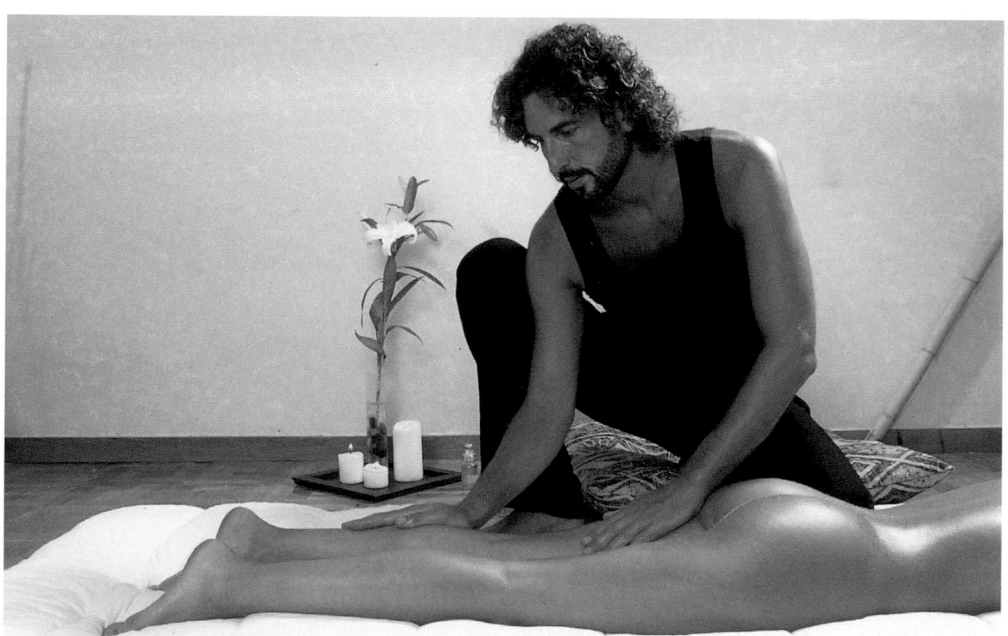

**12. Friction:** *Slide your hands up and down over the leg, starting at the buttock. This movement will generate heat and reactivate energy circulation.*

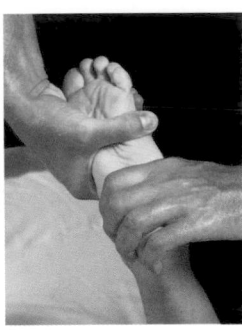

### 13. Knead the feet:
*Knead one foot and then the other as though you were wringing out clothes.*

### 14. Open the feet:
*With upward movements of the thumbs, open the entire sole.*

### 15. Stimulate the feet:
*Using your knuckles, flick along the entire foot to stimulate the area.*

### 16. Knead the heel: *Alternating both hands, knead the heel to relax it. This very important area is where the entire body weight accumulates.*

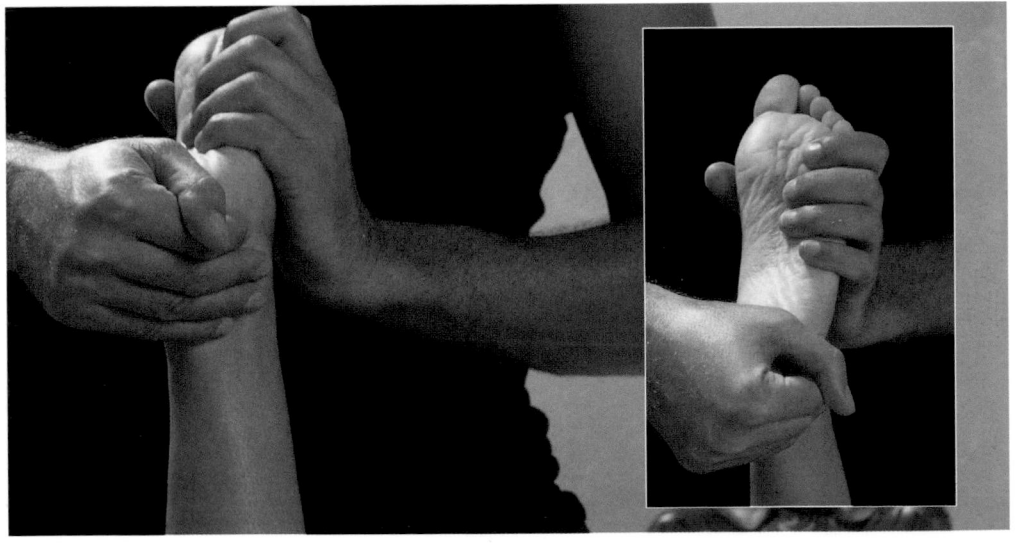

# THE PAIN RELIEF TRILOGY

There are three unique main points that can eliminate all kinds of ailments. Working on them, sedating, or stimulating them contributes to restoring health and brings almost instant pain relief because they regulate energy circulation. These points are as follows:

- Stomach 36: the divine indifference
- Large intestine 4: the great eliminator
- Liver 3: total relaxation

## ST 36

Throughout the centuries, Eastern cultures have demonstrated their love of beauty; case in point is the name ST 36 was given: divine indifference, which contains in itself a philosophy of life.

This point is one of the most important ones when it comes to circulating energy, so it is often used in acupuncture and shiatsu. It is used to treat almost every disease.

It is found at the intersection of two lines: two inches (six centimeters) from the protruding part of the patella and one inch (three centimeters) away from the tibia. Although these measurements vary according to height, weight, and bone size of each recipient, it is a hollow bone that responds to pressure.

Once located, press on it with your thumb, applying 6 to 8 pounds (3 to 4 kg) of weight on it for a few minutes.

## LI 4

LI 4 is located in the gap between the bones of the thumb and forefinger. Pressure almost always feels painful here.

This point governs the large intestine meridian, and it is often used to relieve headaches, toothaches, earaches, and shoulder pain, as well as digestive disorders and circulation problems of the arms.

## LV 3

The third point of the liver meridian is located in the gap between the bones of the big toe and the second toe. It is particularly useful for treating liver and stomach problems or eye disorders, but it is also used for a variety of other problems.

### Suggestions

- Use all three points in every session.
- As with all shiatsu points, press for three to five minutes to tone, and for five to seven minutes to sedate.
- Be aware that you are working with energy, so always assume a meditative, thoughtful, and perceptive state toward everything that happens.
- Do not use shiatsu points on pregnant women, and always remember that every recipient is God in human form.

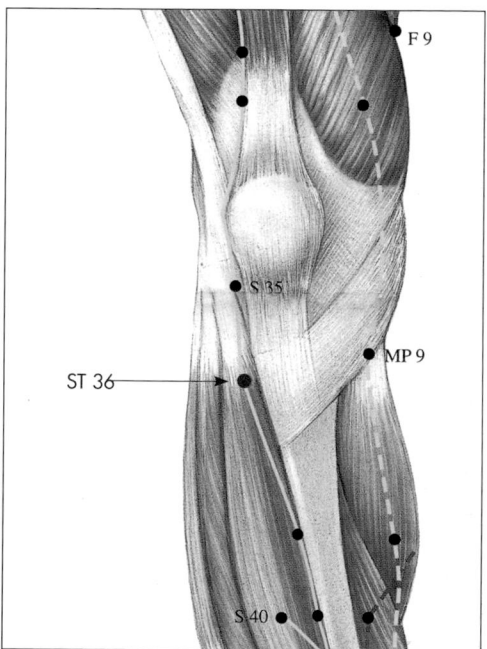

*ST 36, the divine indifference.*

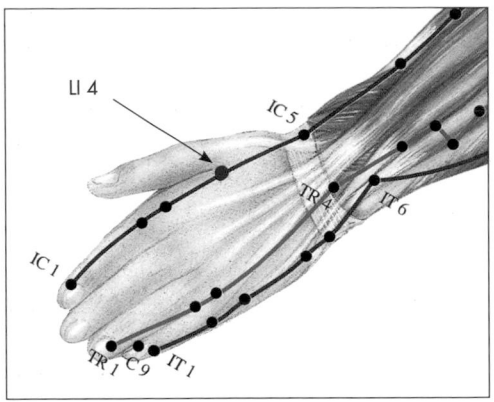

*Large intestine, the great eliminator.*

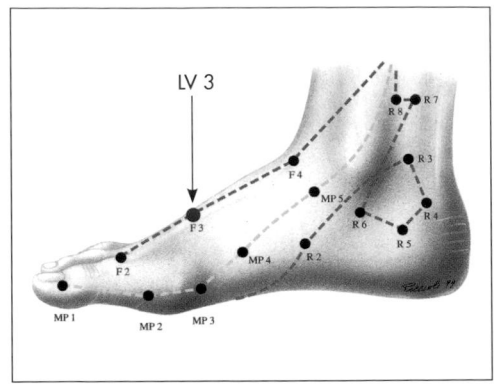

*Liver 3, total relaxation.*

## ZEN SHIATSU POINTS TO TARGET SPECIFIC PROBLEMS

Below you will find a detailed list of points that counteract certain ailments and problems. Look them up on the meridian charts to familiarize yourself with their locations (starting at page 119). Memorization comes with practicing, learning, and loving your work.

---

### MAIN DISORDERS AND THEIR TREATMENT THROUGH ZEN SHIATSU

**Asthma:** BL 13, BL 17, BL 23; CV 17; LU 5, LU 6, LU 7, LU 9; ST 36; GB 21, GB 34; LI 4; LI 10.

**Sciatica:** BL 25, BL 36, BL 37, BL 54; 30 VB, GB 31, GB 34, GB 40; ST 30, ST 31, ST 34.

**Diarrhea:** ST 25, ST 36; SP 9; CV 6; BL 23, BL 25, BL 32; KI 16.

**Headache and migraine:** GB 8 GB 20, GB 21; BL 10, BL 17, BL 60;
LI 4; LU 6 LU 7; LV 3; GV 20; TE 3 TE 5; ST 36.

**Neck pain and trapezius:** GB 20, GB 21; BL 10, BL 11; SI 3, SI 11, SI 12, SI 14; LU 7; LI 4; LI 11; HT 3.

**Shoulder pain:** LI 4; LI 11 LI 14; LI 15; TE 14; SI 9, SI 10, SI 11, SI 12, SI 14.

**Elbow pain:** LI 10 LI 11; GB 34; LU 5.

**Pain in the tow:** LV 3; 4 SP.

**Pain in the thumb:** LI 4; LU 10.

*Rotate the thumb and pull vigorously several times mobilizing the joints.*

**Ankle pain:** GB 34, GB 40; ST 41; KI 3, KI 6, KI 7; SP 6; BL 60.

**Wrist pain:** LU 7; HT 7.

**Pain in the lower back:** BL 23, BL 25, BL 32, BL 36, BL 37, BL 40, BL 54, BL 57, BL 60; GB 30; GV 4.

**Knee pain:** ST 34, ST 35, ST 36; KI 10; LV 8; BL 40, BL 57; GB 34; SP 9, SP 10.

**Constipation:** ST 25, ST 36; LI 4; BL 25.

**Insomnia:** SP 6; ST 36; HT 7; LU 6 LU 8; KI 1; LV 3.

**Irritable bowel:** ST 25, ST 36; CV 6 CV 12; SP 6; LI 4; LI 10 LI 11; KI 16; BL 20, BL 21, BL 25, BL 32.

**Sinusitis:** LI 4; LI 20; BL 2; LU 5.

---

## HARA: CENTER OF VITAL ENERGY

Hara or *dantian* is a power center that is very important in the East. It can be divided into two zones: the upper hara (in the stomach) and lower hara (3 inches below the navel).

This point is the center of life and death, hence its designation as a point where to commit suicide, the so-called *harakiri*.

If the hara is well-balanced, we get to enjoy good health, self-esteem, vitality, smooth breathing, positive attitude towards living, creative drive, determination, and good mood. However, this point also holds psychological remnants: repressed anger, worry, anxiety, low emotions, fear, sexual repression, and low self-esteem. All these deteriorate the hara and overload it with negative energy.

Massaging this point is called *ampuku* and its purpose is to unlock, clean, and boost energy. This technique moves and releases low energy, first through urine, and then through breathing, fasting, and any other technique that is put into practice.

To do the *ampuku* technique, imagine a clock and place one hand at 12 o'clock, on the pit of the stomach, and the other at 6 o'clock, below the navel, on the lower hara. Apply gentle pressure on these two points using three fingers (Figure 1), rotate counterclockwise to sedate, and clockwise to stimulate.

Locate 1 o'clock to the right of 12 o'clock, at a distance of two finger-lengths, and continue this way until you get to 5 o'clock. Work on these points using your right thumb (Figure 2). The remaining points (7, 8, 9, 10, and 11 o'clock) are also worked on with the thumb.

Two important things can happen in this zone: palpitation or crackling. Palpitations indicate that it has gotten enough energy and we must switch to the next point; while crackling (like when you are hungry) indicates that it is welcoming energy through stimulation and we can continue.

Work on each point for one or two minutes, pushing and pulling, or rotating with the thumb.

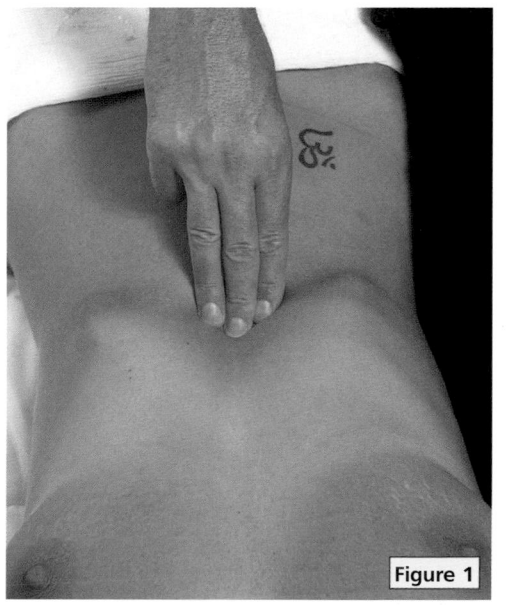

Figure 1

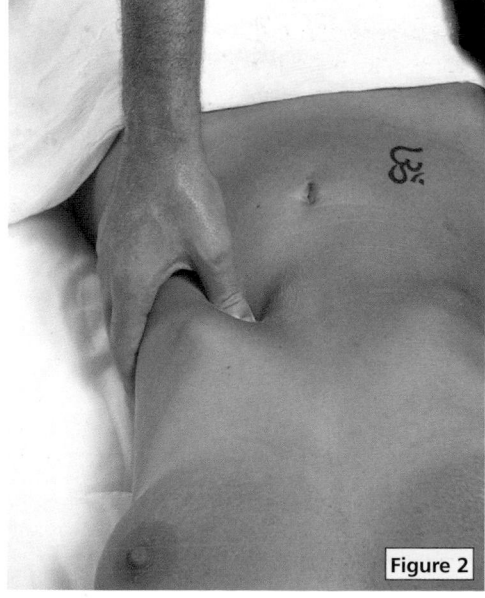

Figure 2

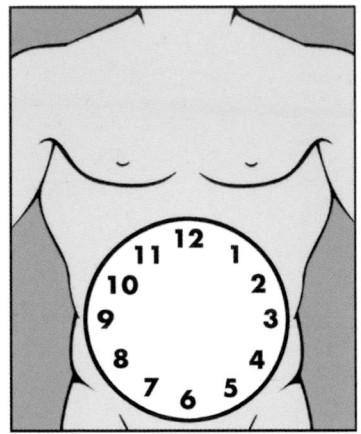

- It is a delicate zone, so you should be cautious when working on it. Remember that you are stimulating not only the internal organs, but also old emotional conflicts and unresolved feelings.
- Use it specifically to counteract low energy, depression, stress, nervousness, anxiety, fears, worry, and low sexual energy.

## SHIATSU ON THE FACE AND HEAD

The head has the most yang in the body and it keeps all energy needed for daily mental activity. Massaging it helps relieve tension caused by thoughts, especially negative thoughts.

Thought is energy. When a thought is held for long enough, it forms an idea that in turn becomes a belief. Beliefs keep us from truly living and experiencing life.

The purpose of my work is getting people to give up their beliefs and start living in the present. Conflicting beliefs have led to countless deaths and unnecessary wars. Consumed with stereotypes and false pretenses for the future, humans have lost the ability to live in the present. The unknowable future causes anxiety and concern, while living in past memories makes us feel melancholy. The present is eternity.

The education we received, as well as fear itself, projects our thoughts forward into the future or backward into the past: "You have to study so you can become somebody"; "Save money so you can take care of yourself later"; "Life used to be better"; "If you do not have a degree, no one will respect you"; etc. These messages have destroyed the minds of people and caused divisions among them, offering them something that they will never attain: being the best in comparison to their peers. The future always has the same pattern.

Both Zen and shiatsu place a special emphasis on the fact that the mind does not stop to savor the delights of the present.

The head massage silences the mind and stops the messy uninterrupted flow of thoughts. The recipient can come closer to living in the present by practicing breathing. This massage also works on the head's nerve endings, allowing the yin and yang energies throughout the body to become harmonized and act as a team.

For cerebral, deep thinkers who are concerned with their future, start the massage at the head. This is where they have accumulated an excess of energy (stress).

### Benefits

- Increases the supply of fresh oxygen to the brain.
- Relaxes the nervous system and eliminates fatigue brought on by mental stress and exhaustion.
- Improves circulation of the protective element that is the cerebrospinal fluid, which is our lifeblood.
- Increases the secretion of growth hormones and enzymes necessary for the development of brain cells.
- Increases *qi* energy levels in the brain.
- Slows down hair loss, baldness, and premature graying.

# SHIATSU ON THE FACE AND HEAD

**1. Opening of the head and back of the neck:** *Grab the head with both hands and glide them gently, first one and then another, along the nape. This technique allows the recipient to start "opening up" the contents of the head.*

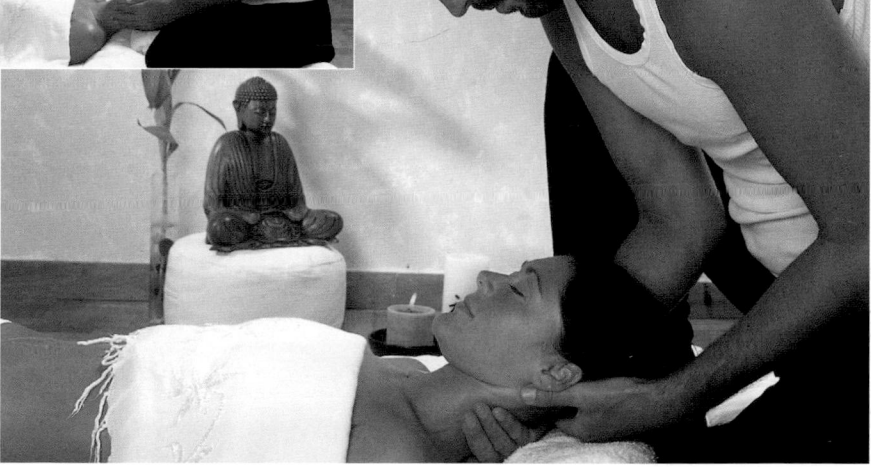

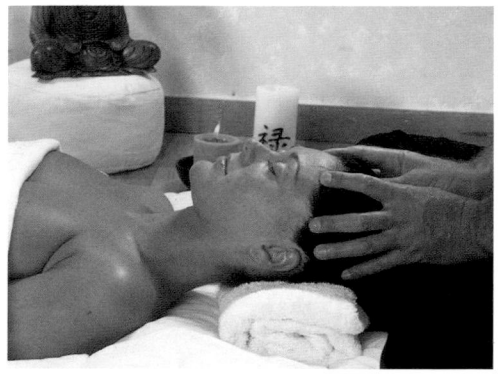

**2. Stimulate the scalp:** *With all ten fingers, massage the entire scalp as if you were washing the head. This will stimulate all the nerve endings of the skull and relieve tension. It also helps move and release stagnant yang energy. It is very pleasant.*

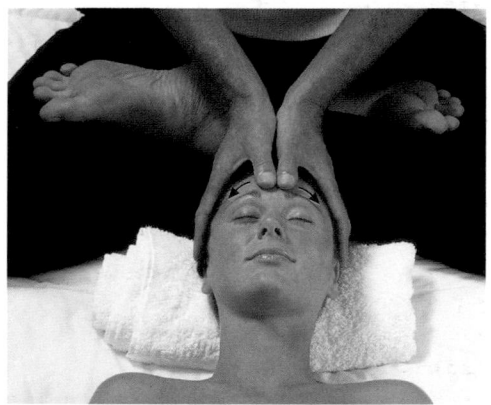

**3. Forehead opening:** *Open the forehead with both thumbs, from the third eye outward. This helps relieve continuous thought flow by centering the recipient.*

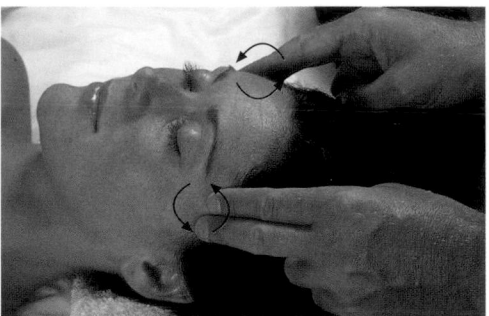

**4. Circles:** *With your index and middle finger, make very gentle circular movements on the temples.*

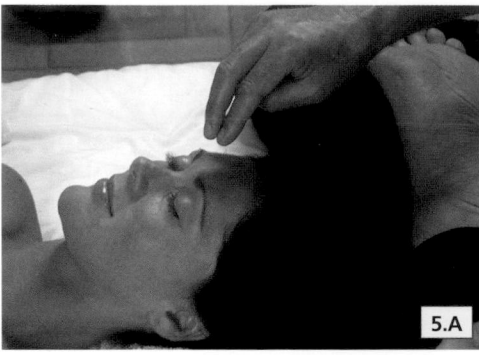

5.A

5.B

**5. Taps:** *With the index and middle finger, tap gently several times on the third eye.*

**6. Press on the eyes:** *With your thumbs, press lightly and smoothly under the eyes.*

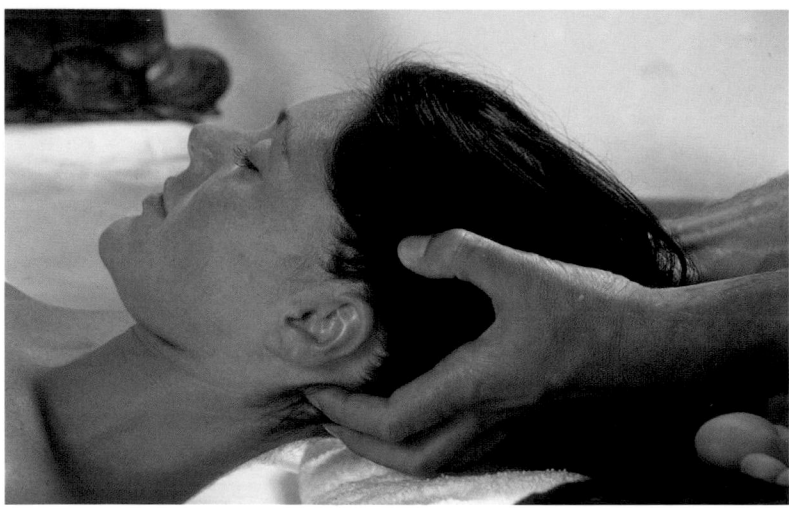

**7. Slide along the neck:**
*With both hands, actively massage the neck.*

**8. Lip opening:** *Massage the lower and upper lip under the nose, opening with both thumbs. This last area is important because it joins the conception vessel and the governor vessel.*

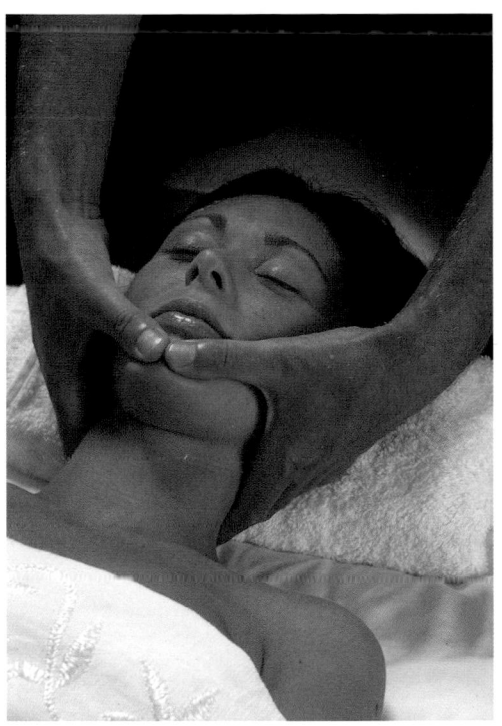

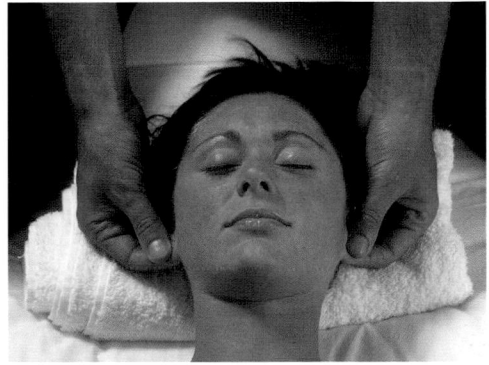

**9. Press the ears:** *Stimulate both ears simultaneously, starting at the lobes. Just like feet, ears hold all of the body points.*

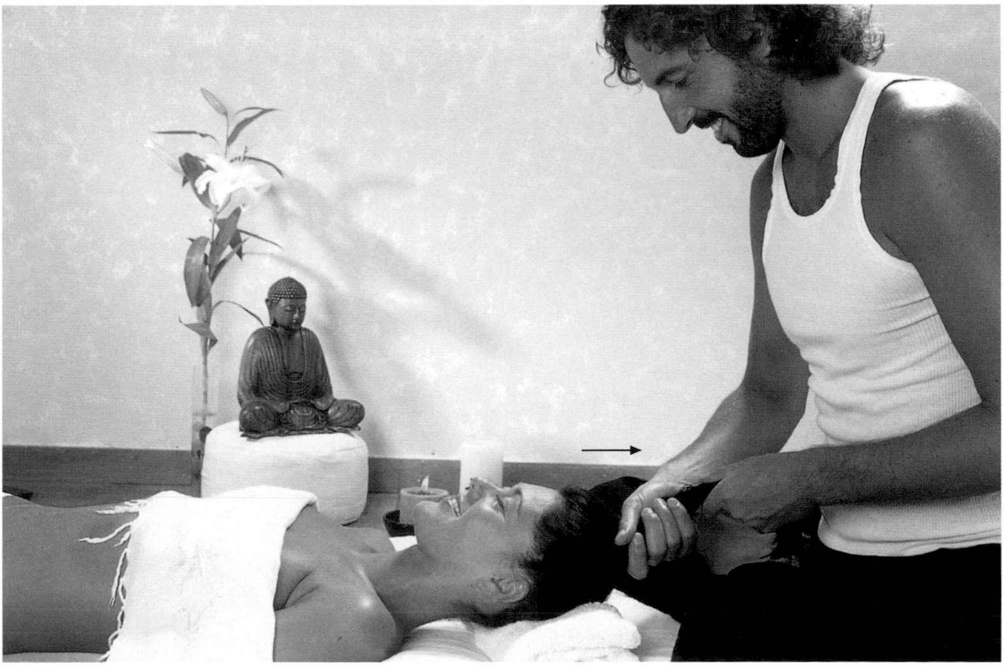

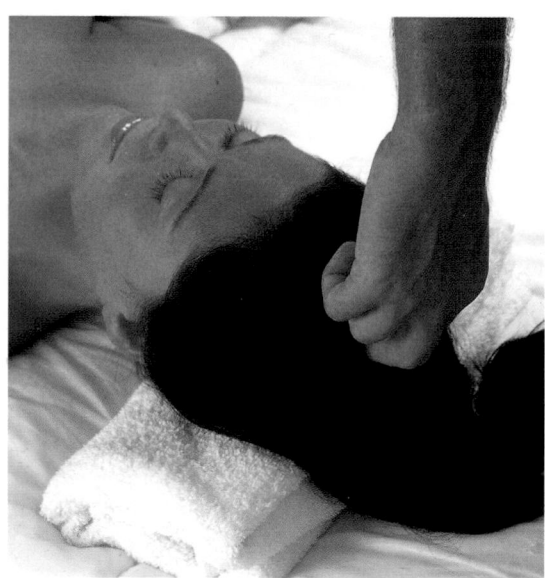

**11. Stimulate the middle of the head:** *Gently press your thumb on the middle of the head, from the hairline to the top of the head.*

**13. Press the neck:** *Using both middle fingers, press the hollow area of the neck. This will relieve headaches.*

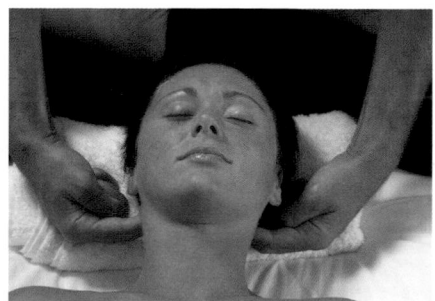

**12. Tap the crown:** *Using the index and middle finger, tap on the crown area (seventh chakra).*

### 14. Pinch the eyebrows:
*Using your index finger and thumb, pinch along the eyebrows.*

### 15. Relax the face:
*Slide your hands gently from the chin to the top of the skull. You must perform this massage with love and gentleness. Then place your hands on the recipient's closed eyes for a minute, visualizing that their head is full of light and serenity.*

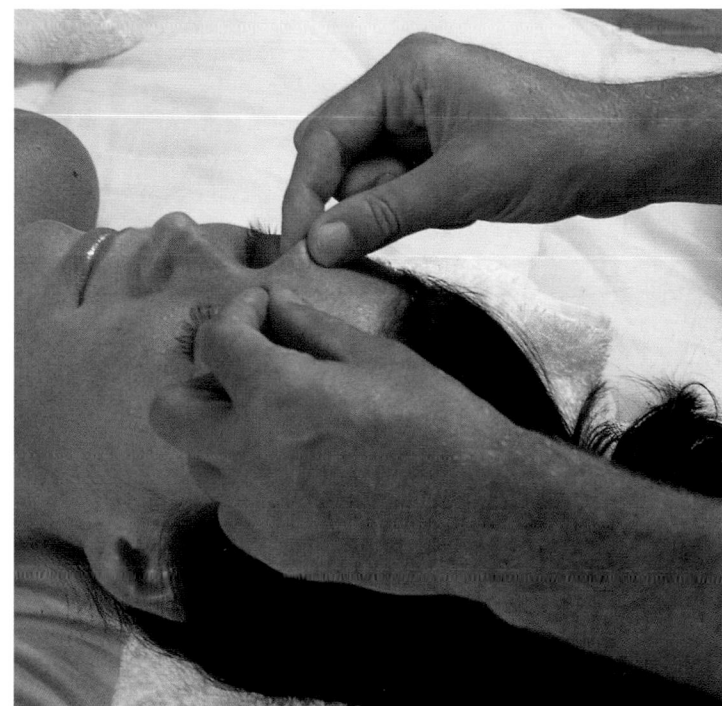

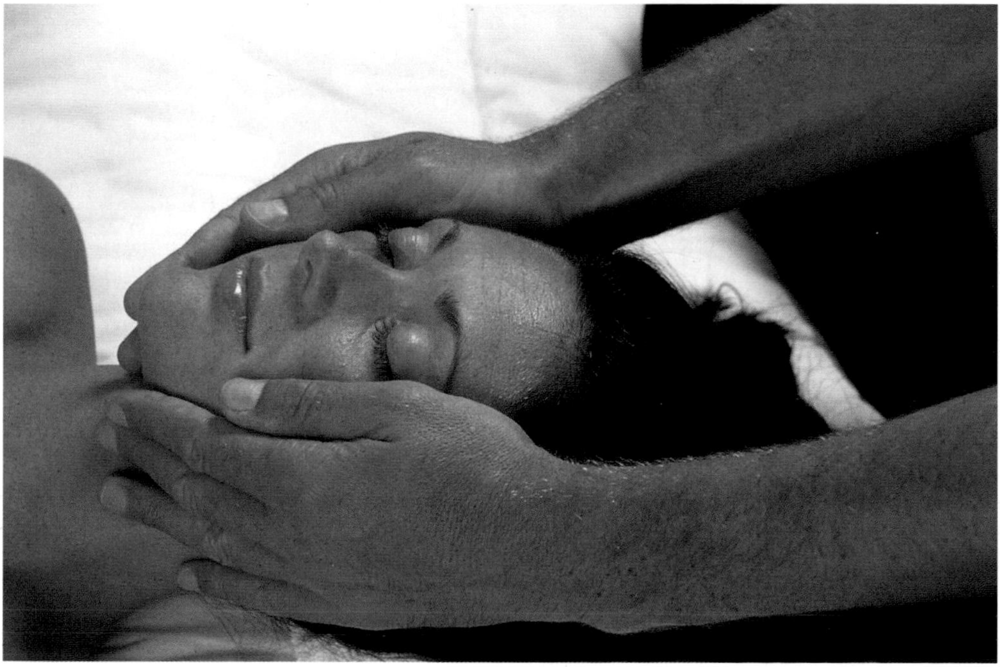

## THE KEYS TO ZEN SHIATSU

Holds help decompress joints and strengthen muscles. They also have a beneficial effect on the meridians because the movements stimulate the them and activate the flow of *qi*.

### Benefits

- Opens the meridians.
- Stretches the muscles and releases all blockages.
- Unlocks energy and emotions.
- Creates a sensation of well-being, ease, and relaxation.
- It is especially beneficial to athletes and physically and emotionally rigid people.
- Works as a warm up for other techniques.
- Is excellent after physical activity or when we are very tired.

### Suggestions

- Do not practice holds on anyone who weighs more than you.
- Not recommended for pregnant women.
- For all holds, make a good foundation with your legs, inhale before straining, and exhale when you stop.

### Face down

Apply each hold five times.

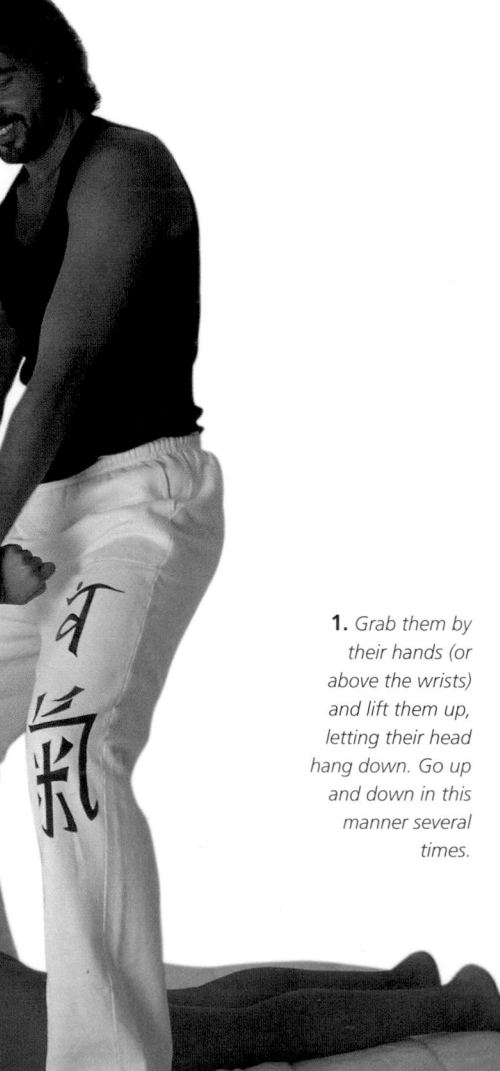

**1.** *Grab them by their hands (or above the wrists) and lift them up, letting their head hang down. Go up and down in this manner several times.*

**2.** *Take one arm and the opposite foot and lift simultaneously. Then switch. This allows for an excellent stretch.*

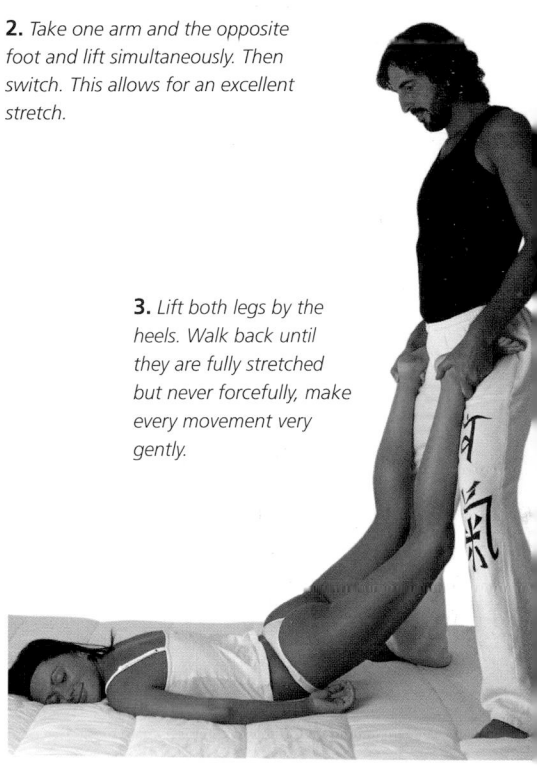

**3.** *Lift both legs by the heels. Walk back until they are fully stretched but never forcefully, make every movement very gently.*

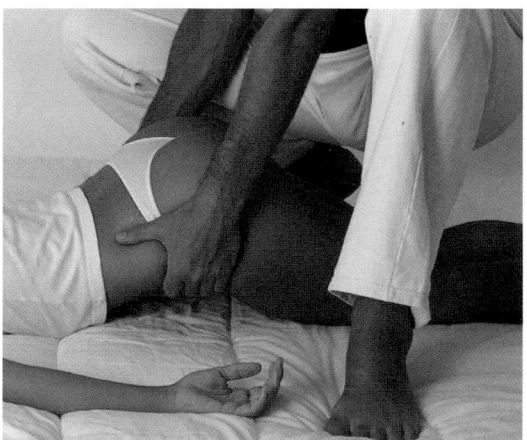

**5.** *Stand behind the legs and bring both heels up to the buttocks. This hold stretches the quadriceps deeply.*

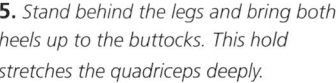

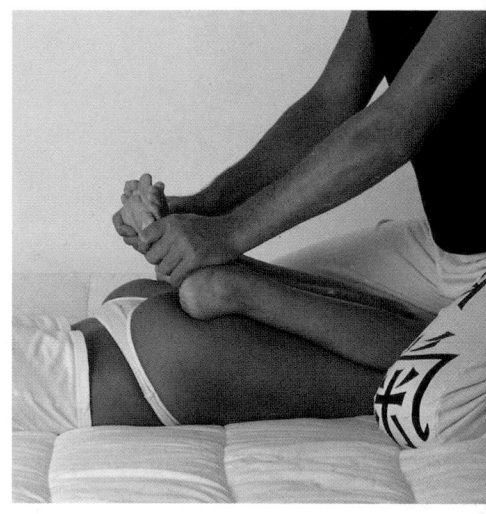

**4.** *Hold the hip bones and lift then lower them several times to decompress blockages in the area of the sacrum and hip. Then make small rotations. This technique is important because many people feel "anchored" in this area due to repression, sexual fears, and traumas.*

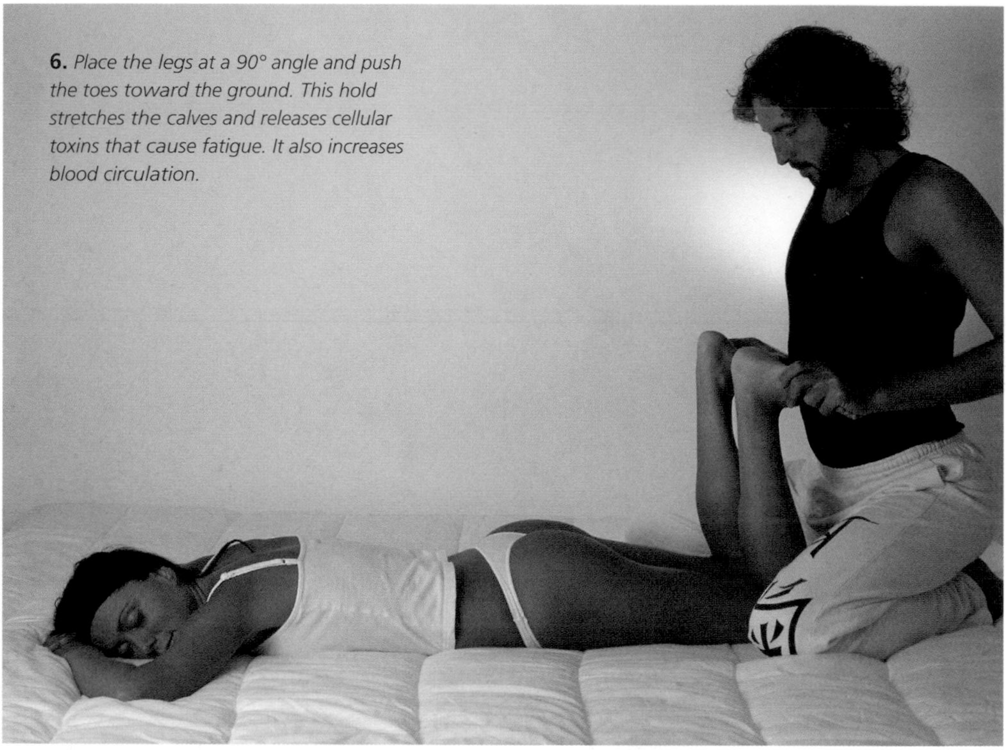

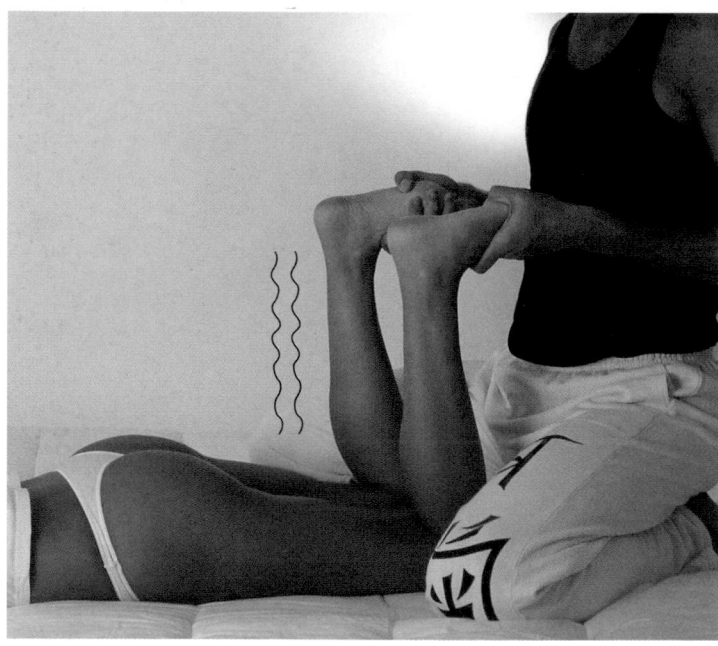

**6.** *Place the legs at a 90° angle and push the toes toward the ground. This hold stretches the calves and releases cellular toxins that cause fatigue. It also increases blood circulation.*

**7.** *Grab each foot by the toes and move them sideways. Loosen and relax the leg muscles. This movement is very pleasant for the recipient.*

**8.** *Position yourself above the recipient's head, grab both arms, and bend backwards to stretch them.*

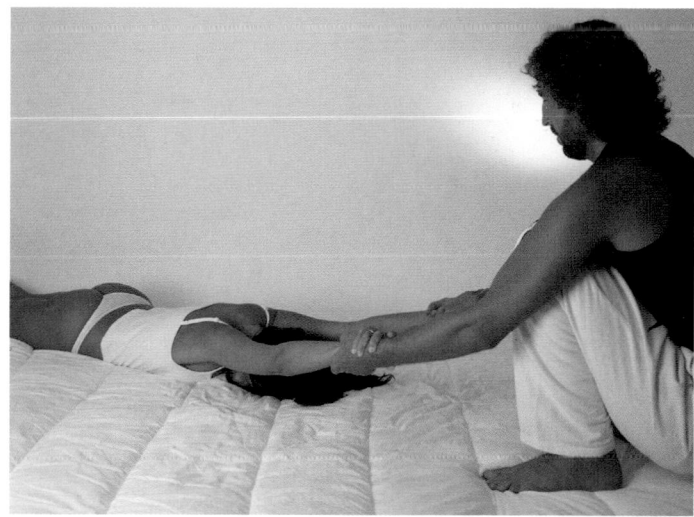

**9.** *With clasped hands and arms at the neck, grab both of their elbows and lift them simultaneously.*

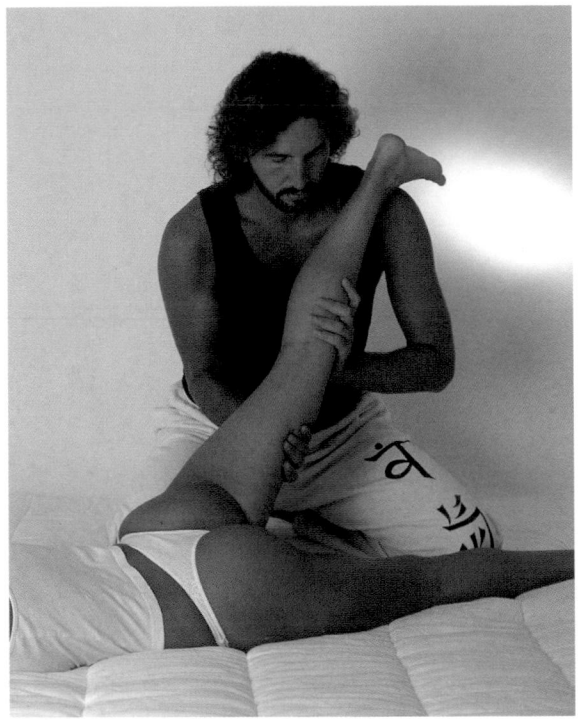

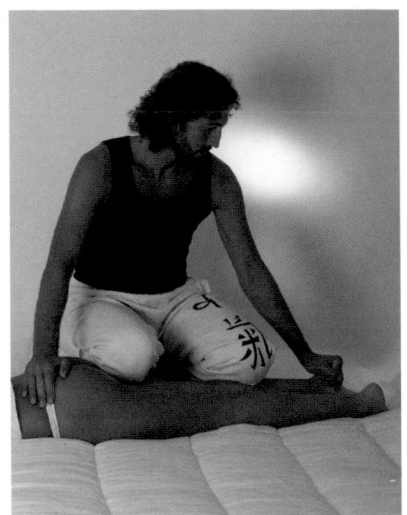

**11.** *While kneeling, gently place a hand on the recipient's sacrum. Then place one knee on the biceps femoris and the other knee in the middle of their calf. With your other hand, press down on the heel area. This helps to relieve sciatic pain.*

**10.** *Kneel and place one leg on your shoulder, grab it with both hands to raise and lower it gently. This hold deeply stretches the leg joint.*

## Face up

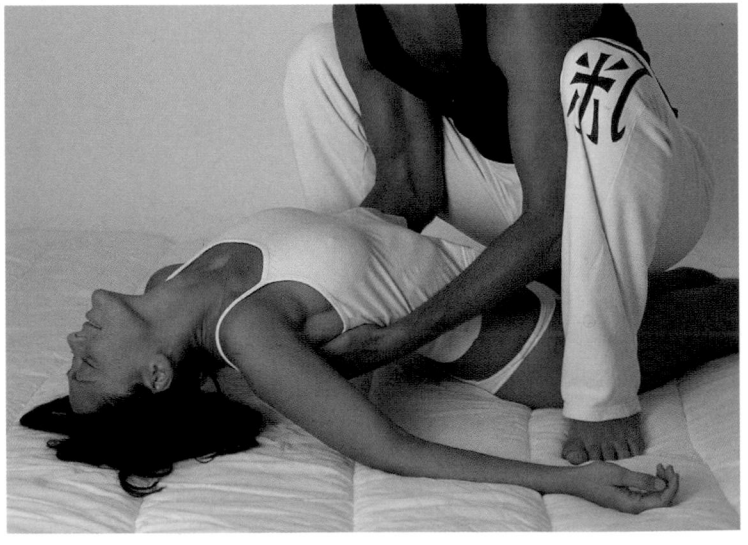

**12.** *Run your hands under the recipient's back and lift up to open and arch the chest area. Let their head fall back, relaxed, allowing greater energy flow and the opening of the throat. It also deepens breathing.*

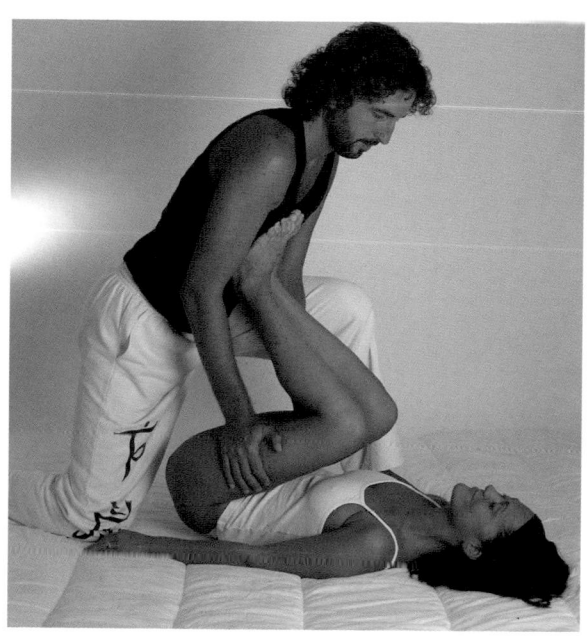

**13.** Grab their ankles and bring their knees up to their chest. This hold massages the digestive organs.

**14.** Grab their ankles and shake them lightly while their legs are kept straight and elevated. This hold is very pleasant, easing tension and relaxing the area.

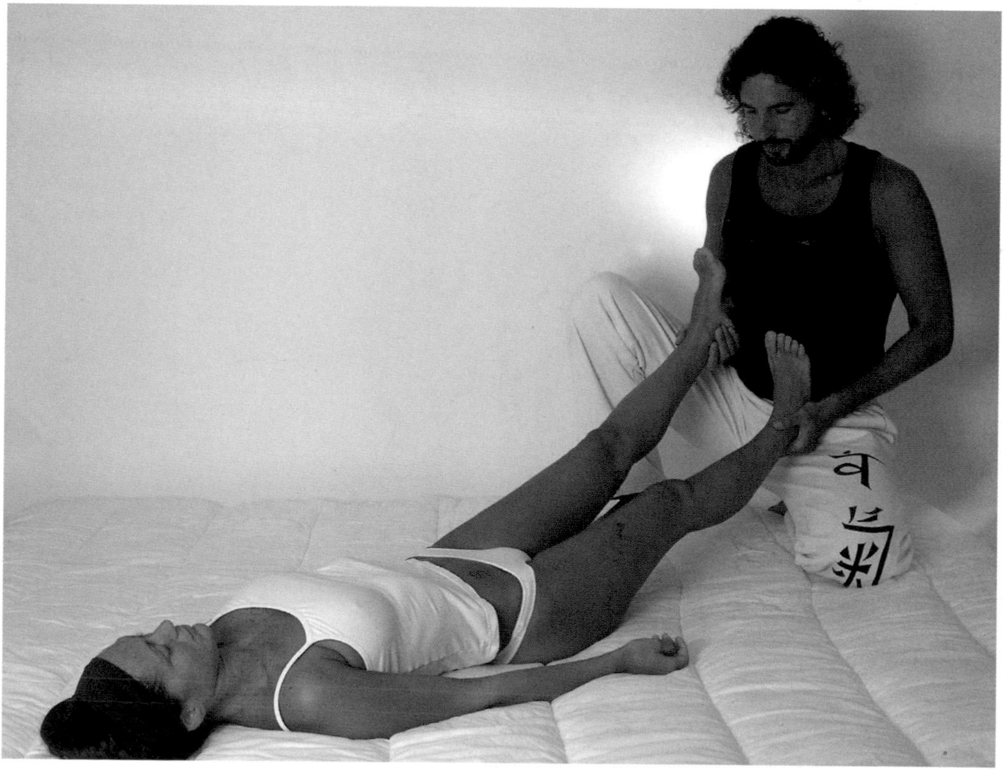

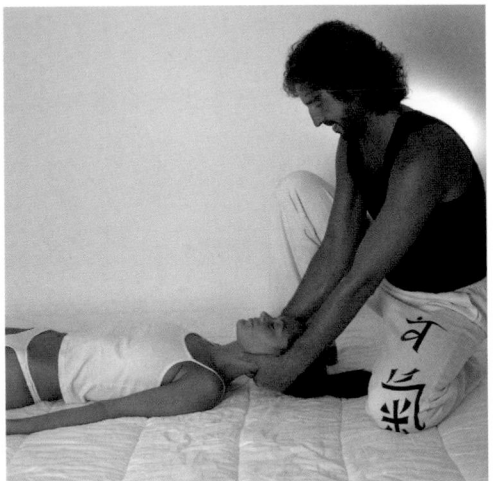

**15.** *Sit behind the recipient and slide your hands down their neck, stretching the vertebrae as much as possible, but without causing pain.*

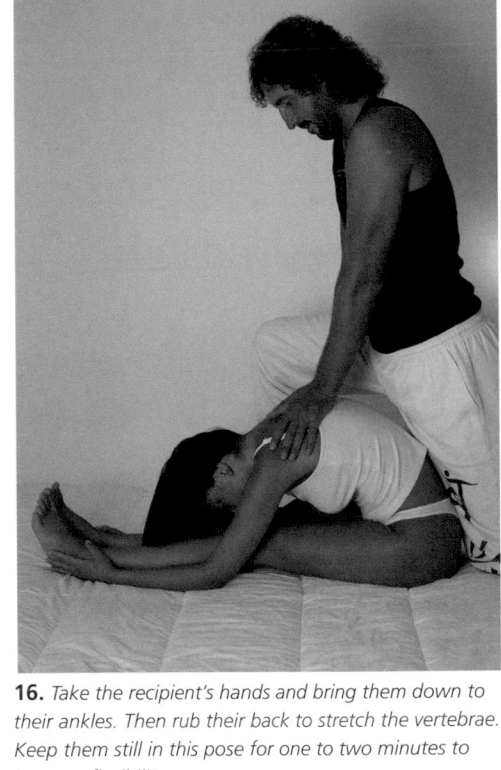

**16.** *Take the recipient's hands and bring them down to their ankles. Then rub their back to stretch the vertebrae. Keep them still in this pose for one to two minutes to increase flexibility.*

**17.** *Grasp the hands and raise the arms above the head. Make sure you put one of your legs behind the spine to support it and keep it upright. This hold helps stretch the spine and arm muscles.*

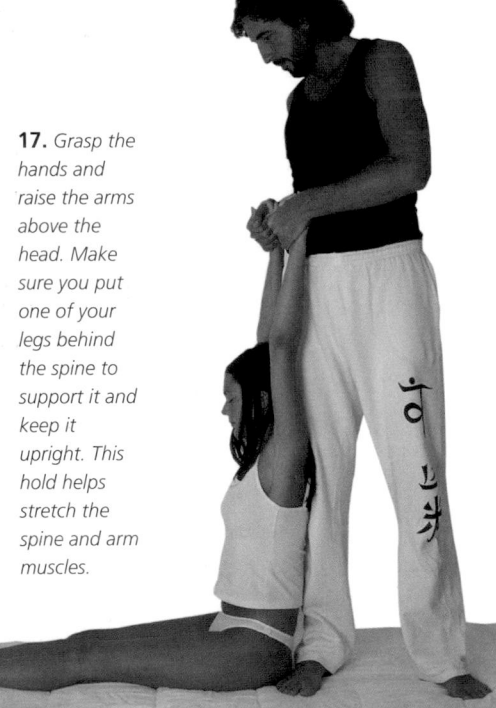

**18.** *This hold is similar to number eight, although in this case the recipient will be facing up.*

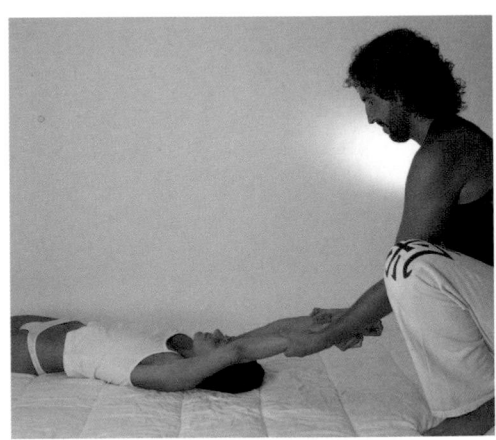

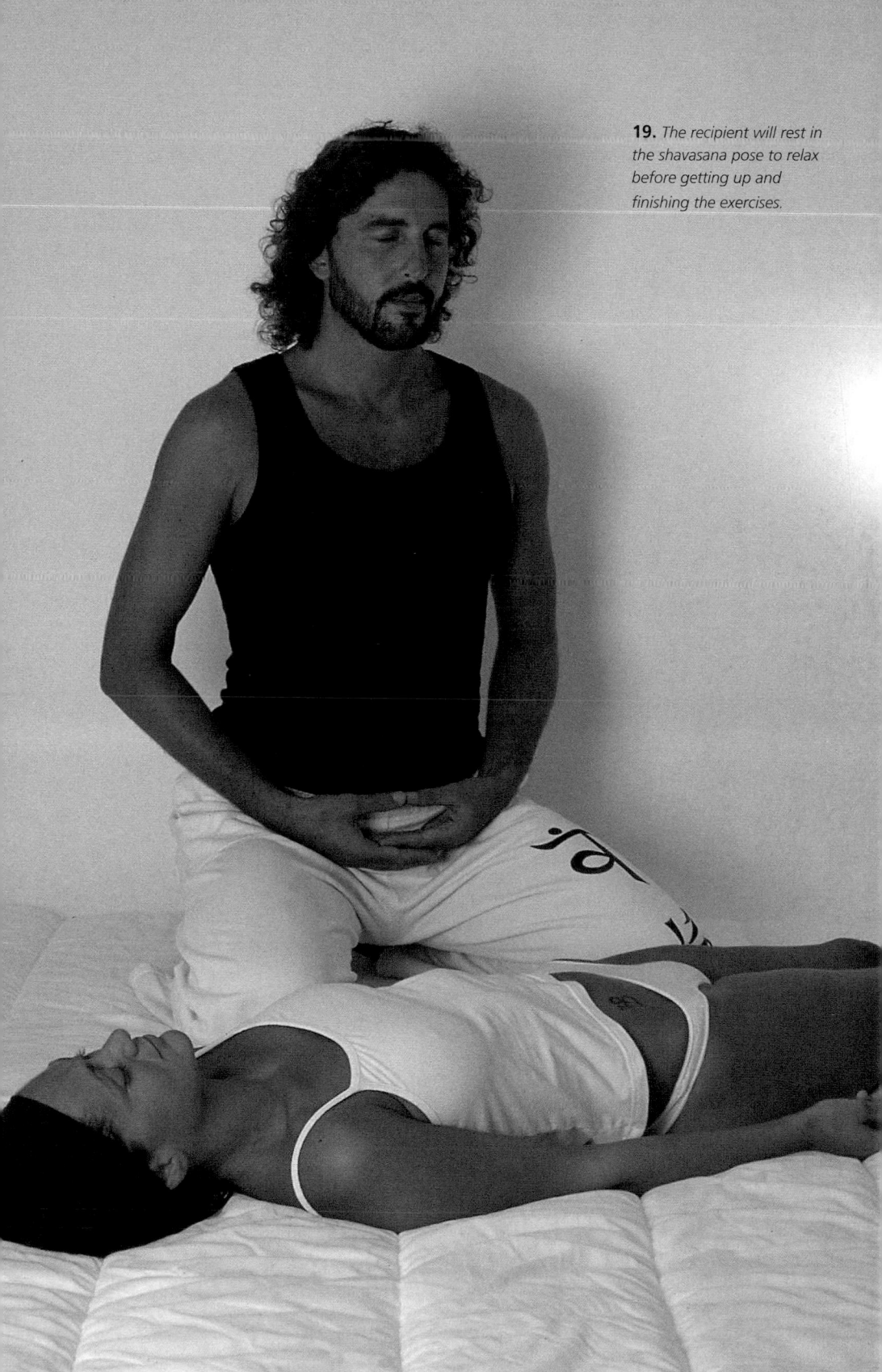

**19.** *The recipient will rest in the shavasana pose to relax before getting up and finishing the exercises.*

## WORKING THE POINTS ON THE UPPER BACK

Today, seven out of ten people suffer from problems and pain in the upper back area. This is because it is an area of the body that retains a lot of pain brought on by poor posture, mental stress, emotional conflicts, stiffness, and blockages that we create around us.

The affected area is of vital importance for the proper functioning of the mind. It also holds old emotions that accumulate between the shoulder blades.

Applying shiatsu to this area decompresses obstructed *qi*, stirring up and activating circulation. Blood flow will also improve, resulting in a feeling of lightness, freedom, and increased energy as it goes from the head to the body. Using your thumbs, press and hold on the points in a bilateral manner, from the neck down. Do a counterclockwise circular motion to sedate each point.

- SI 10: Located on the inner top edge of the shoulder blade.

- SI 12: Located on the outer top edge of the shoulder blade.
- LI 15: Located on the middle of the deltoid.
- LI 16: Also called the "shoulder pit," this is a point for decompressing the entire upper back. It resembles two holes at the top of the shoulder.
- BL 10: Located between GB 20 and GV 15.
- BL 11: Located on the first dorsal vertebra.
- BL 12: Located on the second dorsal vertebra.
- BL 13: Located on the third dorsal vertebra.
- GB 12: Located on the back of the skull, two thumbs behind each ear.
- GB 20: Located on the openings of the bottom of the skull. It feels like slumps that are an inch under the previous point and an inch from the top of the cervical vertebrae.
- GB 21 and TH 15: Two points that are close together in the middle of the trapezius.
- GV 15 and GV 16: Located on the center of the spine, at the start of the neck (in the middle and bottom of the skull).

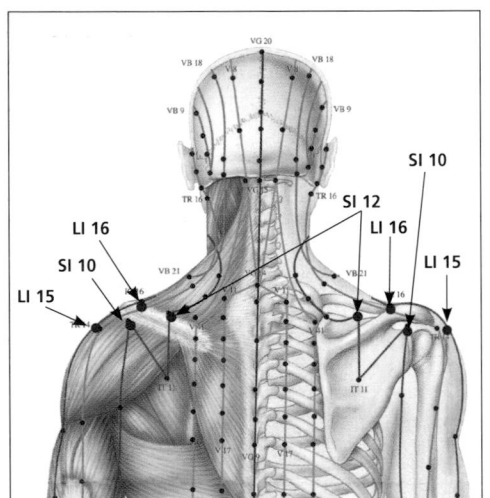 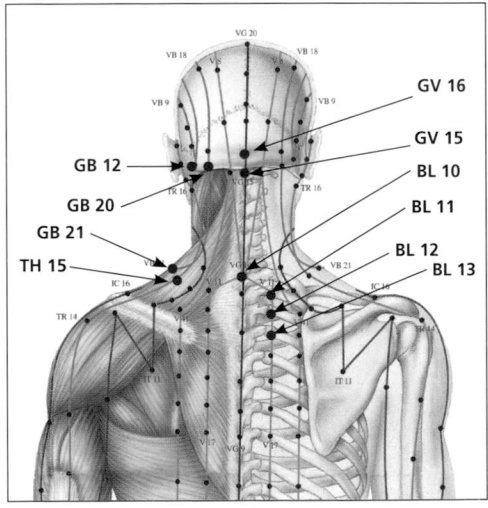

*Shiatsu points to work the upper back area.*

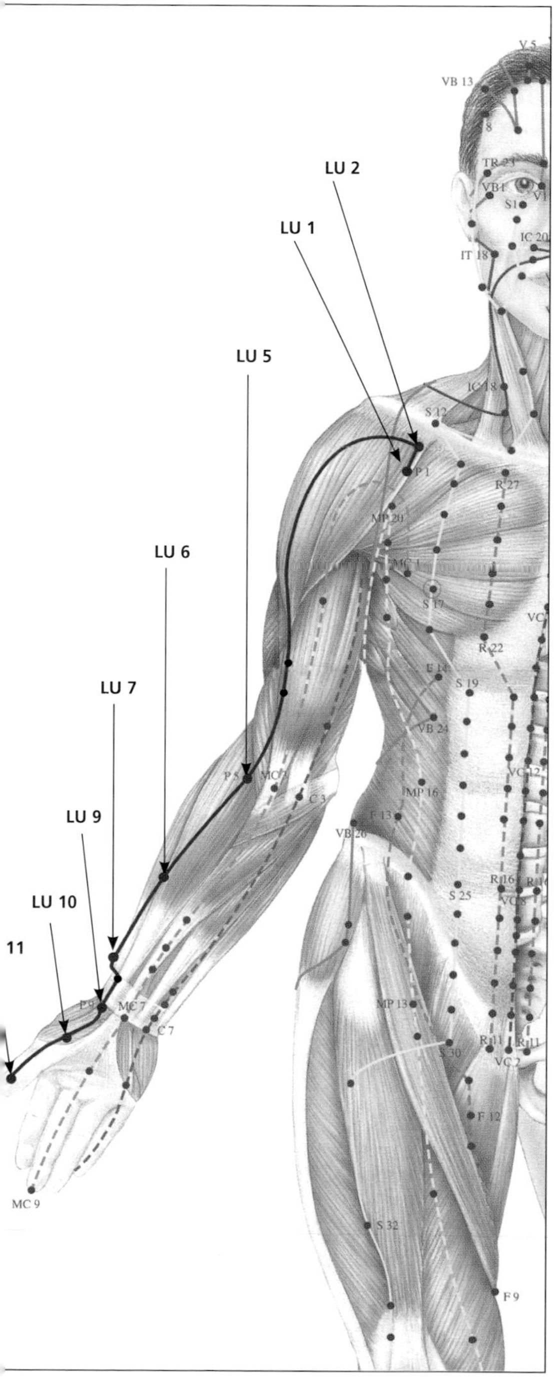

## THE MERIDIANS AND THEIR POINTS

### *Lung meridian*

**POINTS:** 11

**Yin meridian**

**ROUTE:** Inner arms.

**SUITABLE FOR:** Breathing problems, colds, bronchitis, cough and asthma; shoulder and arm pain.

Specific points for particular problems:

- **LU 1:** Colds.
- **LU 2:** Coughing.
- **LU 5:** Lung problems, coughing, sore throat with fever; elbow pain.
- **LU 6:** Asthma attacks and coughing.
- **LU 7:** Fever, cough, neck pain, and headache.
- **LU 9:** Asthmatic coughing; pain and paralysis of the wrist.
- **LU 10:** Asthma, sore throat; sore thumb.
- **LU 11:** Sore throat.

### *Large intestine meridian*

**POINTS:** 20

**Yang meridian**

**ROUTE:** Upper arms to the side of the nose.

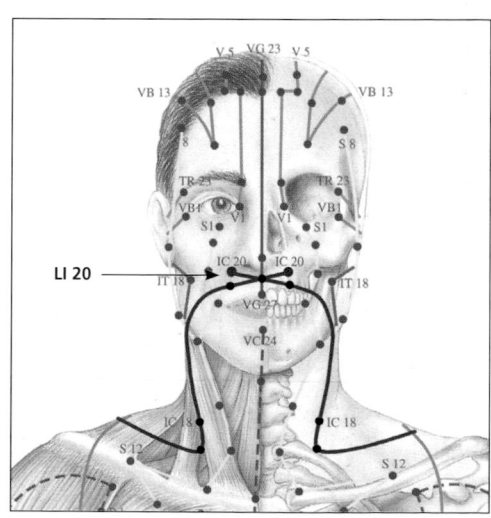

*Large intestine meridian.*

*Lung meridian.*

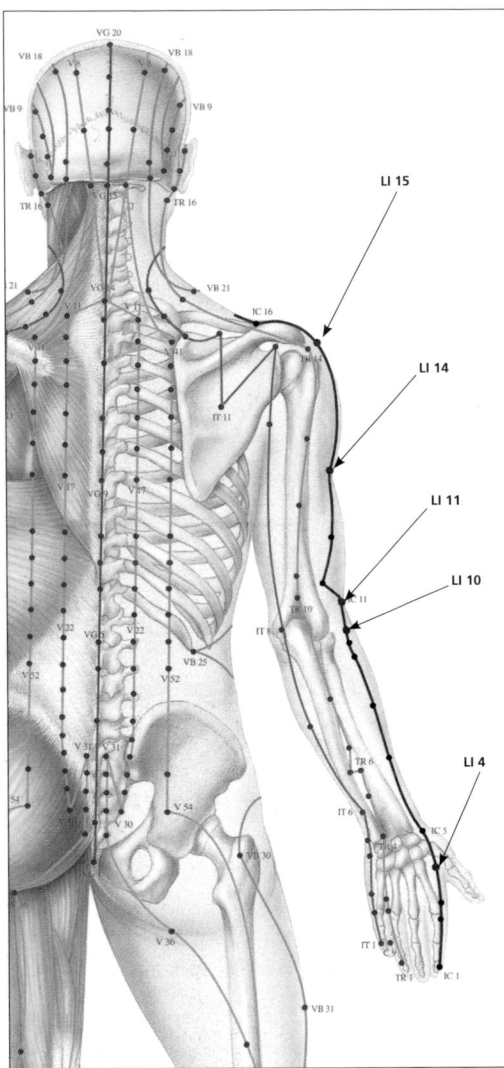

*Large intestine meridian.*

**SUITABLE FOR:** Pain in the abdomen, mouth, and throat, headache, rheumatic pain on the shoulder, nasal congestion, constipation, lowering high fever.

Specific points for particular problems:

- **LI 4:** Treats most head problems: facial pain, headache, toothache, nasal discharge, congestion, and poor hearing; thumb pain, constipation, and paralysis of the hand. This is one of the strongest points for overall wellbeing. Do not use during pregnancy.
- **LI 10:** Intestinal and stomach pain; indigestion and diarrhea.
- **LI 11:** Fever brought on by colds and flu. Skin conditions, eczema, and urticaria. Abdominal pain and diarrhea. High blood pressure.
- **LI 14, LI 15:** Pain in the upper arm and numbness in the deltoid region.
- **LI 20:** Nasal discharge, sinus, and facial paralysis.

## Stomach meridian

**POINTS:** 45

**Yang meridian**

**ROUTE:** From head to the second toe. Front of the body.

**SUITABLE FOR:** Digestive diseases, vomiting, bloating, and stomach pain; facial paralysis, headaches, and nosebleeds. Sore knees.

Specific points for particular problems:

- **ST 6:** Toothache, facial paralysis.
- **ST 7:** Poor hearing.
- **ST 21:** Muscle spasms in the abdomen and diarrhea.
- **ST 25:** Constipation and irregular menstruation.
- **ST 29:** Hernia, irregular menstruation, uterine prolapse, and male impotence.
- **ST 31:** Pain in the abdomen, legs, and hips.

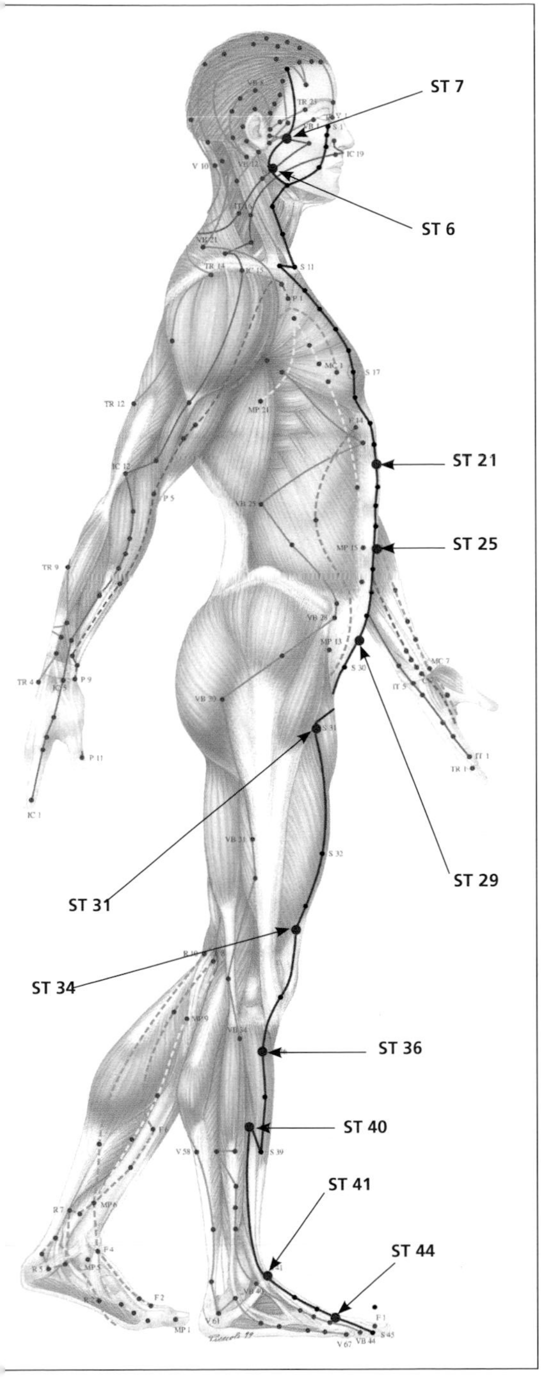

- **ST 34:** Sore knees and stomachache.
- **ST 36:** Stomachache; gastric and duodenal ulcers; diarrhea and constipation; water retention. Any kind of prolapse, irregular menstruation, and knee pain. This point is the most powerful and effective of all. It strengthens the immune system, strengthens the kidneys, and regulates the spleen and stomach, improving digestion.
- **ST 40:** Phlegm, congestion, and colds.
- **ST 41, ST 44:** Ankle pain; headaches.

### Spleen–pancreas meridian

**POINTS:** 21

**Yin meridian**

**ROUTE:** From the foot to the chest, under the armpit.

**SUITABLE FOR:** Abdominal bloating, stomachache, vomiting and diarrhea; swelling of the legs, menstrual problems; insomnia.

Specific points for particular problems:
- **SP 4:** Depression, abdominal pain, and insomnia.
- **SP 6:** Diarrhea, abdominal swelling; hemorrhoids; hernia; insomnia and restless sleep. Menstrual irregularity. Impotence and premature ejaculation, difficulty urinating.
- **SP 9:** Gastric pain, edema, and diarrhea.
- **SP 10:** Itchy skin, eczema, psoriasis and urticaria. Irregular menstrual cycle.
- **SP 15:** Improves condition of the intestine.

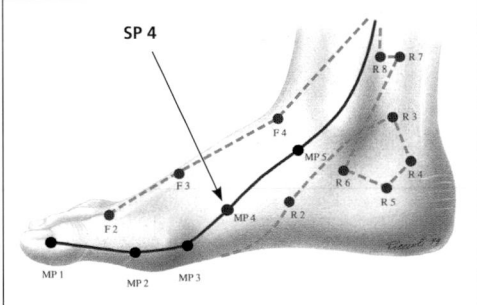

*Stomach meridian*

*Spleen–pancreas meridian.*

121

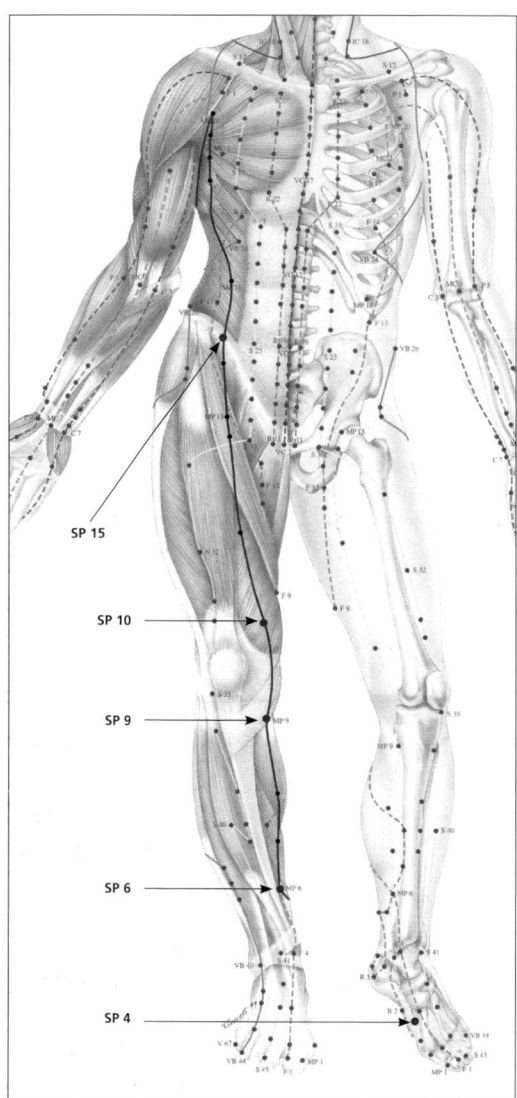

*Spleen–pancreas meridian.*

## *Heart meridian*

**POINTS:** 9

**Yin meridian**

**ROUTE:** From the chest to the pinky.

**SUITABLE FOR:** Heart problems, insomnia, depression, pain of the wrist and elbow.

Specific points for particular problems:

- **H 3:** Local pain in the elbow and atrophied arm muscles.
- **H 7:** Worried mind, insomnia, and light sleep; depression, pain and heart palpitations; speech problems.

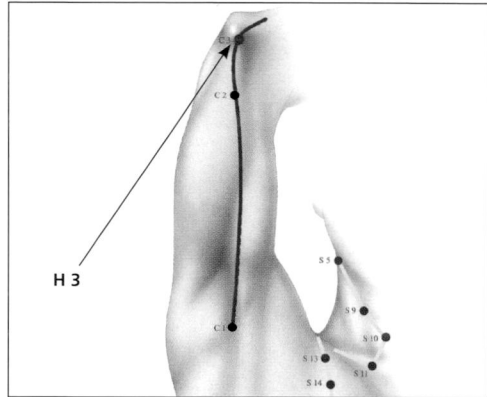

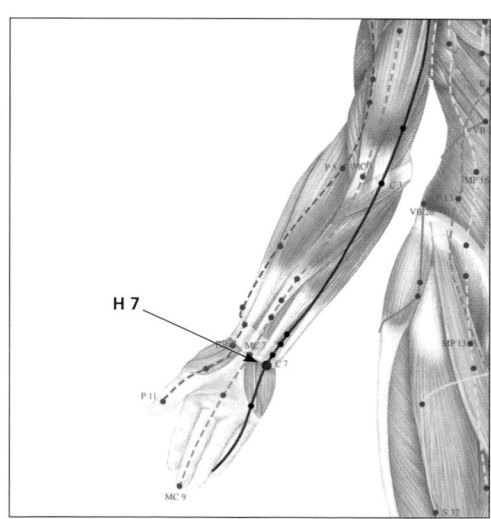

*Heart meridian.*

## Small intestine meridian

**POINTS:** 19

**Yang meridian**

**ROUTE:** From the little finger to the head.

**SUITABLE FOR:** Deafness; neck pain.

Specific points for particular problems:

- **SI 3:** Pain in the outer hand and arm; paralysis of the little finger and neck stiffness.
- **SI 8:** Pain and numbness of the arm.
- **SI 9:** Lack of mobility in the arm and shoulder pain.

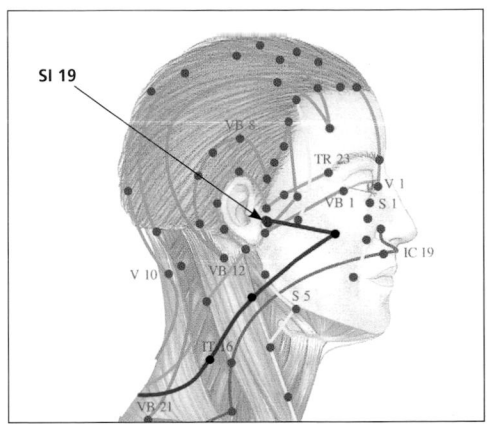

*Small intestine meridian.*

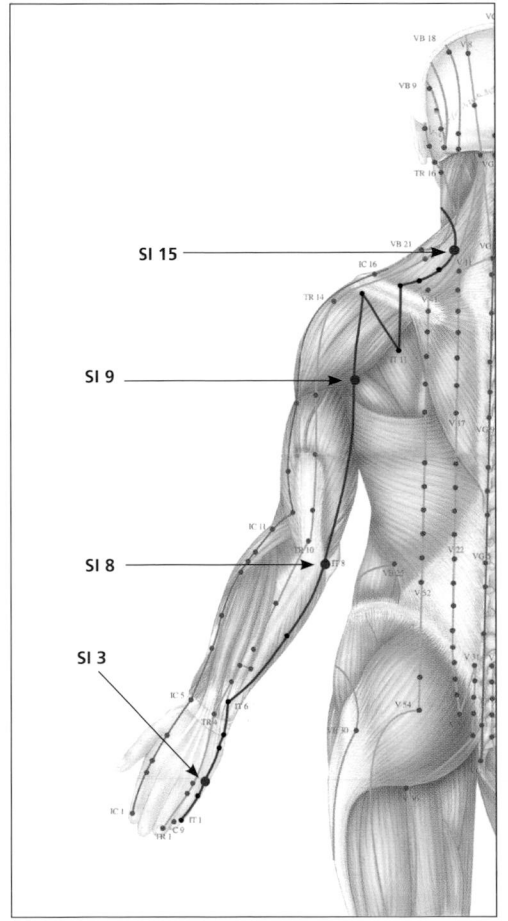

*Small intestine meridian.*

- **SI 15:** Numbness in the neck, shoulder pain, and backaches.
- **SI 19:** Treats ear problems.

## Bladder meridian

**POINTS:** 67

**Yang meridian**

**ROUTE:** From the sides of the eyebrows, behind the back and legs, to the little toe.

**SUITABLE FOR:** Headaches. Sprains, lower back pain, aching thighs, poor circulation in the legs, and cold feet.

Specific points for particular problems:

- **BL 10:** It relaxes tense muscles at the base of the skull, reduces pain, and eases tension.
- **BL 11:** Helps eliminate *qi* blockages in the bones and joints of the neck, shoulder, and back.
- **BL 13:** Treats asthma, coughing, and bronchial problems.
- **BL 15:** Cardiac disorders, anemia, epilepsy, chest tightness, and insomnia. It calms the mind.
- **BL 17:** Blood circulation disorders and urticaria.
- **BL 20:** Removes tiredness, lack of energy, indigestion; relieves vomiting and diarrhea.

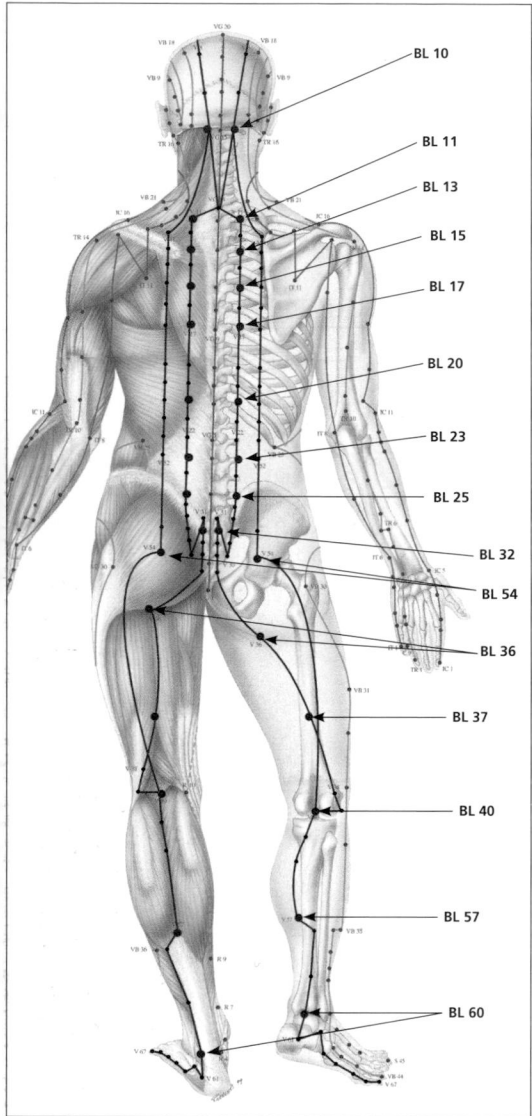

*Bladder meridian*

- **BL 23:** Improves proper functioning of the kidneys, relieves chronic pain in the lower back. Relieves hearing problems, ringing in the ears, and poor hearing.
- **BL 25:** Relieves sciatic pain, letting *qi* flow through the lumbar region, sacrum, and buttocks. Regulates the large intestine, effectively treats diarrhea and constipation.
- **BL 32:** Relieves lower back pain. Treats infertility, excessive vaginal discharge, and uterine disorders.
- **BL 36:** Relieves leg pain and sciatic nerve pain.
- **BL 37:** This point is very effective as a treatment for pain in the lower back, sciatica, and lower legs.
- **BL 40:** Acute pain in the calves. Eases lower back pain.
- **BL 54:** Treats pain in the lower back, sciatica, and heel.
- **BL 57:** Acute pain in the calves.
- **BL 60:** Pain caused by ankle sprains and heel problems. Relieves headache, lower back pain, and sciatica.

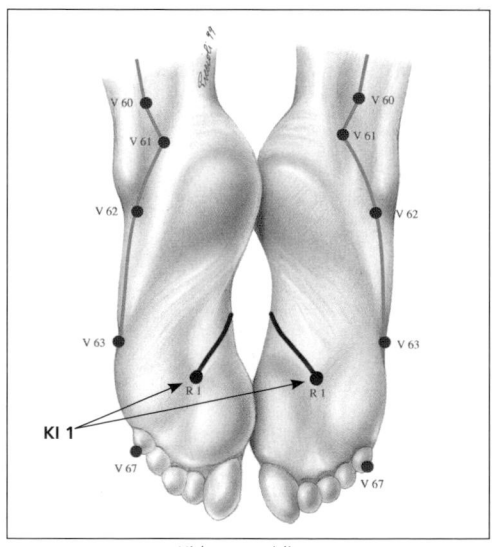

*Kidney meridian.*

## Kidney meridian

**POINTS:** 27

**Yin meridian**

**ROUTE:** Starts at the bottom of the foot, goes up the inner leg, and across the abdomen to the chest, ending under the collarbone.

**SUITABLE FOR:** Coughing, back pain, sprains, pain in the joints of the legs, edema, asthma, cold hands and feet.

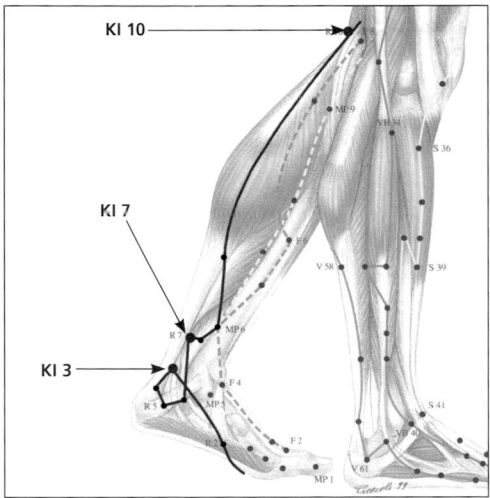

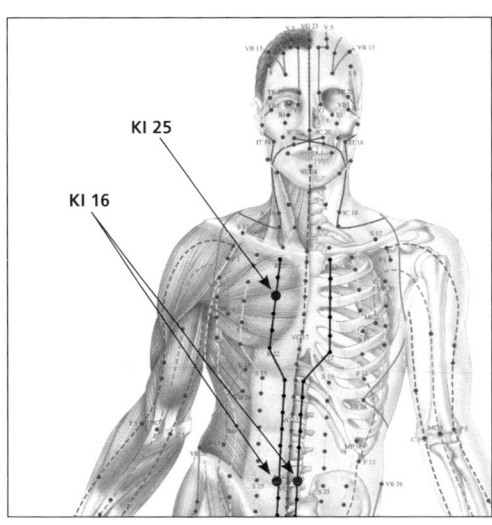

*Kidney meridian.*

Specific points for particular problems:

- **KI 1:** Fainting, shock, agitated mind, epilepsy, convulsions in children, and acute pain such as toothache. Aids sleep and appetite.
- **KI 3:** Pain in the lower back, frequent urination, ringing in the ears, poor vision, insomnia, and irritability.
- **KI 7:** Edema and night sweats.
- **KI 10:** Problems with the ligaments in the knees.
- **KI 16:** Abdominal pain and diarrhea.
- **KI 25:** Coughing fits, asthma, and cardiac stress.

## Circulatory and sexual meridian

**POINTS:** 9

**Yin meridian**

**ROUTE:** From the chest, through the middle of the arm, to the middle finger.

**SUITABLE FOR:** Heart palpitations, vomiting, anxiety, mental confusion, unstable emotions, sprains in the arm joints, heart and chest problems, and anxiety.

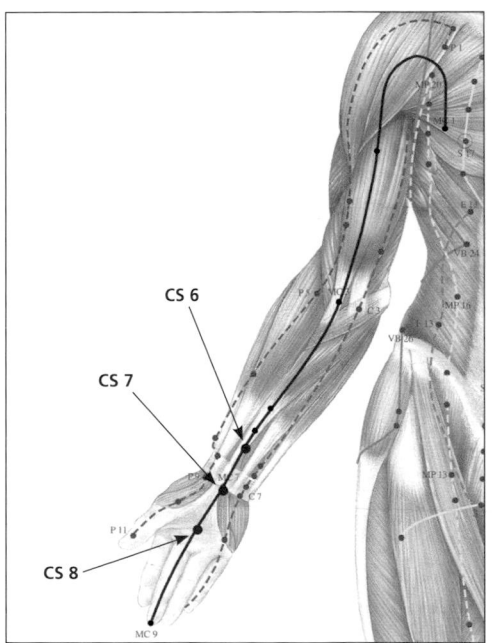

*Circulatory and sexual meridian.*

Specific points for particular problems:

- **CS 6:** Nausea, dizziness; emotional pain resulting from love conflicts, concerns; insomnia, irregular heartbeat.
- **CS 7:** Anxiety, heart palpitations; wrist pain and paralysis of the fingers (especially the thumb, index, and middle).
- **CS 8:** Restless and disturbed mind, and cardiac pain.

## Triple heater meridian

**POINTS:** 23

**Yang meridian**

**ROUTE:** Starts on the ring finger, crosses the back of the hand and arm, runs through the dorsal midline, through the shoulder to behind the ear, and then to the outer corner of the eyebrow.

**SUITABLE FOR:** Headache, deafness, ear problems; eye pain; tonsillitis, rheumatic pain, arm pain; pain at the hips, neck, and joints of the arm, wrist, and elbow.

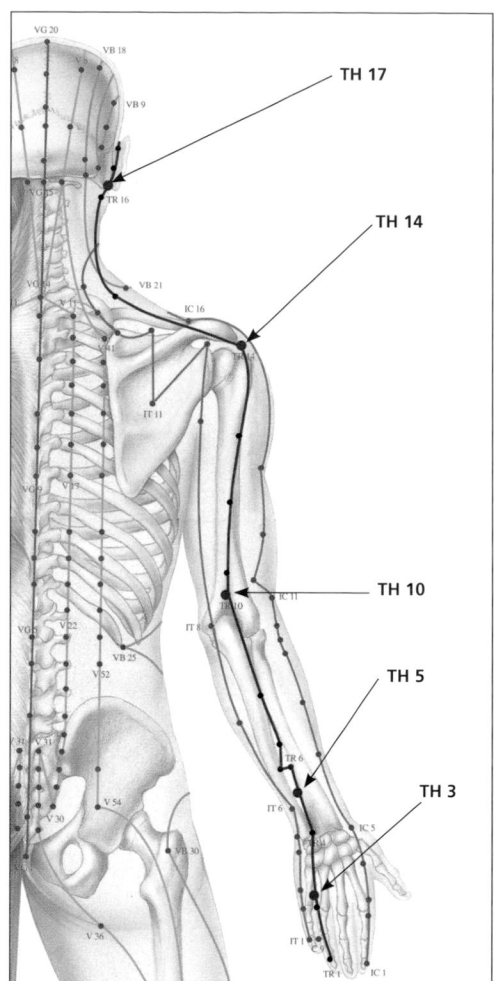

*Triple heater meridian.*

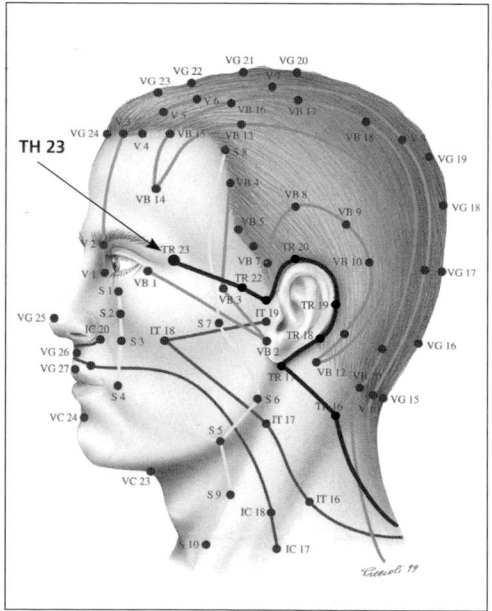

*Triple heater meridian.*

Specific points for particular problems:

- **TH 3:** Ear disorders, poor hearing; migraine, general pain, and paralysis of the hand.
- **TH 5:** Shoulder pain, headache, hearing problems, fever or colds.
- **TH 10:** Pain in the elbow.
- **TH 14:** Pain and lack of mobility in the shoulder.
- **TH 17:** Ringing in the ears, deafness; facial paralysis, toothache, neuralgia in the lower jaw.
- **TH 23:** Headaches, dizziness, facial paralysis, and conjunctivitis.

## Gallbladder meridian

**POINTS:** 44

**Yang meridian**

**ROUTE:** Starts at the outer corner of the eye, goes to the ear, outlines the ear three times, reaches the neck, crosses the clavicle, reaches the armpit, and zigzags down the side of the torso. Then it passes over the outer leg to the outer corner of the fourth toe.

**SUITABLE FOR:** Headache, deafness, muscle disorders, eye pain, intercostal neuralgia, hip pain, biliary colic, knee pain, liver problems; pain in the neck, shoulder, leg, knee, and ankle.

Specific points for particular problems:

- **GB 1:** Eye problems.
- **GB 2:** Ear problems.
- **GB 8:** Migraines.
- **GB 14:** Facial paralysis, headaches, and tightness in the eyelids.
- **GB 20:** All kinds of headaches; problems of the eyes, ears, and nose; tense neck muscles and neck problems. Cold and flu, Parkinson's disease, epilepsy, and facial paralysis.

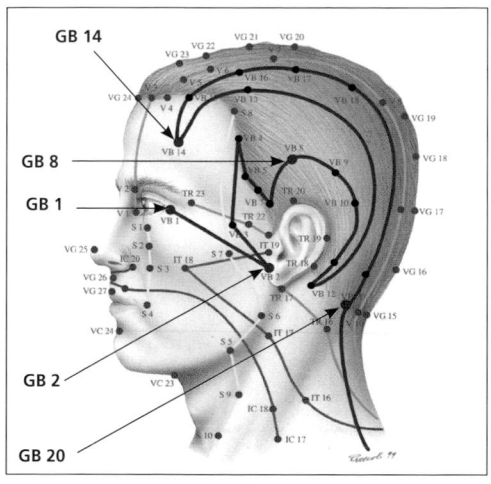

*Gallbladder meridian.*

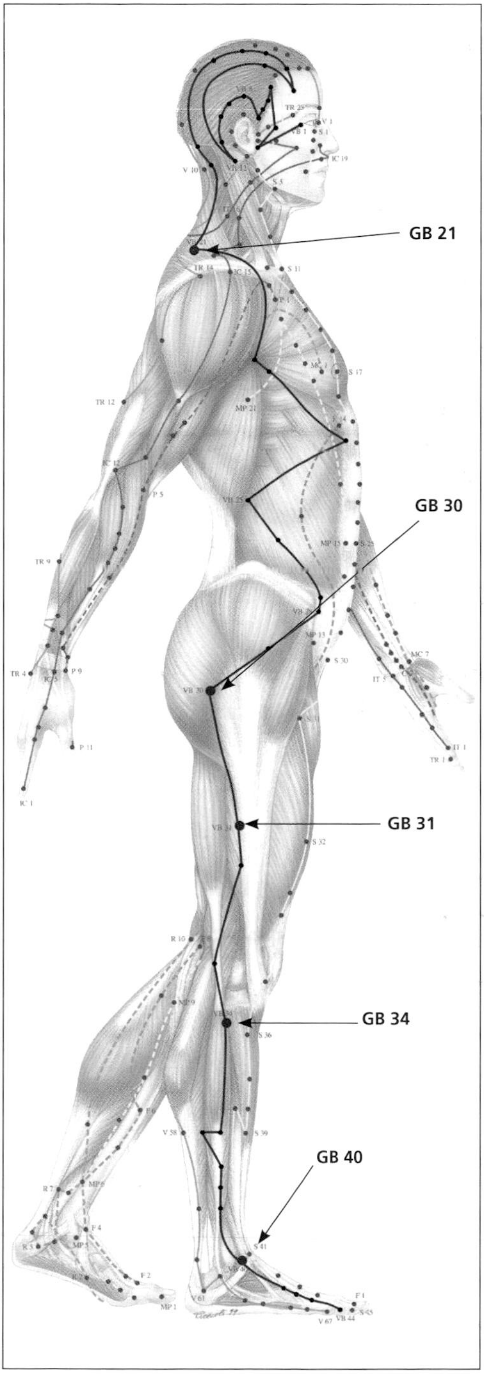

*Gallbladder meridian.*

- **GB 21:** Neck problems and shoulder pain.
- **GB 30:** Lower back pain, sciatica, pain in the hip region, weakness in the lower leg.
- **GB 31:** Paralysis in the thigh and sciatica.
- **GB 34:** Cramps and spasms in the lower leg, ankle and knee pain, neck pain, sciatica and pain in the muscles of the hip. Overall, this point works as a muscle relaxant.
- **GB 40:** Chest muscle pain, and sprained ankle.

## *Liver meridian*

**POINTS:** 14

**Yin meridian**

**ROUTE:** Starts at the toe, ascends the inner tibia, the inner thigh, and the abdomen, goes through the intercostal space where it ends.

**SUITABLE FOR:** Back pain, diarrhea, pain in the female genital area, urinary retention, anger, headaches, dizziness and facial spasms.

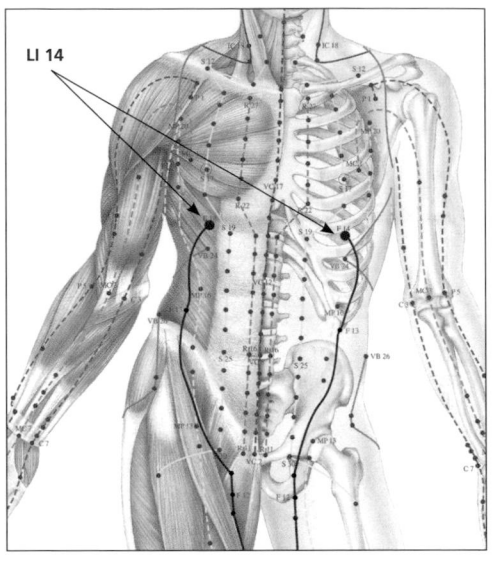

*Liver meridian.*

Specific points for particular problems:
- **LI 3:** Calms down emotional problems, especially anger. Headaches and migraines, liver problems, hepatitis, irregular menses, and gallbladder problems.
- **LI 5:** Excess of libido, impotence in men. It is important for the external genitalia.
- **LI 8:** Knee problems.
- **LI 14:** Vomiting, abdominal pain.

## *Governing vessel meridian*

**POINTS:** 28

**Yang meridian**

**ROUTE:** Starts at the end of the tail bone, goes up the spine to the neck, continues to the head then down the face to the upper gum.

Specific points for particular problems:
- **GV 4:** Lower back pain. Asthma, epilepsy, and schizophrenia.
- **GV 20:** Headaches, and ringing in the ears.
- **GV 26:** Resets consciousness.

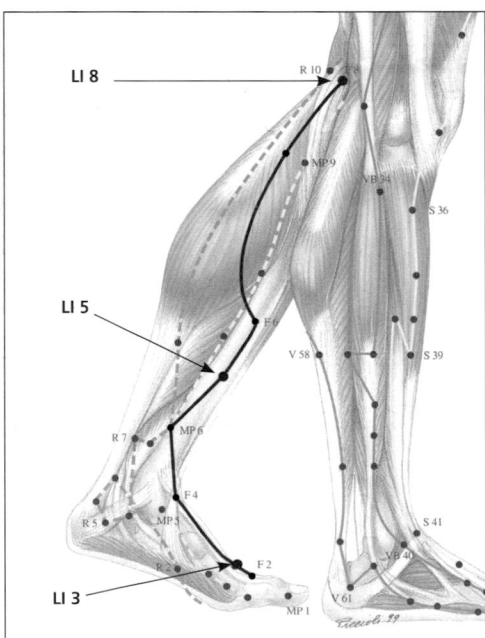

*Liver meridian.*

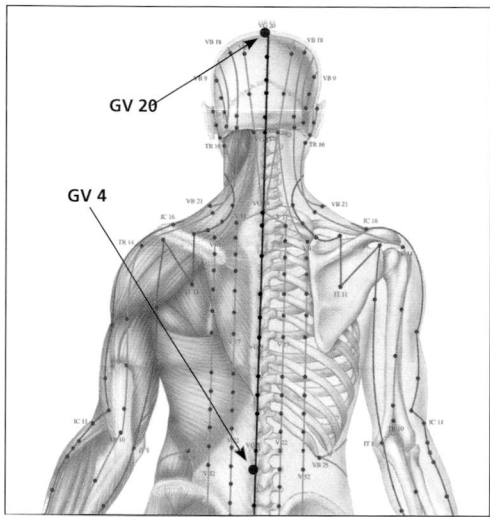

*Governing vessel meridian.*

## *Conception vessel meridian*

**POINTS:** 24

**Yin meridian**

**ROUTE:** Starts in the genital area (between the anus and genitals) and goes up along the midline to the chin.

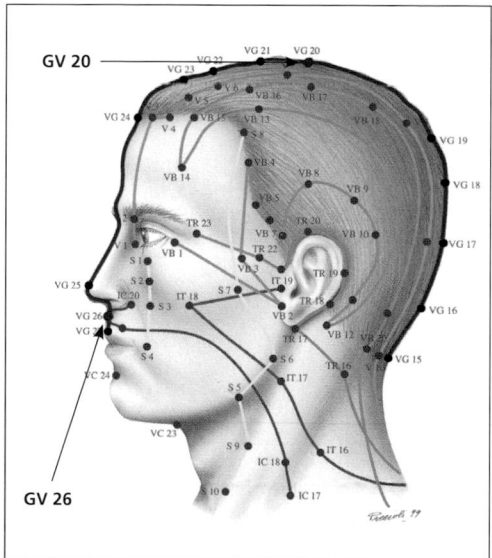

*Conception vessel meridian.*

Specific points for particular problems:

- **CV 3:** Retention and dripping of urine, impotence, seminal discharge, irregular menstruation, and reproductive problems.
- **CV 6:** Prolapse of internal organs, kidney weakness; all *qi* deficiencies.
- **CV 12:** Stomach pains, vomiting, nausea, flatulence, and hiccups.
- **CV 17:** Cardiac chest pains, asthma, and coughing.

This point has great calming effect.

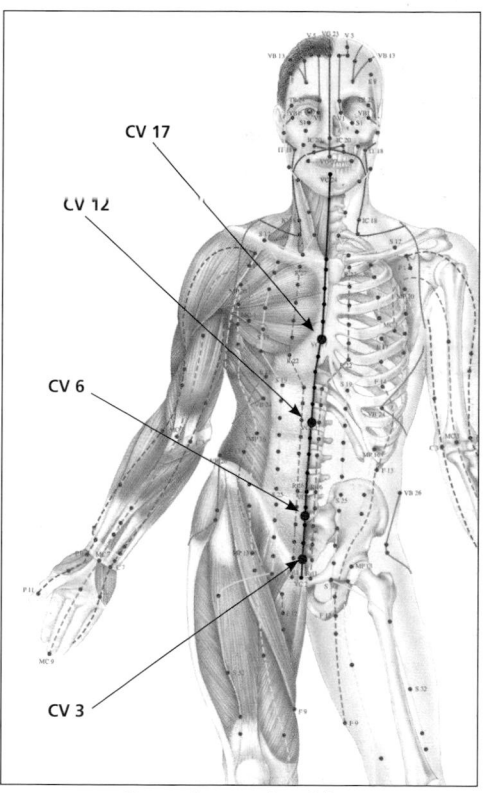

*Conception vessel meridian.*

# Tantric massage

Tantric massage originated during a so-called golden age of India, in which the body was respected, meditative sex was enjoyed, pleasure in all its aspects was emphasized, and mankind was encouraged to cultivate art and contemplate beauty.

Tantra is intimately linked with the sacred consciousness. The sixty-four arts of the *Kamasutra* ("wisdom of desire") show that the individual must master many topics, among which are the art of massage. Massage is considered to be one of the tantric arts and to be essential for the overall development of the individual.

Sex is also considered an art. Unfortunately, closed minds tend to misunderstand tantra and have ignorantly categorized it simply as sex.

Tantra is not only sex; rather, it is a complete and transformative lifestyle. It is a change of attitude and vision.

Tantra uses massage as a way for two people to experience primordial unity. It is from this union that the two complementary polarities are formed: Shakti, the Feminine, and Shiva, the Masculine. Both cosmic principles live in harmony within the body, as well as in the whole universe, and by conscientiously preserving such harmony we can manage to stay healthy.

Tantra is a path to awaken the potential of love (*prema*) and attach it to the innate intelligence (*prajna*) that everyone has within.

The principles of tantric massage are as follows:

- Emphasis on unity, on the one hand, between the physical body and the universe and, on the other hand, between the individual soul and the universal soul, through the use of touch and all other senses.
- Stimulation, sedation, or harmonization of each of the seven chakras in the body's energy system.
- Work on the chakras in the back, front, and feet.
- Tantric massage awakens the senses through stimulation.
- It can activate the psychosexual energy called kundalini, and make it move throughout the entire body, providing a wave of pleasure and connection.

For this, Tantric massage uses the following techniques:
- Specially powerful cleansing breaths.
- Visualization.
- Special oils prepared for each chakra.
- Harmonizing sounds (favorite music and mantras).
- Using colors, gemstones, and crystals.

According to tantra, depression, stress, conflicts, and many diseases are rooted in an unfulfilled basic desire. So its aim is to create a healthy balance by paying close attention to the realization of desires for each individual. The physical body is looked after, venerated, and respected as the temple of the soul. The individual soul (*jiva*) needs to be in a strong, healthy, and flexible physical body, so that the universal soul (*atman*) can manifest itself creatively.

The tantra formula consists of bringing together awareness and energy. Tantric massage consciously seeks to distribute *kundalini* energy around the centers of life in each individual. By applying this massage, we explore the body in an effort to create a healthy emotional balance as well as unity with the divine within the male or female body, so as to transcend the mind into a state of silence.

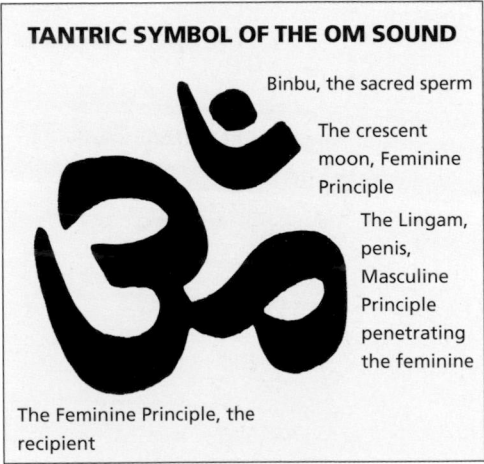

**TANTRIC SYMBOL OF THE OM SOUND**

Binbu, the sacred sperm

The crescent moon, Feminine Principle

The Lingam, penis, Masculine Principle penetrating the feminine

The Feminine Principle, the recipient

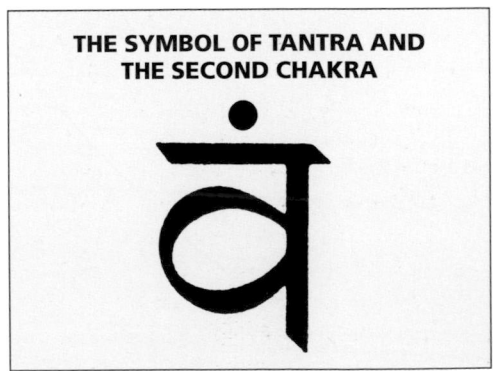

**THE SYMBOL OF TANTRA AND THE SECOND CHAKRA**

## THE BIG BANG: RAIN OF LIGHT ON THE CELLS

Scientists refer to the beginning of creation as the Big Bang, the great explosion; the Bible says, "In the beginning was the Word." Obviously a sound emerged from that word.

Personally, from a tantric point of view, I think the beginning was "an explosion of joy, an orgasm of the Divine, merging the Male and Female Principles." And this explosion continues to expand; it did not end in seven days: creation happens every day, because it is alive.

The petals of a rose (female) and its stem (male), day and night, cold and heat . . . everything is in balance. Tantra encourages living in an orgasmic state; that is, happily, in ecstasy with the morning, midday sun, dusk, night, stars, moon, sea, earth, fire, and everything that happens creatively.

In tantric massage the therapist will guide energy and use it to create internal access to higher levels of festive, orgasmic pathways of perception.

Orgasm is not linked only to the sexual. When you listen to your favorite music, your hormones explode, your emotions get excited, you feel happy, you sing, you are one with life, you feel positive, you want to create, you feel enthusiasm.

So tantric massage is an invitation to experience a state explosion of light in your cells, a state of joy.

Scientifically, it has been shown that when someone feels well and happy, their glands produce happiness hormones, called endorphins. Through my tantric experience, I believe that humanity does not live happily because it fails to use its intelligence to look inward. We have fought over land ownership even though none of it belongs to any of us. We worry about events that have not happened yet and we do not know if they will ever happen. We critique instead of create. We give into fear instead of surrendering to love.

People need to live with tantra, enjoying everything without attachment, guiding their destiny to soar freely, understanding that life is a natural cycle with positive and negative phases, enjoyment, singing, and crying. Using everything God and Goddess have put in your life to make you happy.

Below, I describe different ways of working with massage in a tantric manner.

## THE SEVEN PRINCIPLES OF TANTRIC MASSAGE

This massage will help the recipient feel these seven principles of life within them:

1. The Principle of the Body.
2. The Principle of Movement and Dance.
3. The Principle of Breathing.
4. The Principle of Fire and Arousal.
5. The Principle of Pleasure and Love.
6. The Principle of the Union between Shiva and Shakti.
7. The Principle of Silence, Ecstasy, and Unity.

For example, someone with a rigid personality, who values only their own opinion as truth, is a tense and stiff individual who is detached from the principle of dance and movement. Given that in life everything is moving, dancing, and playing with energy, this person "thinks" they know everything and is left deprived of life experience, which is precisely what is needed in tantra.

Each principle will try to awaken the natural wisdom that has fallen asleep, that is to say, whatever pushed him away from himself. These principles can be shared with your partner or with anyone, just remember these four points: respect, awareness, depersonalization, and silence of the mind.

## 1. THE PRINCIPLE OF THE BODY

The first principle consists in making conscious contact with the body. People with cerebral tendencies send their energy up to their head, forgetting the legs, spine, sacrum, and pelvis.

The Principle of the Body will bring us back to unity, starting at the first step.

To get started, the recipient is placed face down. First, rub their naked body with oil as you press with your fingers and your entire hand. You can use sandalwood, rose, jasmine, and lotus oils, or any combination I describe in chapter 4. Remember to emphasize the sense of touch so that the recipient's senses begin to awaken.

### BACK AND FACE DOWN

Each technique shown below is to be repeated four to five times, on both sides.

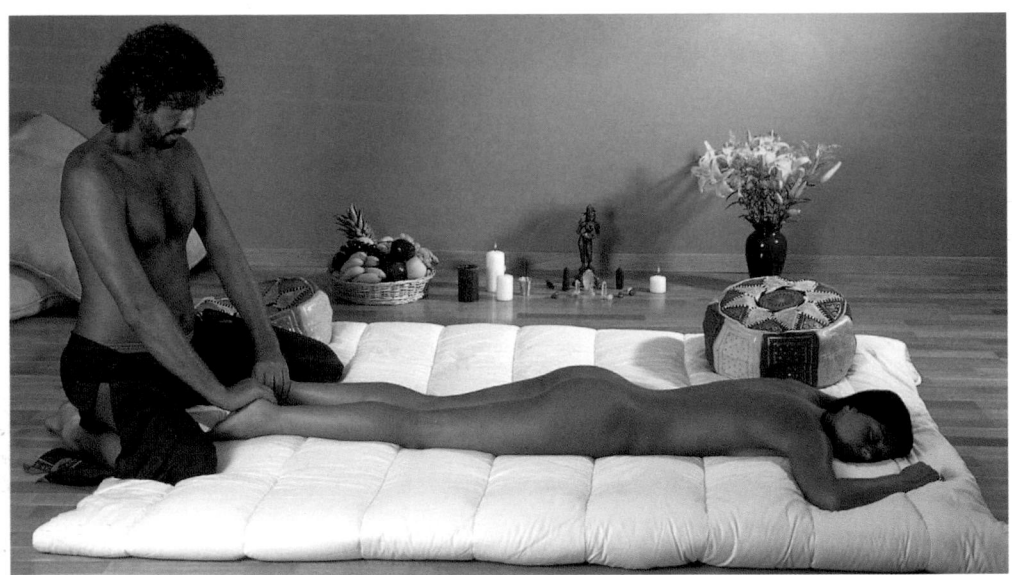

**1. Stimulate the sole of the foot:** *Rub the entire bottom of the foot. In doing so you stimulate multiple bodily organs.*

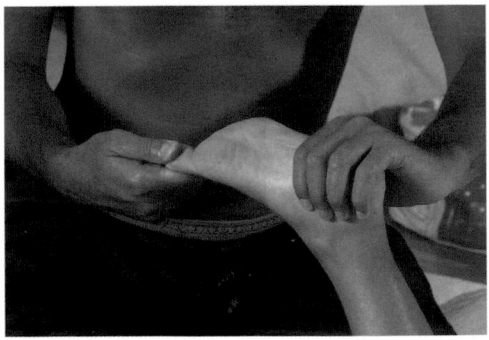

**2. Toe presses:**
*With the thumb and index finger, apply pressure to each of the toes.*

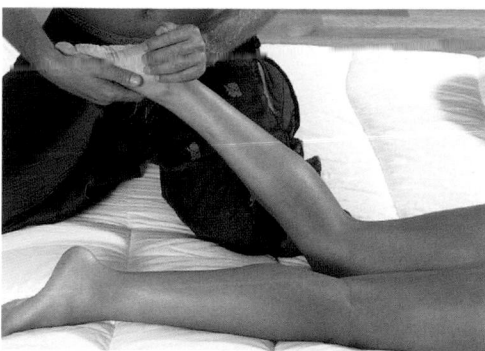

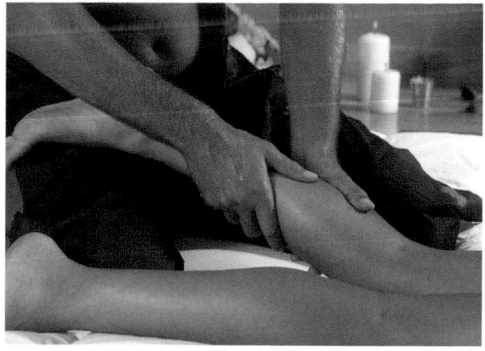

**3. Rub the ankle and instep:** *Vigorously rub the ankles, heel, and instep.*

**4. Knead the calf:** *Slide your palms over the calf and shin, kneading the area.*

**5. Knead the biceps femoris:** *With open hands, knead the back and upper leg.*

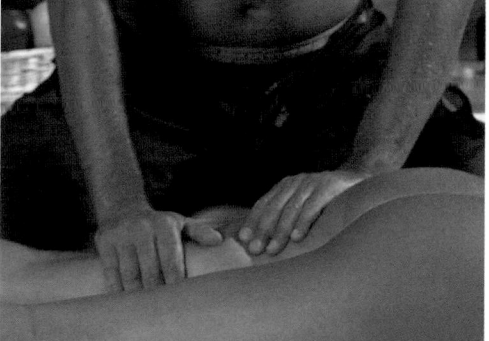

**6. Knead the buttocks:** *Tone the buttocks by kneading. This technique releases blocked kundalini energy. It is very common for the recipient to feel a wave of energy that rises to the head.*

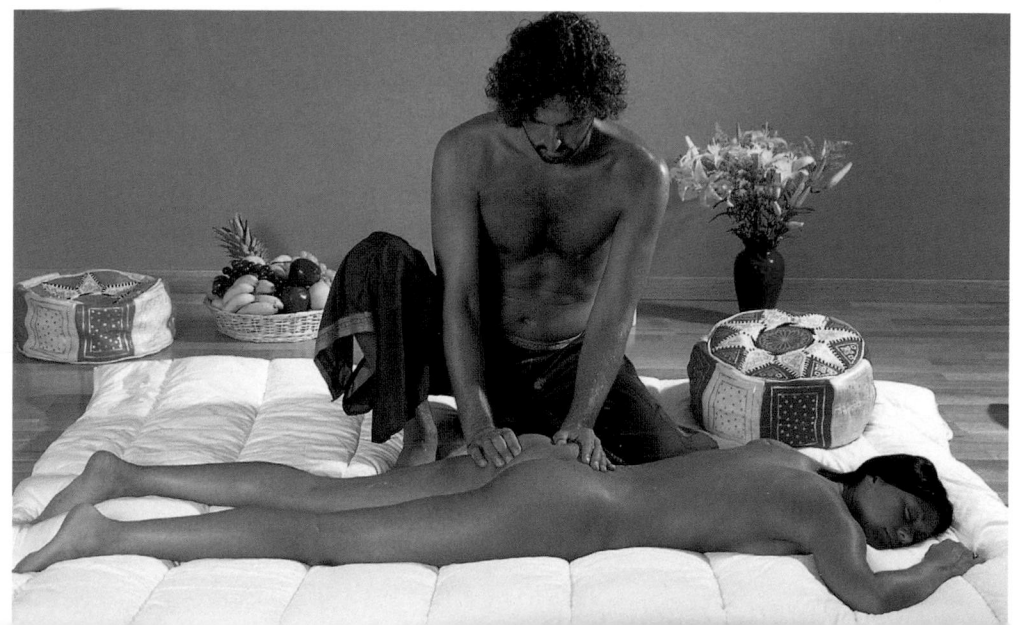

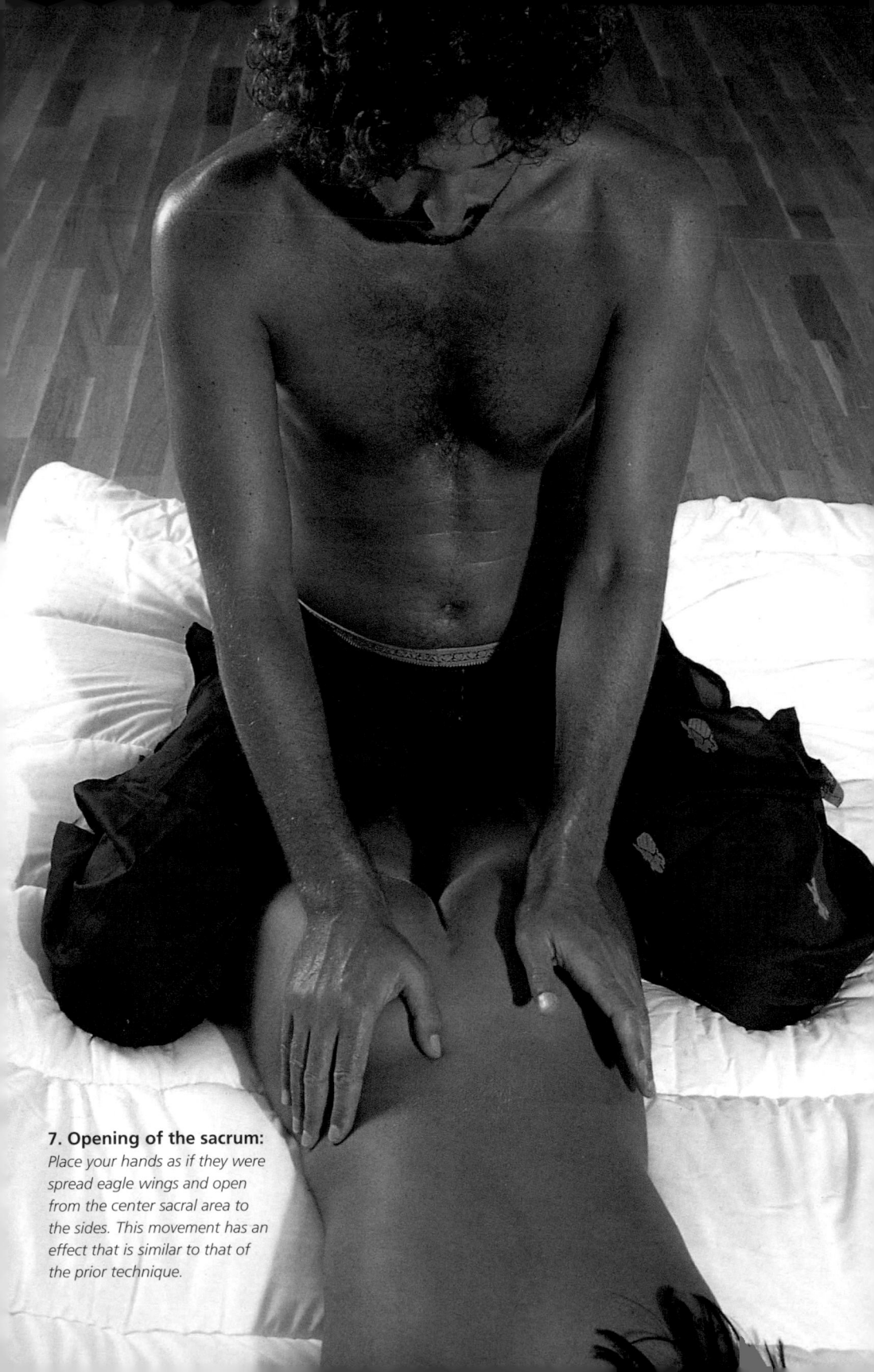

**7. Opening of the sacrum:**
*Place your hands as if they were
spread eagle wings and open
from the center sacral area to
the sides. This movement has an
effect that is similar to that of
the prior technique.*

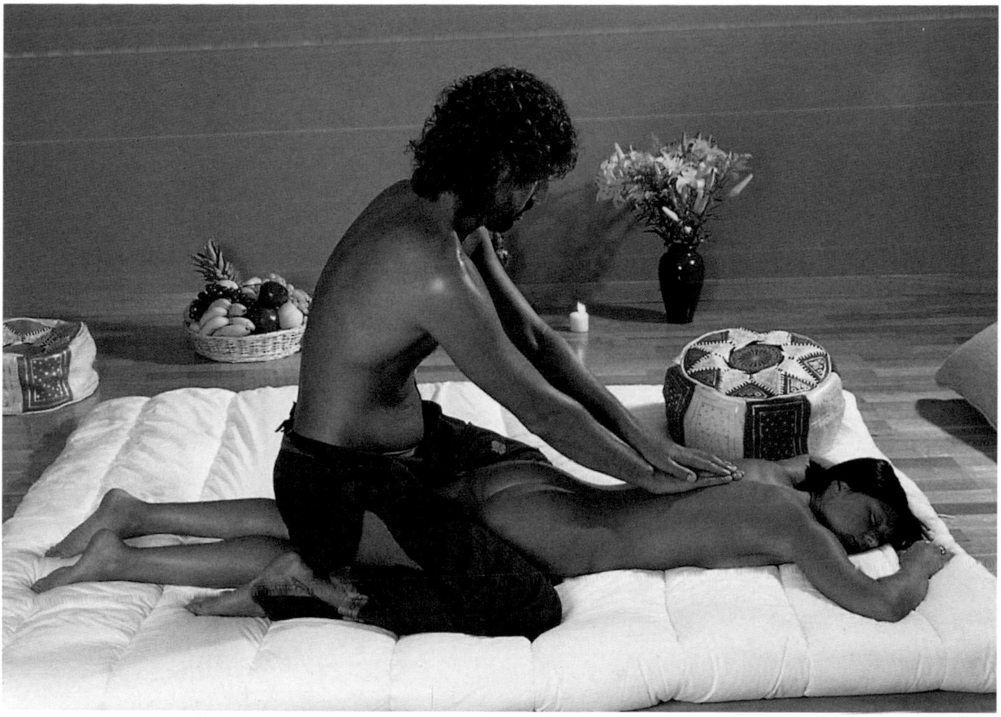

**8. Rub the spine:** *Placing your hands flat like a board, go up from the sacrum to the neck while generating heat.*

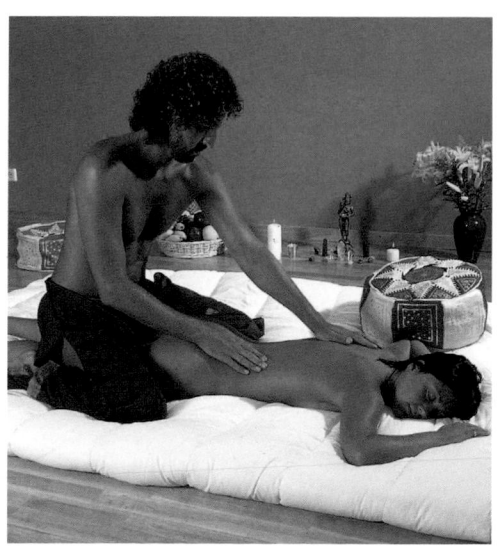

**9. Stimulate the back:** *Slide both hands across the entire surface of the back.*

**10. Release arm tension:** *Using both hands, knead the arms gently.*

**11. Gliding with the hands:** *This technique is very important because the hands are extremely sensitive. Gently glide your hand over the recipient's hand while stimulating the fingers and nails. Feel their body language as their sensitivity begins to awaken. It is very common that recipients who lack affection will unconsciously hold your hand for a while.*

**12. Shoulder kneading:** *With the base of the hands, knead the deltoid area where a lot of tension tends to accumulate.*

**13. Gentle stimulation of the hair:** *Caress the head, kneading it gently. Then move their contracted energy so that they can let go of worries, and fill the void with relaxation. Finally, run your hands through the hair and then grab it to release any tension. This technique gives great pleasure and a feeling of surrender.*

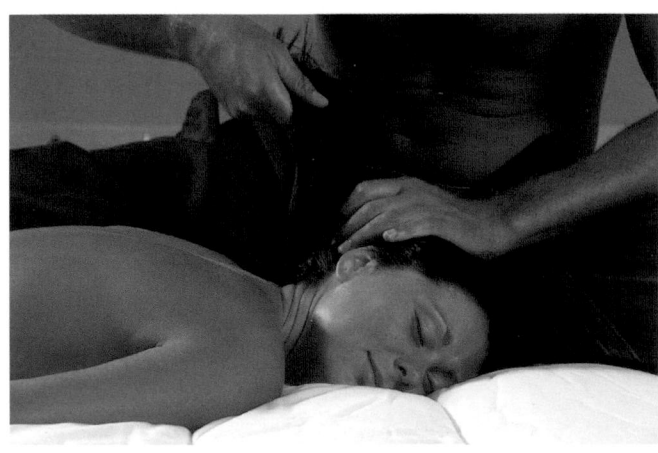

## Face up

**14. Gliding your hands across the whole face:** *Softly and delicately touch and glide your hands on the face without forgetting the forehead, eyebrows, eyelids, nose, mouth, and ears.*

**15. Kneading the neck:** *Glide three fingers of each hand (index, ring, and middle) from the nape (seventh cervical vertebra) to the neck.*

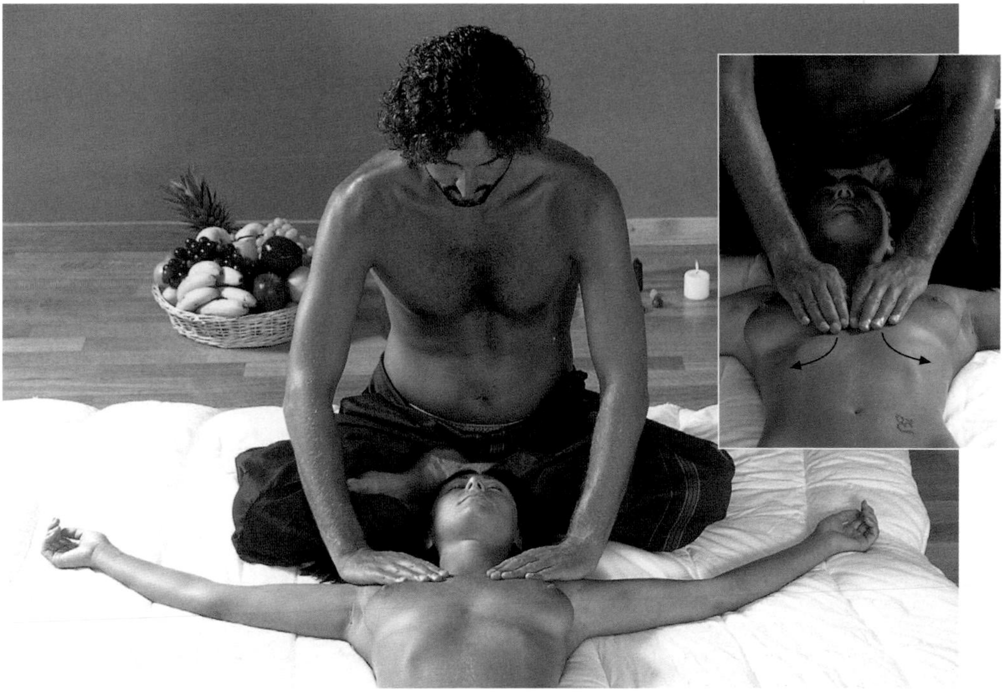

**16. Open the chest:** *Make opening movements across the surface of the chest, and make circles around the breasts.*

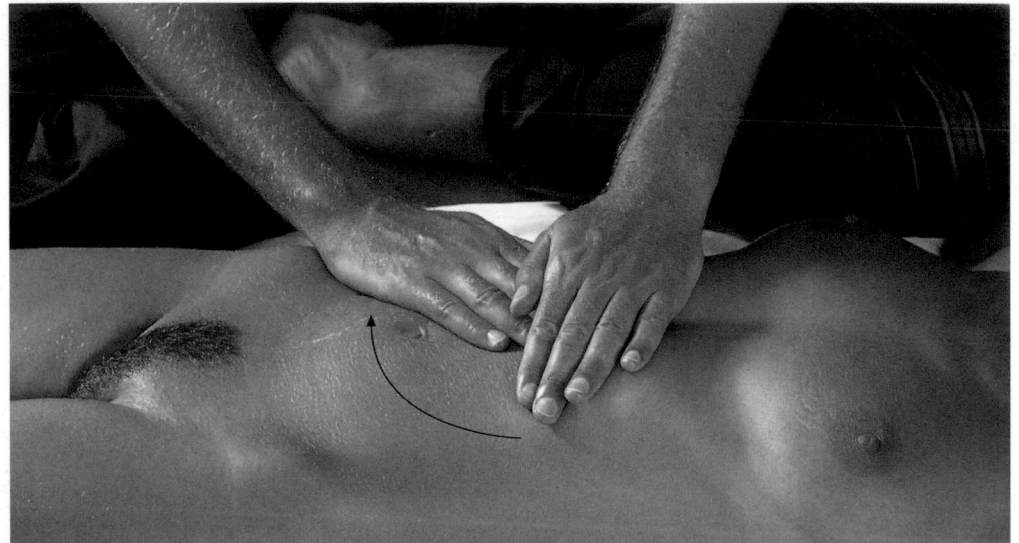

**17. Relaxation of the abdomen:** *Draw very soft circles on the abdomen.*

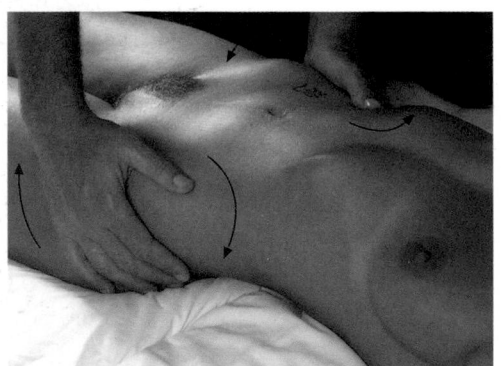

**18. Gliding your hands along the hips:** *Glide your hands outward over the second chakra, reaching the hip, pubic area, and leg opening. It is very common for the recipient to experience sexual arousal during this movement, so it is important that you make them breathe deeply in order for this awakened energy to get distributed to the other chakras.*

**19. Gliding your hands along the leg:** *Run your hands over the legs, quadriceps, knee, tibia, and ankle.*

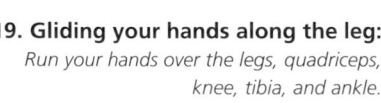

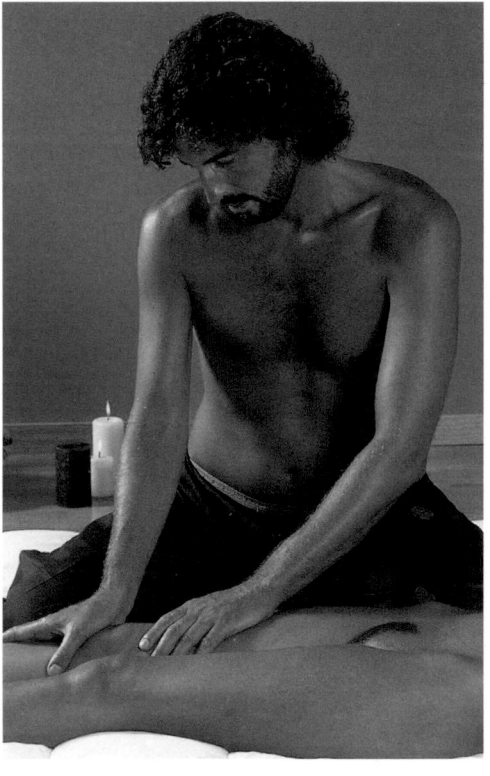

**20. Relax the body:**
*Finally, caress and gently press on each area of the body for a few seconds. Start on the feet and end at the head. The recipient should lie on their back at all times.*

## 2. THE PRINCIPLE OF MOVEMENT AND DANCE

Work on moving the body's joints to release energy blockages.

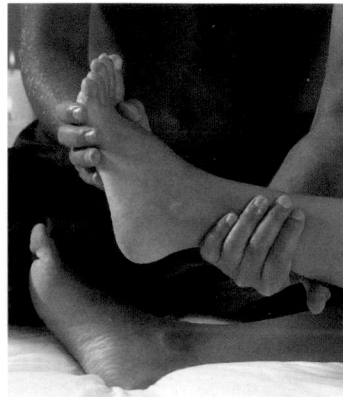

**1. Ankle move:** *With one hand on the ankle and one on the sole of the foot, move the entire foot in circles, in both directions, to release muscular tension. Then bend them forward and backward by grabbing the toes.*

**2. Knee move:** *Grab a foot with both hands and then flex the leg until it reaches the chest. Repeat several times, making sure that you handle the knee very gently.*

**3. Pelvic move:** *Use both hands to grab the pelvis below the sacrum and make circular movements from side to side.*

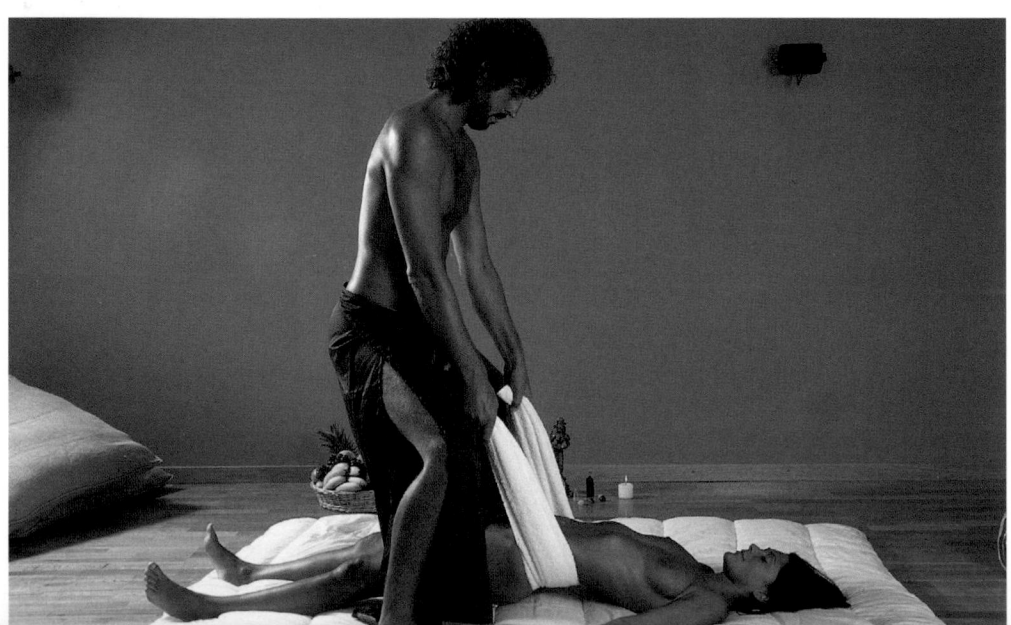

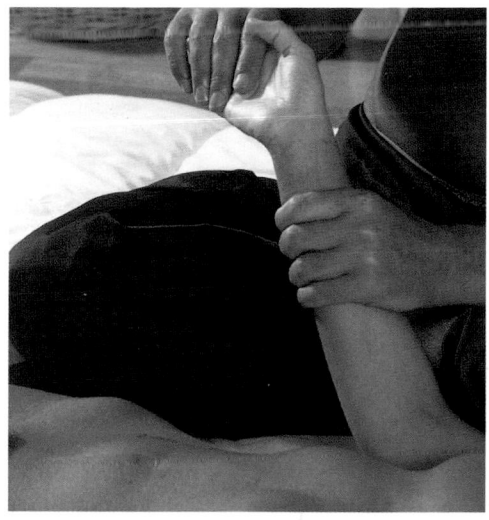

**4. Flex the spine:** *With hands on the back, lift the spine on an inhale and lower it on an exhale. This technique opens up the chest as it unlocks and flexes the vertebrae.*

**5. Wrist move:** *With one hand holding the recipient's fingers and the other placed on the elbow, make circular movements with the wrist, first in one direction then the other.*

**6. Elbow move:** *Grab the shoulder with one hand and the forearm with the other to move the elbow joint.*

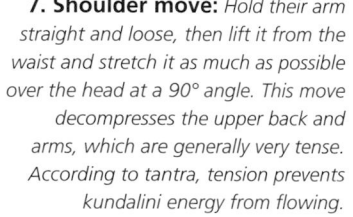

**7. Shoulder move:** *Hold their arm straight and loose, then lift it from the waist and stretch it as much as possible over the head at a 90° angle. This move decompresses the upper back and arms, which are generally very tense. According to tantra, tension prevents kundalini energy from flowing.*

## 3. THE PRINCIPLE OF BREATHING

Throughout this principle, practice a series of breathing techniques that cleanse, energize, and relax.

### *Cleansing breathing*

Inhale deeply through your nose and exhale out the mouth as you empty out the lungs. Fill your lungs with fresh air to benefit the pulmonary alveoli, increase blood oxygenation, and improve the functions of your heart and brain.

Do this for four or five minutes and then be sure to stop and breathe gently through the nose, then repeat this process following any other cleansing techniques.

### *Energy breathing*

This breathing technique is done in three stages: inhaling (*puraka*), holding (*kumbaka*) and exhaling (*rechaka*). Inhale through the nose for five to seven seconds, hold it in for five seconds, and finally exhale for nine or twelve seconds, depending on your lung capacity.

**1. Slide upward:** *Place your hands on each ankle and gently go up the legs, chest, shoulders, and arms, until you reach the hands. Start cleansing breathing for three cycles of five minutes each, with intervals of abdominal breathing for relaxation. Continue with the same technique.*

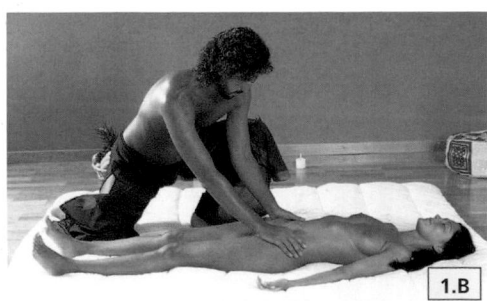

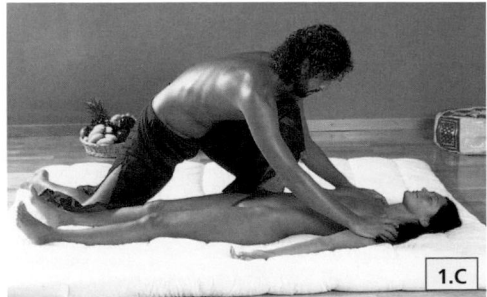

Adding the holding phase, this breathing helps to store *qi* energy or *prana* throughout the body. According to tantra: "Your thoughts can move energy wherever you want it or toward a particular activity." You can guide energy to any particular chakra you want to strengthen, or take seven breaths (one for each chakra, starting at the bottom, moving up, and ending at the seventh). You can also visualize how the orange-colored energy rises from the sacrum to the top of the head, like a flame.

### *Relaxing breathing*

Inhale and exhale as you inflate and deflate the abdomen. Also known as abdominal breathing, diaphragmatic breathing, or belly breathing.

The top of the lungs do not engage much since this breathing is done using the diaphragm.

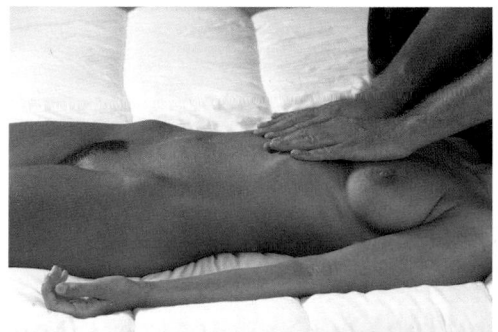

**2. Opening the chest and abdomen:** *Press gently, making opening movements over the chest and abdomen. Do seven breathing cycles.*

**3. Connect the chakras:** *Place one hand on the first chakra and the other at the top of the head, while doing abdominal breathing. Then place one hand on the second chakra and the other on the fifth; then finish by placing them on the third and fourth chakra. Stay on each chakra for one minute.*

## 4. THE PRINCIPLE OF FIRE AND AROUSAL

According to tantra, living energy in the body, *kundalini*, is a fiery energy. Just as air fuels fire, *kundalini* energizes us internally.

Fire has its own characteristic of joy, contentment, excitement, sexual energy, spiritual inner fervor, enlightenment, courage, and passion. This element helps people recover their ancestral power and their body and soul connection to the magic of nature. Be aware of energy and its awakening, keeping a conscious purpose without attachment.

Tantra sees each woman as Shakti in the female body, and each man as Shiva in the male body. For this technique, you need to practice mutual respect, intelligence, and consciousness. Do not let your mind block you with its own prejudices or temptations. Simply feel how life energy moves within you. Return to your natural state filled with peace as you contemplate being a creature of light.

**1. Stimulation of the mouth:** *Slide two fingers (index and middle) gently along the contour of the lips.*

**2. Nipple stimulation:** *With those same two fingers, stimulate the nipples by delicately touching them and making circles around them. According to tantra, the nipples are the feminine polarity of the male body, while its masculine polarity is the penis. By contrast, the nipples are the masculine polarity of the female body, while its feminine polarity is the vagina. Therefore, during the sexual act both poles come together, above and below, producing spiritual light. Breathe deeply at all times, and stay present with excitement as you awaken your internal energy.*

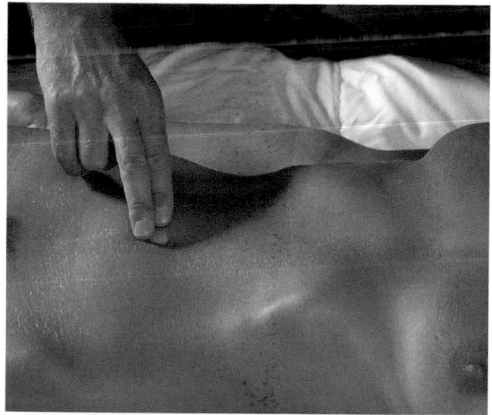

**3. Circles around the navel:** *With the index and middle fingers, tap and glide along this area as you make gentle circles.*

**4. Looking for the jewel:** *Along with the previous technique, respectfully glide your hand over the pubic area, grazing the lingam (penis) or yoni (vagina) without even touching them. In so doing you will awaken the other energy polarity of the body. Breathe and stay conscious of the rising energy level. It helps to visualize an orange stripe that goes up from the first to the seventh chakra.*

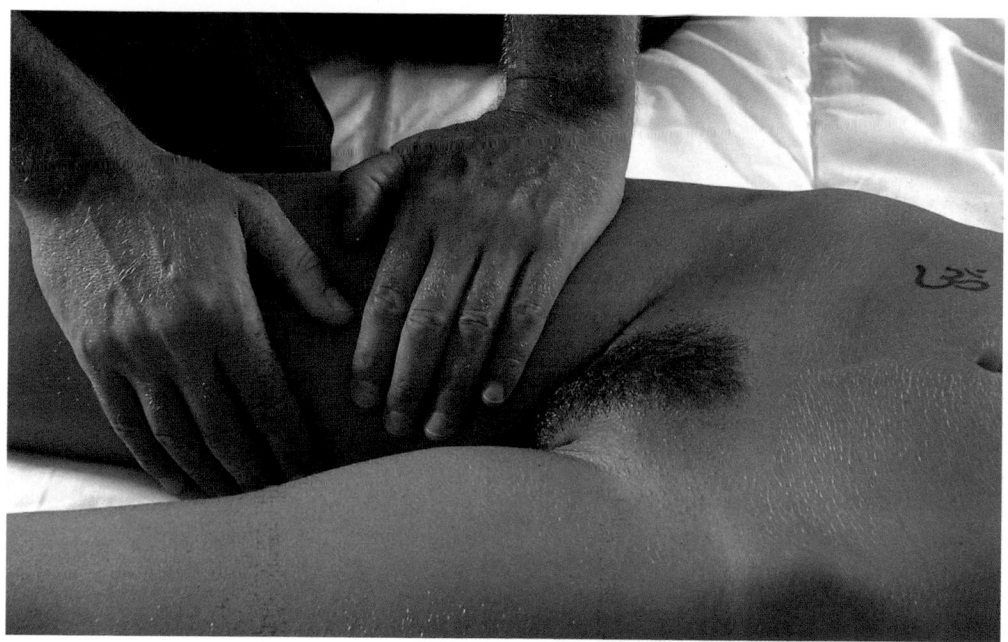

**5. Touch the wrists and forearms:** *Gently glide your fingers on the wrists and forearms as though your fingers were feathers.*

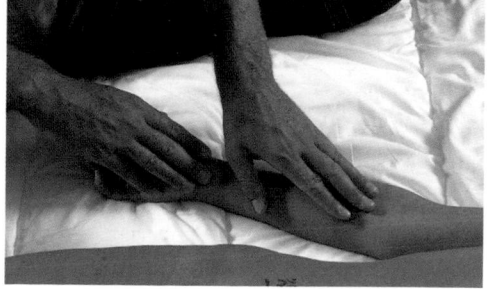

## 5. THE PRINCIPLE OF PLEASURE AND LOVE

According to tantra, it is possible to learn through pleasure.

Religions have encouraged us to suffer, to think of suffering as a way to get into heaven. However, tantra goes hand in hand with pleasure (understood as nourishment for the body) and love (perceived as sublime, delicate, and conscious energy).

Resetting this principle of pleasure and love is of vital importance because too many people live constantly criticizing themselves, ashamed, repressed, and unable to receive the gifts and good fortune that life has to offer.

**Delicate touch:** *Touch gently with your hands around the recipient's body, more like a caress than a massage. Touching and giving affection helps do away with loneliness. Lovingly touching someone can completely change their attitude towards life. It is very common with this technique to see tears flow. Let it happen. Be sure to place your hands on every chakra, joint, and body part. Do this massage with the recipient first facing up and then down.*

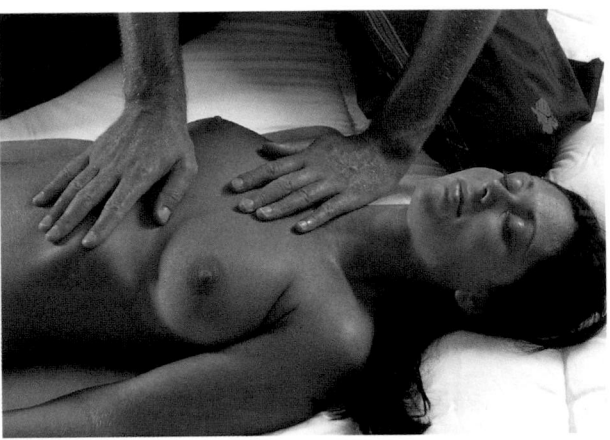

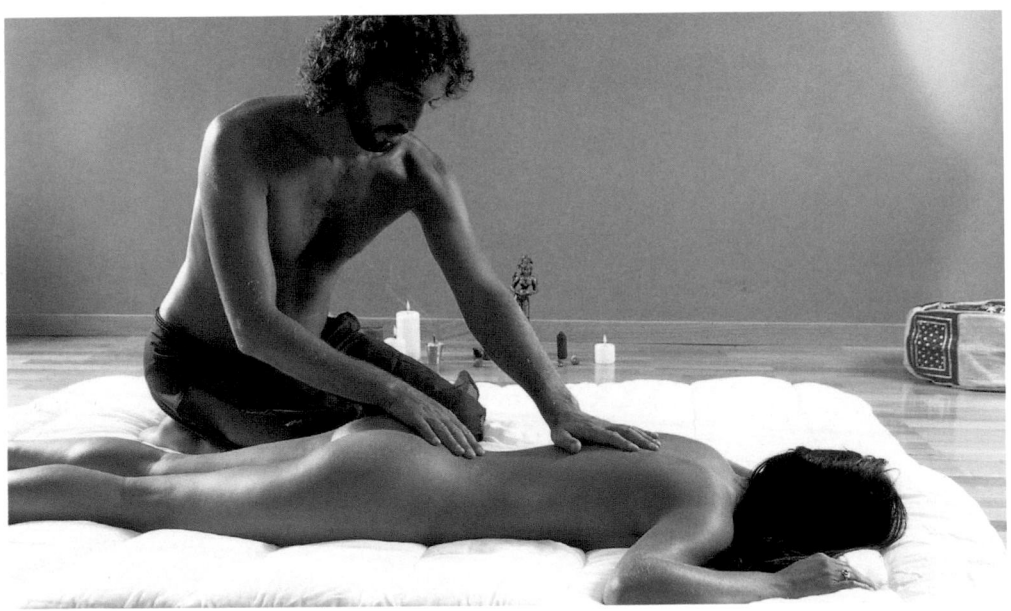

## 6. THE PRINCIPLE OF THE UNION BETWEEN SHIVA AND SHAKTI

These two concepts are understood as Shiva, consciousness, and Shakti, energy, tantra's driving force. The masculine and the feminine.

Any union, however small, represents the union of two principles: seed and earth, fire and air, sexual unity, petals and stem, electric plug receiving electricity, etc. And the Principle of the Union aims to balance both sides.

Shiva and Shakti are present in humans, each ruling a few functions and principles, as shown in the illustration. For women and men, the right side is male, while the left side is female. If a person is too active and not very contemplative or receptive, there will be increased activity on the right side of their body. By contrast, if they live too intellectually or passively, their left side will be most active.

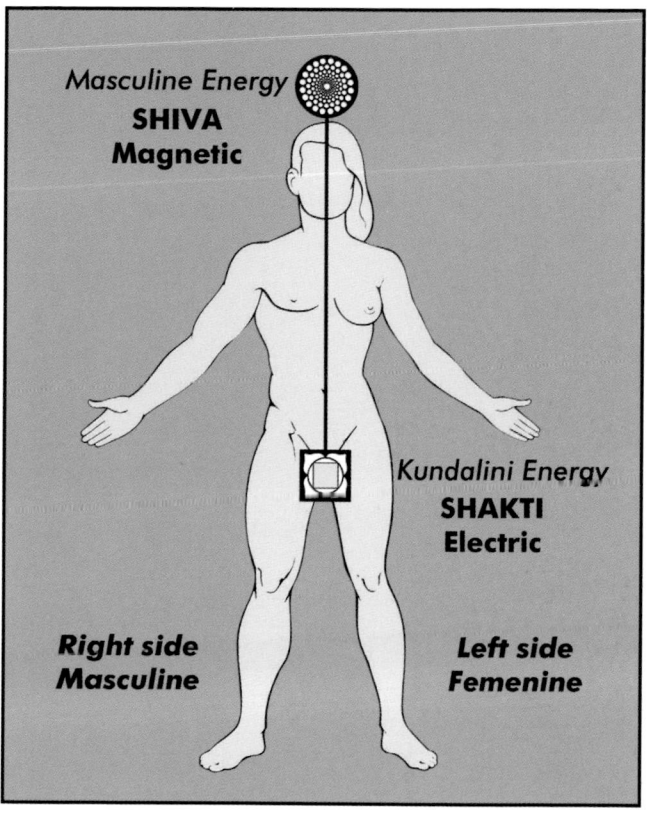

It will also have an influence on body temperature: a person can feel that their extremities are very cold due to lack of activity, not doing sports, and neglecting their inner fire by not using their gifts or individual talents. But someone else may feel a rise in their body temperature if they live very aggressively, at an accelerated pace, with great stress or tension.

Shakti exists in the sexual region of the first chakra, and within it is the divine energy of *kundalini*, represented as a coiled serpent.

Shiva, meanwhile, is latent on the top of the head, in the seventh chakra.

The purpose of tantra is to balance and unite the cosmic couple that lives within. In doing so, Shakti will rise up to meet Shiva.

Electric and magnetic life vibrates between the two ends of the spine, which is where the two halves of the physical body unite.

Repeat the following techniques first with the recipient facing down, activating and meditating on the Shakti, activating and meditating on Shiva, and then place the recipient on their back, but this time without repeating the meditations.

1.A

### 1. Activate Shakti:

*Move your hands up along the left side of the body from the heel, leg, and buttock, up to the shoulder, down the arm, and finally to the hand. Do each movement warmly and uniformly without stopping. Repeat about twelve times while softly guiding the recipient along the following meditation.*

1.B

#### SHAKTI MEDITATION

*Feel how your body is a sacred temple. Inside it is a golden goddess sleeping in the sacrum and she wakes up when you flow with life. With your consciousness, try to awaken the energy of Shakti, the Goddess. Feel how it climbs the left side of your body, feel how she is one with the moon, the sea, the flowers, the breeze, with the senses. Feel that you are vital and receptive energy. Visualize a wave of electricity going up your body. Breathe that energy.*

1.C

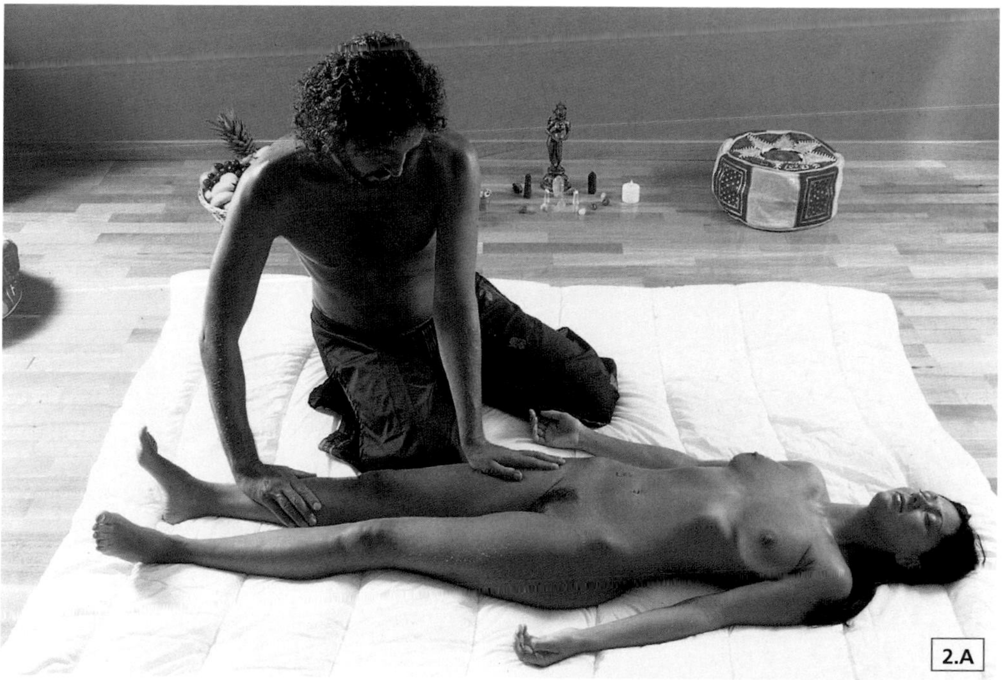

2.A

## 2. Activate Shiva:

*Repeat the same sequence of the previous exercise, but this time do it on the right side of the body. Do this twelve times while softly guiding the recipient along with the following meditation.*

2.B

---

### SHIVA MEDITATION

Feel nature's force, magnetism, and power. Imagine the sun within you as it rises up on the right side of your body. You are fire, you are a volcano, a hot vortex of energy. Feel the warmth and the enthusiasm for life burning in your cells. You generate light. You are a fiery comet, the center of a volcano, a passionate heart. You are love, passion, courage, and adventure. You are a dancer flowing with life. You embody action. Feel the magnetism dancing through your being.

2.C

## 7. THE PRINCIPLE OF SILENCE, ECSTASY, AND UNITY

The final principle aims to push the boundaries of the mind and expand consciousness, immersing the person into a space of peace and quiet, connecting with the natural state of life, the essence, and the raw material that makes up the universe. My teacher Osho said that "existence is made of a substance called delight."

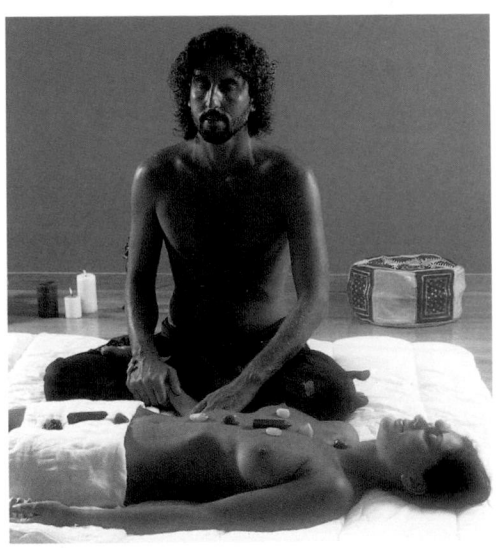

**Relaxing with gemstones:** *As the recipient lies on their back, place a gemstone on each chakra, from the first to the seventh. Then cover them with a sheet or blanket so that their body does not cool off, although this will not be needed in the summer. The recipient will breathe freely and smoothly through the nose at an increasingly slower pace. Play faint background music, while repeating the Beatitudes as a tantric meditation, with a soft voice and at a slow pace. When finished, let him or her enjoy the moment for ten to fifteen minutes.*

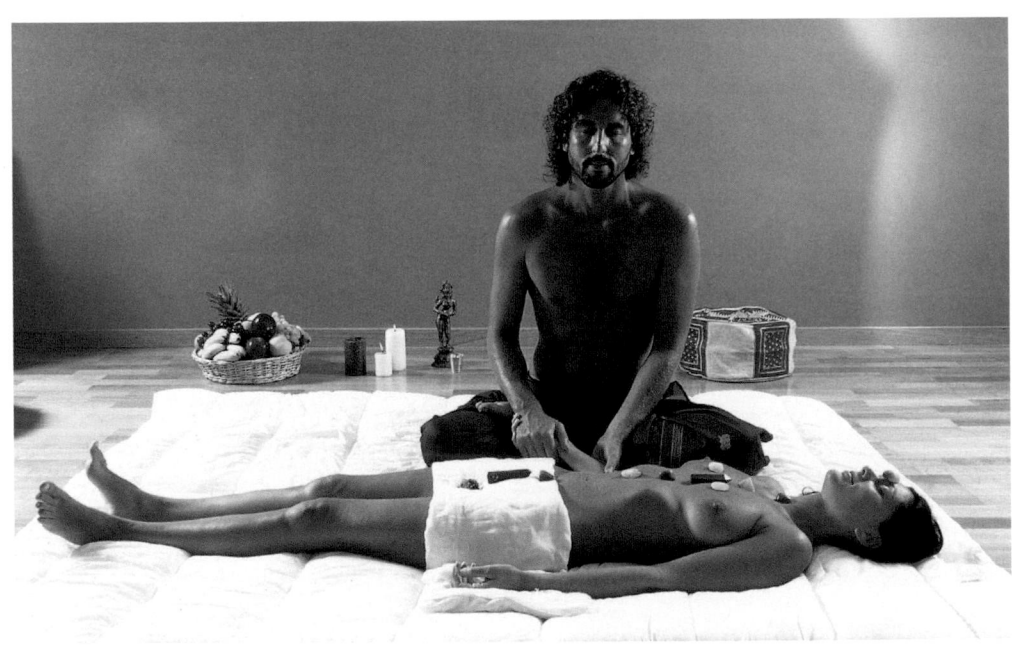

## THE NEW TANTRIC BEATITUDES

*Blessed are those who are positive, for they know the sublime side of life.*
*Blessed are those who do not criticize, for they will have creativity.*
*Blessed are those who are in love, for they are the only ones alive.*
*Blessed are those who enjoy the art of breathing, for they will have an abundant life.*

*Blessed are those who reach an orgasm, for That is the Big Bang in all its essence.*
*Blessed are those who practice meditation, for they will vanquish death.*
*Blessed are those who love and nourish their body, for it is the temple of the divine.*
*Blessed are those who have an open mind, for they are released from false morality and sin.*

*Blessed are the non-dogmatic mystics, for they know the ultimate freedom.*
*Blessed are the lonely, for they can join with others.*
*Blessed are those who are not swayed by beliefs, for they learn from experience.*
*Blessed are those with a healthy heart, for they will have innocence.*

*Blessed are those who understand what they feel, for they will be wise.*
*Blessed are those who act out of selfless interest, for their soul will be filled with joy.*
*Blessed are those who are like children, for playing is the law of life.*
*Blessed are those who fulfill their destiny, for they live in peace.*

*Blessed are those who touch, smell, see, hear, and enjoy, for they feel without repression.*
*Blessed are those who are not afraid, for they are protected by love.*
*Blessed are those who live without guilt, for their roads will open.*
*Blessed are those who make of their life a daily gift, for life will repay them twice.*

*Blessed are those who are simple and celebrate, those who love and sing.*
*Those who dance and create, those who live in the present, conscious seekers.*
*Those who do not adhere to the past nor fear the future, for they shall see God laughing eternally.*

## HARMONIZATION OF THE CHAKRAS

In another session, we will work on the first two chakras from the back and the remaining five from the front of the body. All techniques are to be done for ten to twelve times.

### *Face down*

**First and second chakra**

 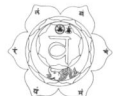

It is important that the recipient do soft cleansing breathing while being massaged. Here we will also add individual visualization exercises and, in some cases, the bija mantra (the "seed" of each chakra's sound), which will be repeated mentally by the recipient.

---

**BIJA MANTRA**
*First chakra:*
*Lam, a red circle.*
*Second chakra:*
*Vam, an orange circle.*

---

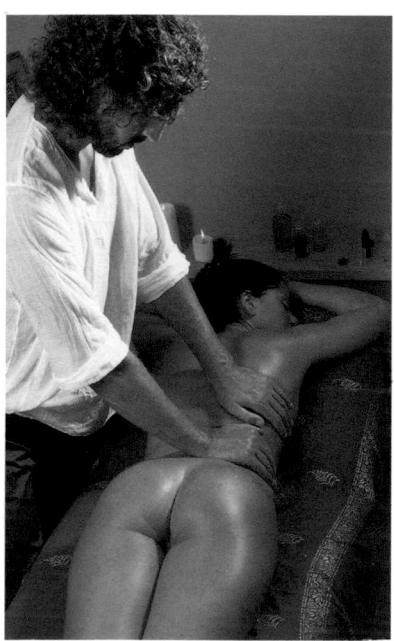

**1. Fiery friction:** *With the basis of both hands, go up about six inches (fifteen centimeters) from the sacrum, while generating heat.*

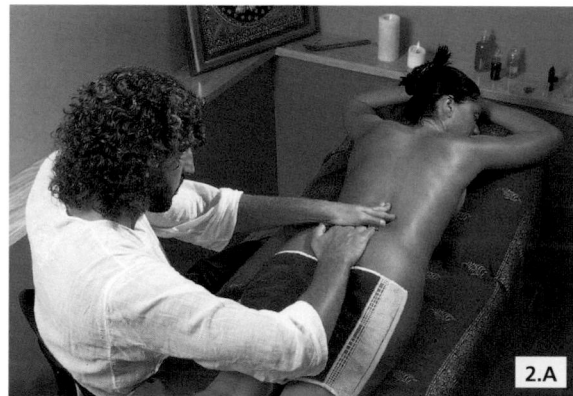

2.A

**2. Circle of fire:**
*With one hand over the other, make circles of four inches (ten centimeters) in diameter in the central area of the sacrum. Warm up the entire area. Remember that clockwise movements invigorate, while counterclockwise movements sedate.*

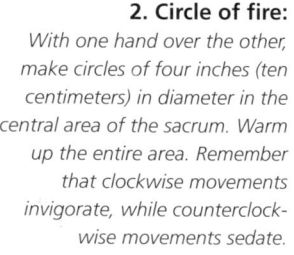

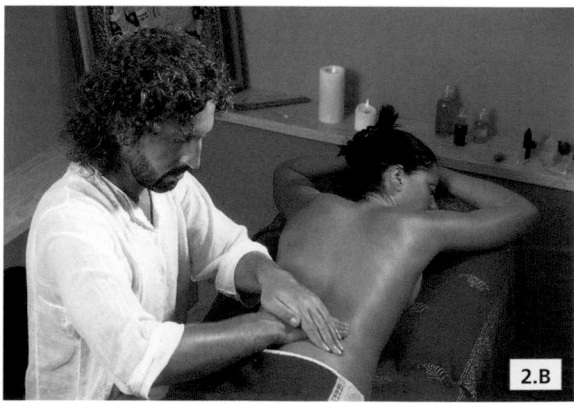

2.B

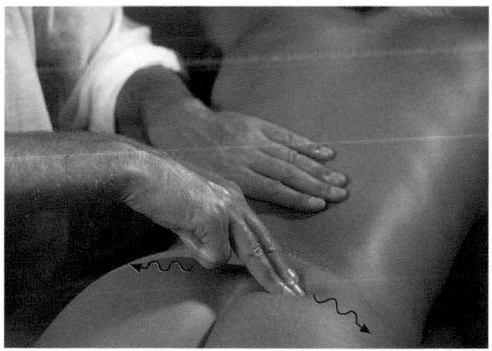

**3. Zigzag movements:** *With three fingers (index, middle, and ring), make zigzag movements from the sacrum to the waist, first in one direction and then the other.*

**4. Opening of the sacred:** *With both hands, open the surface of the sacrum outward and horizontally.*

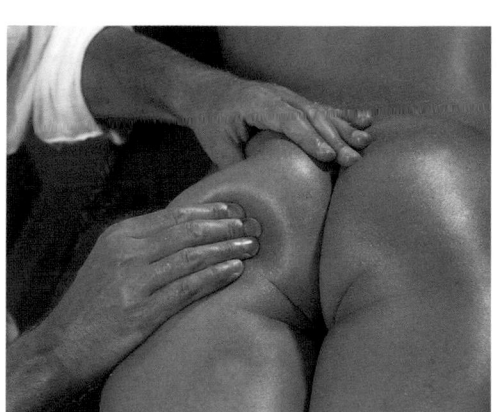

**5. Knead the buttocks:**
*Stimulate this area by circling the buttocks. This releases blocked kundalini energy.*

**6. Stimulate the back:**
*Rest both hands across the surface of the back, and hold and press for about five seconds.*

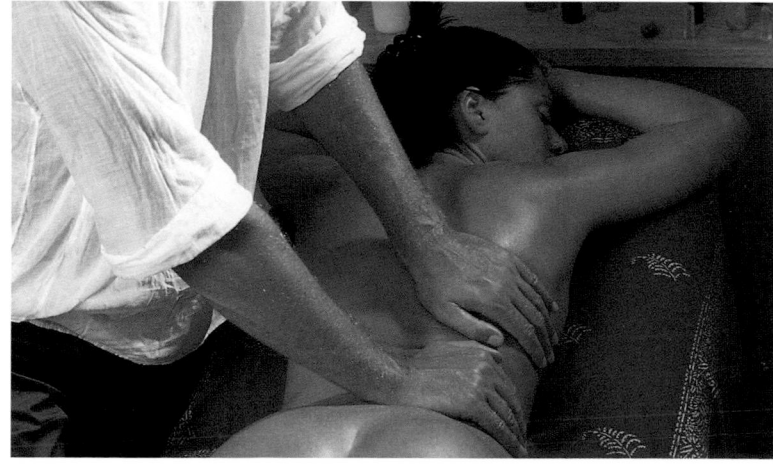

## *Face up*

**Third chakra**

> **BIJA MANTRA**
>
> *Ram,* a yellow circle.

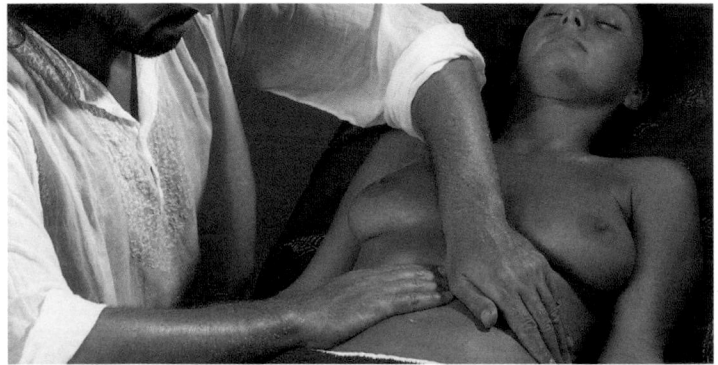

### 1. Opening the solar plexus:

*Place one hand over the other and gently knead the surface of the solar plexus, from the stomach up to the navel.*

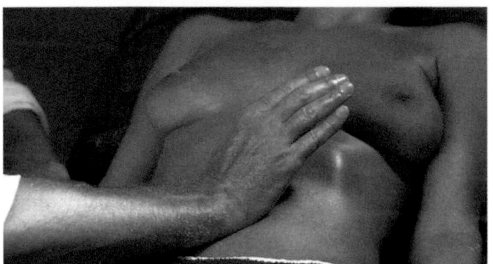

**2. Circle of fire on the belly:** *Make vigorous circles with the base of the hand for two minutes, within four inches (ten centimeters) of the navel. This technique will allow the energy of fire to rise up.*

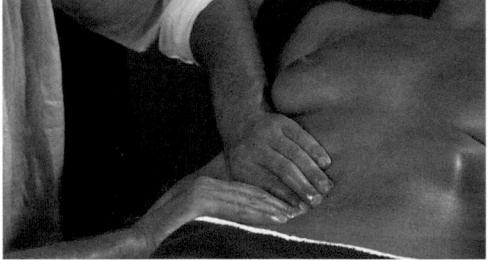

**3. Sustained pressure:** *Using the entire surface of your hands, stretch and press the stomach area by making opening movements. Go slowly as you hold the pressure.*

| MALE | | FEMALE | |
|---|---|---|---|
| 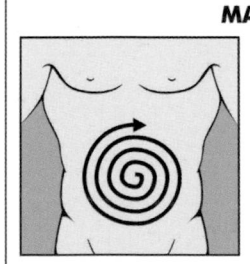 | 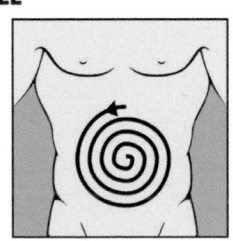 | 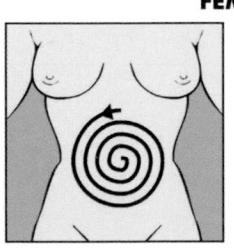 | 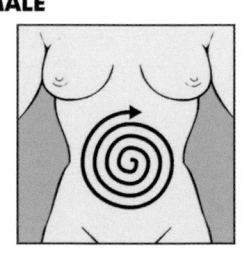 |

**4. Solar harmonization:** *Make circles on the solar plexus and on the coccygeal plexus (second and third chakra), as shown in the illustration. For women, first do it thirty-six times counterclockwise and then twenty-four times clockwise. For men, do it thirty-six times clockwise and then twenty-four times counterclockwise. Let the energy increase evenly.*

**Fourth chakra**

**BIJA MANTRA**

*Yam, a green circle.*

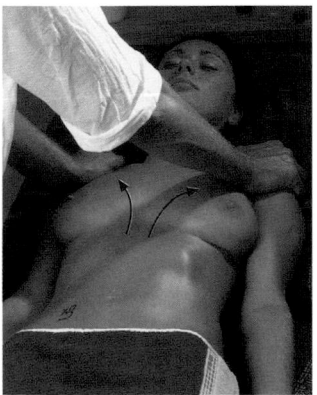

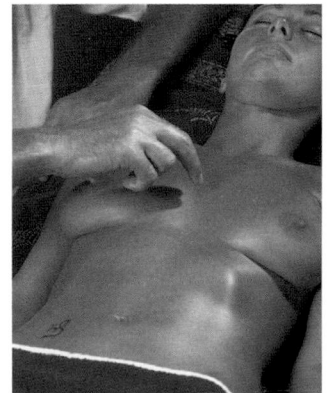

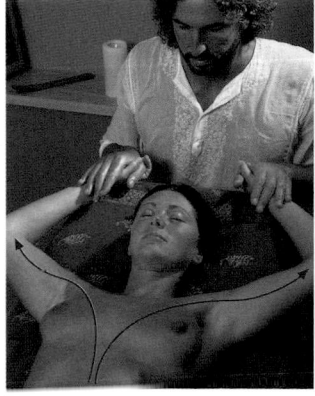

**1. Opening arc:**
*With one hand after the other, open up the area that stretches from the center of the chest to the shoulders.*

**2. Taps:** *With the index and middle fingers of the right hand, vigorously tap on the center of the chest.*

**3. Arm extensions:** *Raise the recipient's arms over their head. Then, with both hands, go over the center of the chest, the arms, and hands These movements offer relaxation, as they cleanse and open the fourth chakra. Remember that you must sit at the head of the recipient so that you can better reach the entire treatment area.*

**4. Hand play:** *Lovingly slide your hands into the recipient's hands so that their sensitivity awakens.*

**5. Fiery circle:** *With the heel of your hand, make energetic four-inch-wide (ten centimeters) circles in the center of the chest for two minutes. Fiery energy rises.*

**Fifth chakra**

| BIJA MANTRA |
| :---: |
| *Ham,* a blue circle. |

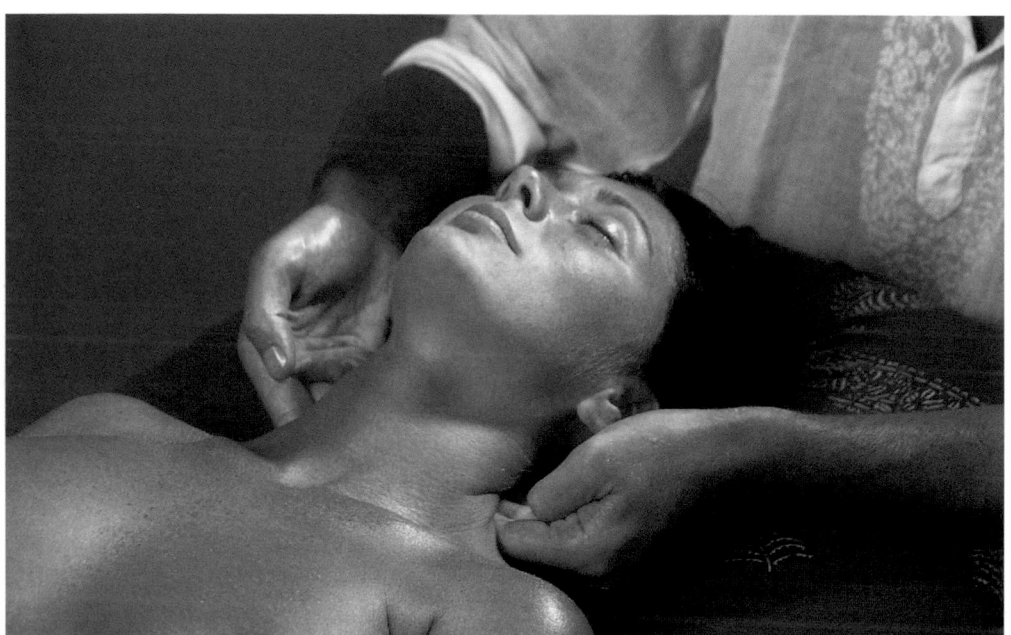

**1. Stretched neck:** *Oftentimes, guilt, inability to express oneself, and keeping in everything we want to say, feel, and think causes blockages in the throat and the fifth chakra. To ease this tension, glide three fingers (index, middle, and ring) along the neck, slightly raising the head.*

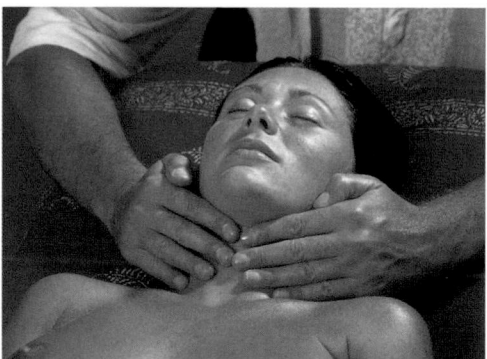

**2. Opening of the throat:** *With the same fingers used in the previous technique, make opening movements very softly over the throat.*

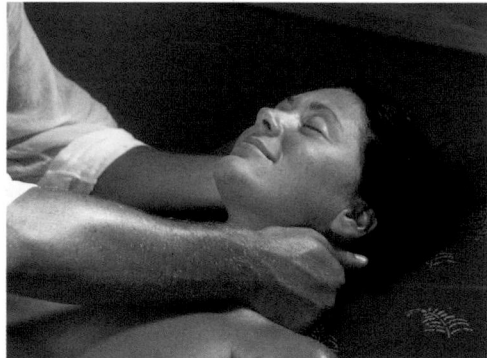

**3. To stimulate and relax:** *With your right hand, stimulate the sides of the neck.*

**Sixth chakra**

**BIJA MANTRA**

*Om*, a white circle.

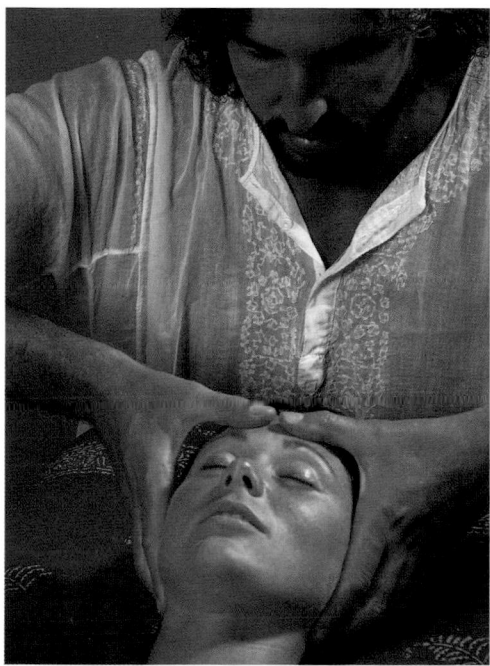

**1. Eyebrow opening:** *With your thumbs, make a gentle and sustained opening movement towards the temples.*

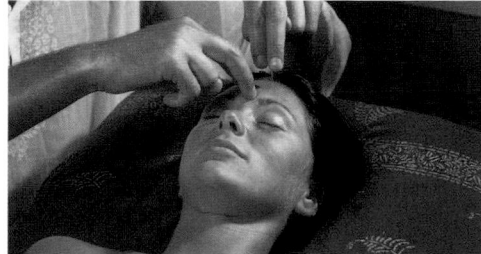

**2. Taps:** *With your right index finger and right thumb, tap gently in the area between the eyebrows.*

**3. Circles:** *Make stimulating circles around the third eye, using three fingers (index, middle, and ring).*

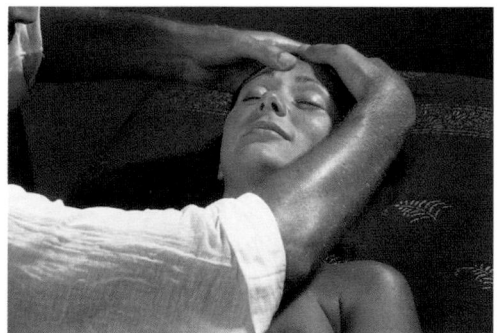

**4. Feather step:** *Glide your thumbs very gently, as though they were feathers, from the point between the eyebrows to the hairline, always straight and upward.*

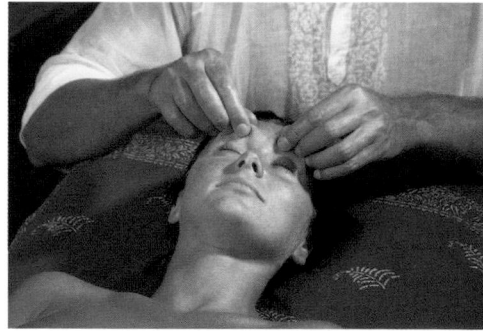

**5. Pressures:** *With the thumb and forefinger, gently press the entire area of the eyebrows.*

**6. The palm of peace:**
*Place the palm of your right hand on the recipient's forehead, with your fingers towards the face. Visualize a flame, a blue-violet circle, or a snow-white dot. Rest your hand there for one or two minutes.*

**Seventh chakra**

| BIJA MANTRA | Visualize a beautiful lotus flower with a thousand petals and a bright sun. |
|---|---|
| *Om*, a violet circle. | |

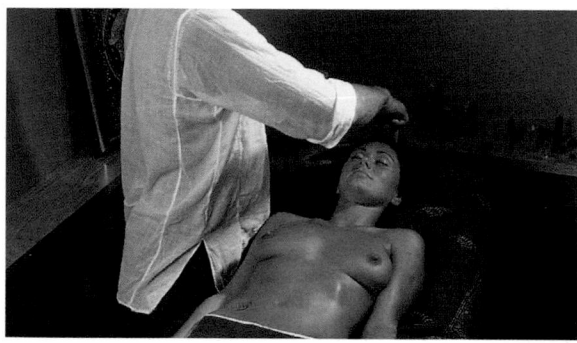

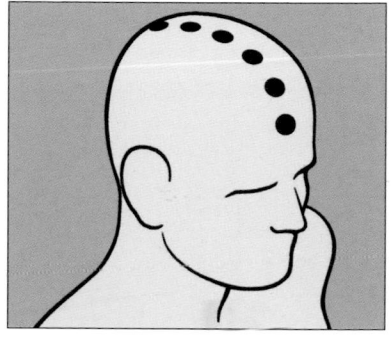

**1. Zigzag movement:** *Make a vibrating zigzag motion with three fingers (index, middle, and ring), so as to stimulate the entire upper head area. It is important that the stimulus be continuous from the forehead to the temples, at least for one minute.*

**2. Pressing:** *Using your thumb, press the points that are in the middle of the skull for about five seconds, as shown in the illustration.*

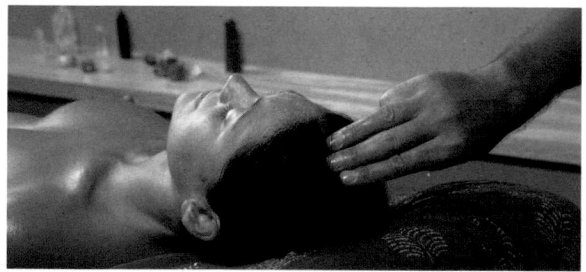

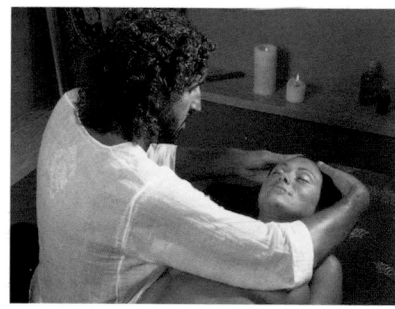

**3. Circles:** *Make stimulating circles on top of the head using three of your fingers (index, middle, and ring).*

**4. Washing the head:** *With the fingers of both hands wide open, stimulate the skull.*

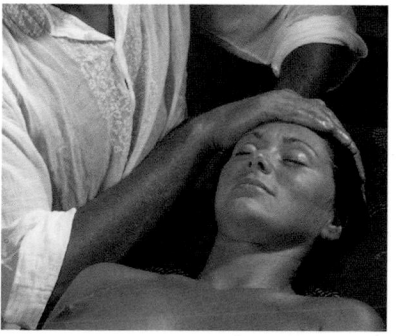

**5. Angel hands:** *Place your hands gently above the crown chakra and keep them there briefly. Breathe softly while visualizing that a cylinder of light floods and bathes the recipient's chakras with divine energy. Then lift your hands and for ten or fifteen minutes to let the recipient enjoy a state of deep peace, harmonization, and inner balance.*

## Suggestions

- Breathing is very important to the success of tantric massages on the chakras. Be sure to guide the recipient by pacing the rhythm of their cleansing breathing, alternating it with gentle breaths. The mind is usually very lazy and tends to forget its connection with conscious breathing.
- Do not let the recipient talk at any time, unless it is to share visions of symbols, images, unknown places, new sensations; everything will be recorded after the session to compare with later sessions. Many facets of the past, current life, or even a previous life can be manifested. Although tantra has no interest in psychoanalysis, we will simply make observations without any judgment.
- It is natural that the person needs more time to "return" to normal waking consciousness. Do not worry, let the recipient take all the time necessary but guide them toward feeling their physical body again.
- Always cleanse any gemstones you use with water and rock salt, or sea water. Then charge them with energy from the sun and the moon. Likewise, rinse your body before the massage.
- Pay attention to any contraindications in performing tantric massage (listed on page 39). Remember, this massage is very strong and powerful since you will be working with the person's consciousness.

- Never stop halfway. If there is catharsis at a certain chakra, guide the recipient out of it through soft breathing, and let them know that their soul is purging something that is no longer needed. Just as the sun comes out after the storm, calm and peace follows any catharsis. Use your voice, your support, and self-control at all times.
- Allow yourself to enjoy everything your recipients share with you about the tantric massage. The benefits and changes they experience will make your soul rejoice.

## MASSAGING THE CHAKRAS ON THE FEET

In general, though more and more people have access to different spiritual paths, most do not know how to relax and meditate. Obviously, if we lived in complete harmony with nature there would be no traumas, muscle contractions, or energy blockages, but we have forgotten to appreciate sunsets, the moon, the stars, the sun, and the body, in our pursuit of material goods, excessive eating, personal pride, excessive sex outside of sacred consciousness, and all the obstacles that slow the soul: greed, selfishness, deceit, etc.

Tantra is an honest, direct, simple, and profound way to return to our roots. Just as the roots of a tree need care, we also need to understand how to care for our own roots: our feet.

| CHAKRAS AND THEIR CORRELATIONS | | | | | |
|---|---|---|---|---|---|
| CHAKRA | SOUND | ELEMENT | GEMSTONE | COLOR | OIL |
| Muladhara | Lam | Earth | Black tourmaline, ruby, and garnet. | Red | Jasmine, cedar. |
| Swadisthana | Vam | Water | Orange stone. | Orange | Sandalwood, jasmine. |
| Manipura | Ram | Fire | Citrine. | Yellow | Lemon. |
| Anahatta | Ham | Air | Rose quartz, green quartz, and emerald. | Green | Rose. |
| Vishudda | Yam | Ether | Aquamarine. | Blue | Mint. |
| Ajna | Om | Light | Lapis lazuli, amethyst. | White | Incense. |
| Sahasrara | Om | Thought | White quartz, amethyst. | Violet | Lotus. |

And the seven chakras can also be stimulated, healed, activated, or sedated by applying tantric techniques to the foot.

This is profound, transformative, and delicate work because you can break barriers, remove blockages, and access alternative states of expanded consciousness. As a result, when people get this tantric massage, oftentimes they feel as though they are "floating" in air. Because the physical body is not the main focus, the energetic body and the other bodies play a more important role in the receiver's awareness.

This is when images can appear along with symbols, sensation of floating or being on the astral plane, memories, premonitions, fears, joys, etc., a whole array of new feelings to fuel the soul's journey may appear.

Basically, at the end of this technique, lightness and peace remains, but it is a journey; a journey into the depths of the unconscious, a cleansing journey. Repressions, blockages, fears, negative attitudes, unresolved conflicts, and multiple barriers to impede the individual's growth can resurface.

Every technique that uses energy, such as massage, is ultimately a shortcut to accelerate personal evolution and inner growth. Therefore, it is extremely valuable as a healing tool.

Although you are working with the feet, this massage is not reflexology, and it is not related to reflexology. However, tantra knows the ancient map of the human body given that spiritual journeys begin from the body and its functions.

It is not recommended that you start tantric stimulus from the feet, but start first with some other type of massage. Reflexology, which is explored in the next chapter, is a good prelude to then focus on the tantric massage from the feet.

The chakra massage is beneficial for people with blockages, fears, traumas, and also for those who wish to reach another state of consciousness.

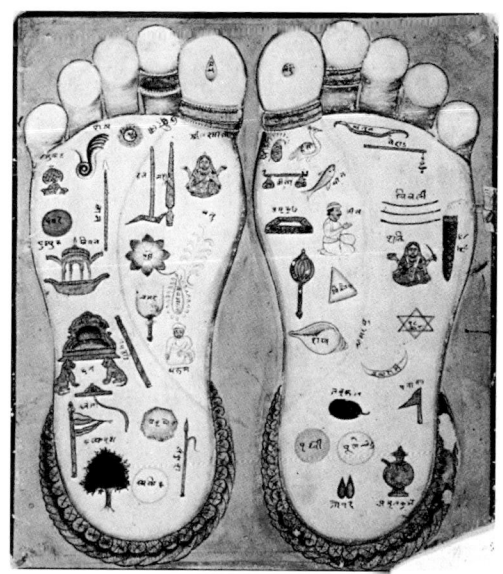

For all, tantric massage will be a relief, a source of joy, a gift to the body, and a bright song for the soul.

It will be a gateway to a meditative state, as never experienced before. This happens because the body is a tide of electric and magnetic circuits, and within it there is a very extensive network of meridians and bioenergetic points.

By pressing points on the feet, we activate the stream of life flowing through these circuits. From thought to action, there is an impact in the different areas of an individual—muscular, skeletal, nervous, organic, emotional, and cerebral—that affects them physically and spiritually.

## Suggestions

All points may show signs; for example, become red, itchy, painful, stiff, crystal. Work on them for several sessions until these symptoms disappear.

All visualizations are to be done for five to seven minutes since this is the amount of time needed to stimulate each energy center.

## Technique

Once the recipient is facing up and fully relaxed, guide them through cleansing breathing while placing gemstones on each of their chakras. Then apply oil to the chakra on which you will be working.

Using your thumbs, stimulate each chakra (shown in the illustrations), making circular movements, ladder motions, pressure, and kneading. Similarly, guide the recipient through the specific visualization corresponding to the chakra that is being stimulated.

Between massaging one chakra and massaging the next, make complete movements around the entire foot so that the connection between the centers of energy is not lost.

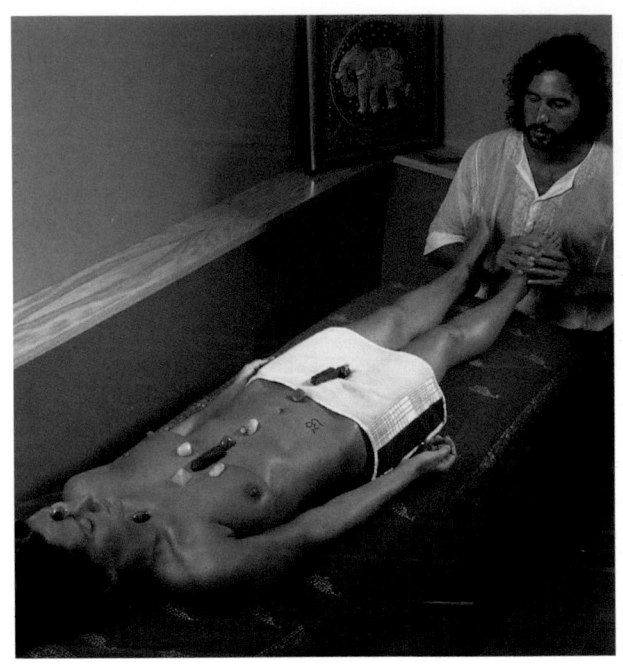

## First chakra

Muladhara is the root chakra and it reflects the following aspects:

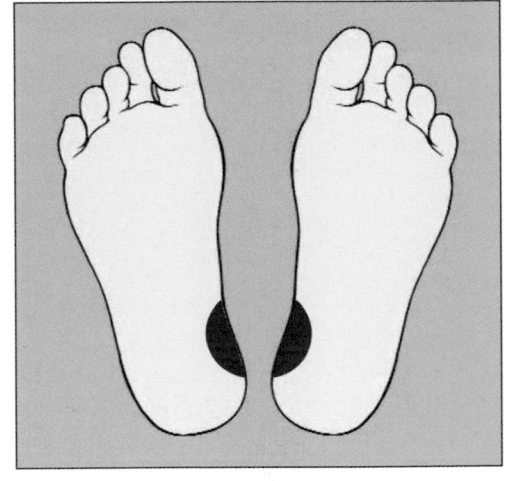

- Economic security.
- State of abundance.
- Survival.
- Material desire for comfort and purchasing power.
- Primary instincts.
- Roots in the Earth (tangible property, contact with nature).
- Rationale, solid human foundations, convictions, personal destiny, using talents and vocation.

People who have not solved the principles above are in conflict with life and have problems in the first chakra. They constantly think of money, self-improvement, buying a home, and watching where to direct the creative energy that God has given them through individual talent; from cooking artistically to carpentry, car repair, writing books, or any way they may be gifted.

Therefore, this chakra will be harmonized through stimulation. Consciousness will focus on abundance, without causing worry. "First seek the Kingdom of Heaven and then everything else will come to you," Jesus said.

Guide the recipient towards abundance through the following meditation:

> *Envision a cornfield, fruits, flowers, mature trees, mountains, and among these, your flexible and healthy physical body walking toward your dream house. See yourself cheerful, carefree, and barefoot, touching the warm soil of the earth. Give thanks internally for the entire life of your physical body, for what it has endured and what it has enjoyed. You can have all the riches of the world, having the wealth of feeling as one with God, the Creator of all the worlds.*

## Second chakra

Swadisthana is the sacral chakra and it reflects the following aspects:

- Sensuality.
- Sensitivity.
- Mobility.
- Sexuality.
- Pleasure stimulus.

People who have not solved the principles above cannot accept joy and pleasure in feeling that they do well in life, and so they have blockages in this chakra.

People who fear or run away from sexuality as a natural part of life repress the element of this center: water. It is known that when water does not flow, it stagnates.

This chakra is linked with feelings and pleasure. There will also be blockages in those who do not accept their sensitivity or who act with rigid patterns of conduct or ethics.

Feed your pleasure whether it is related to food or sex, listen to your favorite music, paint, sing, dance, take baths, light candles, enjoy, laugh, and celebrate. This is the ultimate tantric chakra; use what God has given you to raise your consciousness.

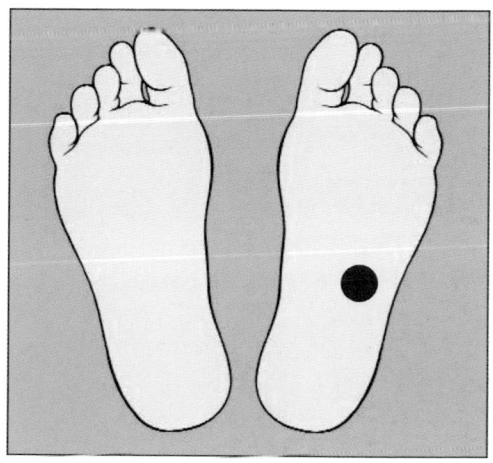

Guide the recipient toward sensitivity through the following meditation:

> *Let yourself feel that your pleasures are being fully realized. How does it feel? Who is preventing you from feeling your body's impulses? Let your imagination dance to the image of love with your lover or beloved, allow yourself to indulge your fantasies, feel the joy of letting pleasure nourish each of your cells.*
>
> *Consciously wash away any blockages that may have been left behind in your sexual awareness from a bad experience. Life is change, acceptance, transformation. Be reborn. You are designed for pleasure. Now it is your moment of pleasure, your mind bathes in pleasure of your own choosing. You are free to do so at this time.*

## Third chakra

Manipura is the solar chakra and it reflects the following aspects:

- Personal power.
- Self-esteem.
- Eating.
- Spiritual fire.
- Willingness.
- Sense of humor.

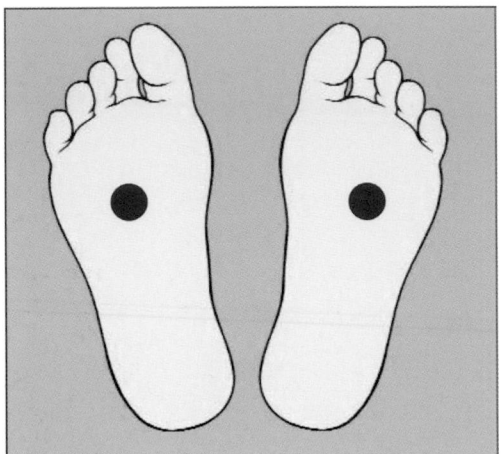

This center needs harmonization for those who have not solved the principles above or are in conflict because they do not use their personal power, whether that is due to having been brought up to obey, to submit to a superior, to not make their own decisions, to not feel capable of being successful in the world, etc. If the solar chakra is active, the person develops a willful behavior with good humor, joy of living, and personal power due to high self-esteem.

This chakra holds onto doubts, worries, fears, anger, and inertia.

Guide the recipient toward a ring of fire through the following meditation:

> *See yourself running with vitality around this circle of fire. You can see an ancient tribe performing powerful rituals with the fire. See yourself singing, dancing, moving the body, causing combustion; you are fire.*
>
> *You are a flame, you are light. Feel the power and heat of this element in your body.*
>
> *Your will and the Divine Will are one and the same. Burn your personality, your character, your habits, and your moral ideas, burn everything that weighs you down, whatever prevents your flames from reaching heaven. Let the transformation happen. You are energy and light, you are fire.*

## *Fourth chakra*

Anahatta is the heart chakra and it reflects the following aspects:

- Love.
- Affection and tenderness.
- Compassion.
- Unity.
- Solidarity.
- Personal relationships.
- Breathing.

People who have not solved the principles above, or are unable to express their love and creative energy, need to work more with this chakra.

If you do not show what you feel, what are you? Where do your feelings and emotions go when you repress them?

Guilt is the worst enemy of this chakra, and unfortunately some religions have instilled guilt three times in this area: the person who feels guilty cannot enjoy, love, feel, or be worthy of being loved.

There are two ways of living: by the heart or by the head. If you let your head block your heart, you become desensitized, lose contact with the divine, and begin to feel isolated.

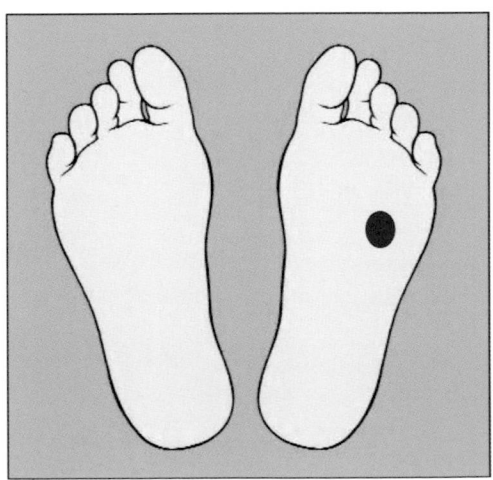

But if the heart and head—hat is to say feelings and thoughts—work together, you can wisely connect love with intelligence.

Guide the recipient on an eagle's flight through the following meditation:

> *Feel as your wings spread and fly. Observe the vastness and openness of the sky, breathe freely and joyously.*
>
> *Love all the earth, feel how a ray of light comes down from your eagle chest to the earth and is then projected through the cosmos.*
>
> *You are flight. You are love. Allow yourself to float in your inner sky.*
>
> *Dive into the sensation of feeling your living heart beating. Your own heart is part of the larger Heart of Life. Give into, join, and become one with everything you feel. Let your heart feel freedom, conscience, and loving unity with God.*

### Fifth chakra

Vishudda is the throat chakra and it reflects the following aspects:

- Creativity.
- Expression.
- Communication.
- Sounds.

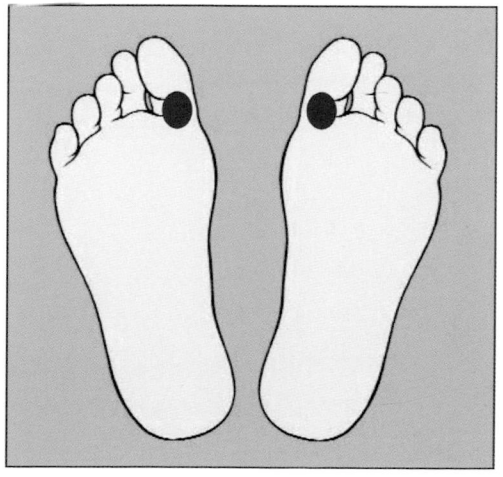

People who have not solved the principles above are unable to express their creativity, their gift, their talent. They will benefit from working on this chakra, the throat center.

If you are told to shut up, hold your position and express yourself clearly and decisively. If you do not spend time doing artistic activities, it is time that you start doing so.

Singing, music, and mantras will help the principle of speech and sound come to light.

Guide the recipient toward the silence of the origins, to nothing, to the immaculate, through this meditation:

> *Let your mind be filled with silence as you empty it of thoughts. Allow for a few minutes of silence. Then sing the sound of sounds, the Word of Creation: Om. Say it mentally and let it spread out.*
>
> *Let the healing sound penetrate over and over again. Feel how the creation of the universe occurs; suns, stars, planets. See how it feels to inhabit a spirit that seeks to make itself known. Let creativity come to you from the depths of your soul. Inspire creation.*

### Sixth chakra

Ajna chakra is the frontal chakra and it reflects the following aspects:

- Imagination.
- Intuition.
- Intellect.
- Design, visualization.

People who have not solved the principles above are too cerebral, use imagination negatively (seeing things that are not there, taking them as real), have no creative life projects, or they are led only by reason. These types of individuals will get the most out of working with this chakra.

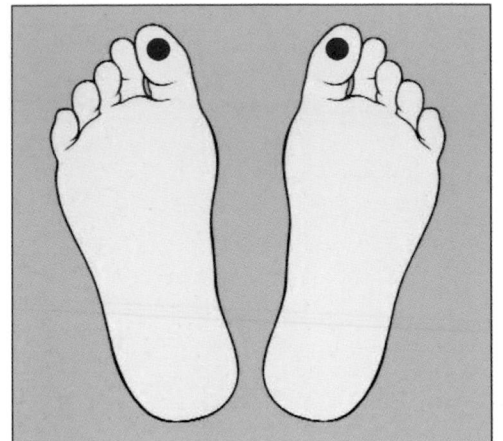
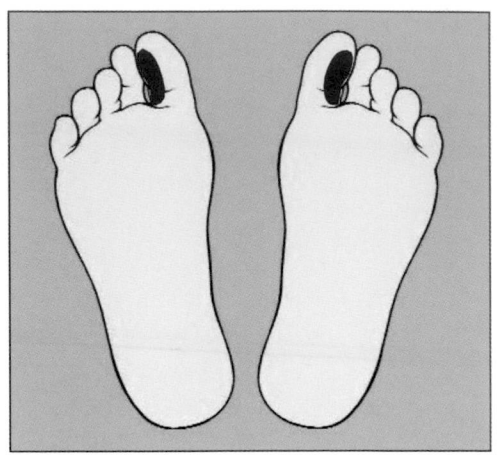

Stimulate the tip of the toes. The inner eye, the Egyptian eye of Horus, the third eye, is the eye of consciousness, the center of balance. Focus your mind on that point: the point where your soul exits the physical body. Then guide the recipient toward the Real using the following meditation:

> *Envision everything that happens within you as though it was a movie and you were a mere observer, without having any involvement. See how your thoughts go by and evaporate. No judgments, no notions, no words. Observe. Clearly contemplate your inner eye full of light.*

### Seventh chakra

Sahasrara is the crown chakra and it reflects the following aspects:

- Illumination.
- Transcendence.
- Free spirituality.
- Connecting with the Cosmos.
- Crown of light that unites heaven and earth through human beings.

People who have not solved the principles above or are in conflict with the (non-religious) spiritual connection with life and the universe will get a lot of benefits from working with this chakra.

The seventh chakra is asleep when there isn't a strong connection with life, and instead there is a feeling of disconnect, loneliness, selfishness, and helplessness.

Early in the morning, we should be thankful that we have another day to live, another gift, and let in gratitude, devotion, love for the magic of creation.

We will open the chakra of the temples so that the divine energy of Shiva can enter and descend to join in love with Shakti, the *kundalini* energy that rises from the first chakra, earth, toward heaven. It unites heaven and earth, Shiva and Shakti, male and female.

Through the following meditation, guide the recipient toward devotion, cosmic love, and everything that exists without a name.

> *Repeat these words as a sublime eco: "I am one with the Tao."*
> *Dive into an ocean of bliss. Feel the small cells, then feel love as an infinite field of consciousness. You are divine consciousness.*
> *You are wonder manifested.*
> *You are the love that always exists.*
> *You are eternal.*

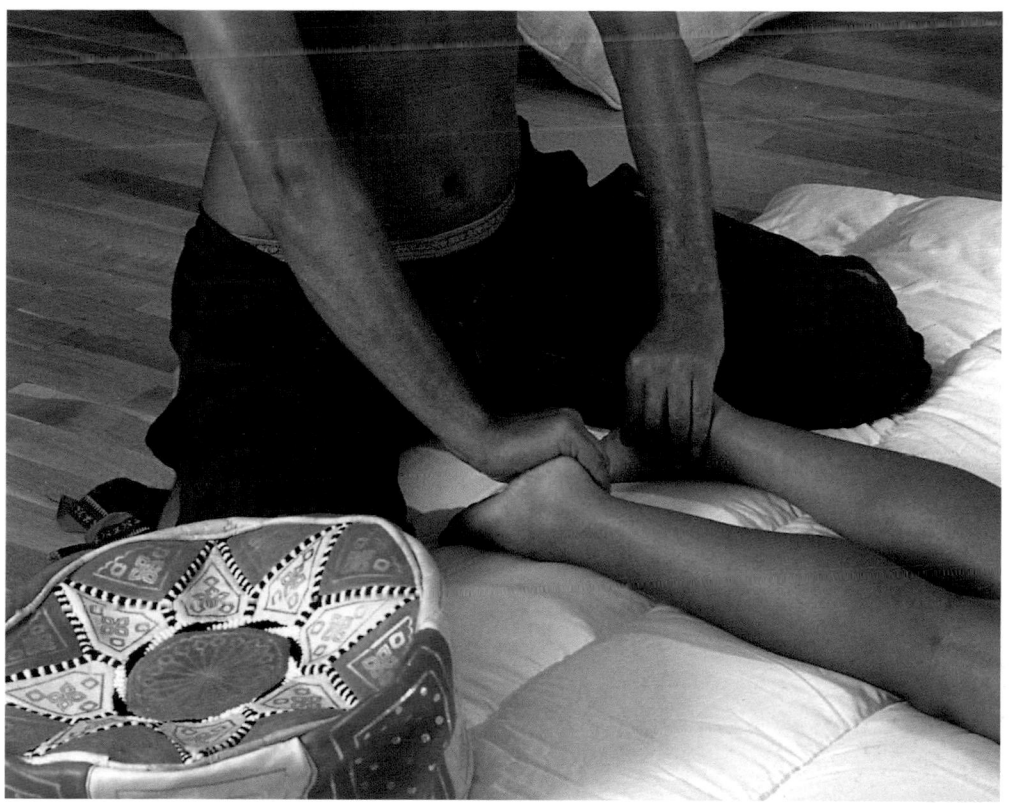

Then let the recipient breathe gently and enjoy this state for ten minutes. Meanwhile, lovingly rub, knead, and soften the entire surface of their feet, instep, and ankle. This is a loving massage. Then remove the gemstones one by one, from the bottom up, and cleanse them in water with coarse salt. They will likely take longer to come back to waking consciousness. If this should happen, then press harder on their feet.

### Suggestions

- Be sure to guide their breathing.
- Between one chakra and the next, be sure to stimulate the entire foot, soles, ankles, and toes to prevent them from cooling off.
- Do not forget that this is a deep massage and it will work on hidden aspects of their consciousness.
- At all times stay centered on your connection with the divine.
- Use the techniques described: circular movements, applying pressure, and kneading.
- Each chakra massage should be done in one session, without mixing them.
- Write down everything that the recipient visualizes and how they feel in each chakra, etc.
- Do not do this massage every day. Let at least twenty-four hours go by where physical and spiritual waste can be eliminated. For massage, apply each chakra's corresponding oil.
- Do not let the recipient talk during guided meditations, unless what they have to say is very important or if they feel unwell.
- Work with love and dedication, with connection and unity.

## TANTRIC MASSAGE FOR COUPLES

There are many tantra techniques that can help strengthen relationships. These range from love-making techniques, stimulation of the chakras, culinary arts, breathing, to the art of meditation and massage. In this book I do not intend to list each and every practical use of tantra, but the reader should be aware that its practice is deep and varied.

Tantric massage for couples aims to create an important exchange of energy. Energy is what nourishes any function of life. Just as an entrepreneur uses mental energy to succeed in business, so too can lovers use energy to make their relationship succeed.

Obviously, tantra energy is different because it involves sexual attraction, as well as the energy of love, tenderness, and meditation. The couple will nourish their relationship by learning how to manage this energy.

*Kundalini* energy requires control: mindful consciousness. When sexual desire arises, it is very common that you forget to massage. Massage can end up as a sexual act if you both want it, but handling it intelligently means that energy feeds the chakra system and raises awareness, perception, and the inner world.

Couples that have been together for a long time and feel as though they lost some passion and eroticism can also learn the secrets of tantric energy.

First, respect some factors:

- Do not hurry.
- Awaken the sense of touch, using a wordless language to reveal the soul's feelings.
- Move with an unencumbered mind.
- Be one with the body, let it be free.
- Do not look at the time.
- Prepare the place for this occasion.
- See it as a game, have fun, enjoy, and be aware of what is happening inside.
- If there is sexual arousal, breathe, stop, and let it run through your cells, organs, and skin. Then return to the massage.

It is important that you both feel energy awakening and that you direct it with your consciousness. "Energy responds to consciousness." Excitement, attraction of the poles is one of the most natural laws that exist on earth, and it is perhaps the most sacred. Therefore, human beings must understand that attraction is the ultimate desire to form "one" by joining two.

The intelligent point is for this energy to lead directly to oneness and connectedness with the universe.

The techniques I offer below are specific to the couple's energy, but all the techniques described in previous chapters can also be used.

### Suggestions

Decorate the room for this occasion. Light some candles, serve a little food and drink, light incense, and play soft music. You can also use a special oil. I recommend sandalwood, musk, and jasmine.

It is very important to breathe deeply through your nose. Breathing is the thread through which energy will reach all corners of the body.

I also recommend that you sit fully nude with your back as straight, yet flexible, as possible.

# TANTRIC MASSAGE FOR COUPLES

**1. Touching the roots:** *Spread oil on your partner's feet and massage, apply pressure, and rub the entire foot. After two or three minutes, switch to the other foot.*

**2. Releasing fatigue:** *Knead the calf gently using all fingers.*

**3. Traveling to your secrets:** *With both hands, press up over the inner thigh to the groin.*

**4. Turning to the sun:** *With one hand, open the third solar plexus chakra, and with the other hand open up the back area. Make circular movements.*

**5. Opening the temple door:** *Apply the same technique but in the fourth chakra, the center of affection, love, feeling, and the united consciousness.*

**6. Taking turns:** *One partner will massage the entire surface of the other partner's arm. It is important to consciously do and not do (wu-wei) and simply relax.*

**7. Spreading your wings:** *With both hands, knead the upper back, from the shoulder blades to the neck. This allows the body to take off into a state of lightness, ease, and relaxation.*

**8. The love boat:** *Sit facing each other with your legs spread open, glide your hands over your partner's arms, while you both gently rock forward and backward.*

**9. The floating trunk:** *One partner will assume the shavasana position (relaxation of the body) and will the other partner massages the head with both hands open to release stress and tension in that area.*

**10. Wave of pleasure:** *Place both hands below the navel and move them up along the solar plexus and heart, branching toward the shoulders and ending at the arms and hands. Hand contact is very important. This technique is performed at all times as if it were an ocean wave. Both partners must breathe deeply, exhaling through the mouth and letting out a sound.*

**11. The dance of Shiva and Shakti:** *Go up along the left side of your partner's body, from the ankles to the pelvis, ending at the arm and hand (which will be stretched over your partner's head). Do this very slowly, three times on each side. Remember that the slower the breathing and the technique, the quieter the mind will get.*

**12. Chakra kiss:** *Sitting with your backs resting against each other, rock your bodies very softly, feeling the beautiful and exhilarating heat in the whole spinal area.*

**13. Friction of the gods:** *Stand with your backs against one another and with your eyes closed, and gently create friction with your bodies. Then glide your hands all over the body, feeling how energy moves from one partner to the other.*

**14. Light rod:** *One partner will lie face down and the other will rub their hands and spine, from the sacrum to the neck, up and down. This will generate a lot of heat and soft energy around the chakras.*

**Final relaxation:** *After the session, both partners will stretch together while holding hands. Their breathing will soften and slow down. If the experience is deepened, after a few minutes both partners will feel their hands become one, losing all sense of separation and division between their bodies.*
*After fifteen minutes, begin to move again, then dance, make love, or do whatever you feel like doing at that moment.*

## CHAKRAS TEST

The following test will help you understand the person who will receive the tantric massage so that you can apply the most suitable type of massage for each chakra. It would also be very useful for you to learn the characteristics of each chakra (see box in page 21).

In any case, this massage presents no risks or problems except for those listed as contraindications in chapter 2 (see page 39).

Answers can be:

- Good (G)
- Regular (R)
- Bad (B)

QUESTION

**First chakra**

**1.** How are your finances?

**2.** What is your relationship with the land and nature? Do you get out often?

**3.** Are you satisfied with your work?

**Second chakra**

**1.** How would you rate your sexual relations?

**2.** Do you tend to drink plenty of water during the day?

**3.** How is your level of sensitivity?

**Third chakra**

**1.** How is your self-esteem and personal power?

**2.** How is your eating and digestion?

**3.** How well do you express strong emotions (fear, anger, anxiety)?

**Fourth chakra**

**1.** How much do you love yourself?

**2.** How is your ability to give and receive love? And relate to others?

**3.** How is your happiness level?

**Fifth chakra**

**1.** How is your creativity level? Do you use it often?

**2.** How is your voice?

**3.** How is your artistic life (from cooking to writing)? Do you do something creative every day?

**Sixth chakra**

**1.** Do you think you have a high level of perception and intuition?

**2.** Do you use your imagination often?

**3.** How well do you remember what you dream?

**Seventh chakra**

**1.** Do you meditate daily?

**2.** How is your spiritual level of oneness with life?

**3.** How is your openness to magic? Do you see the miraculous side of nature?

**ANSWERS**

For your answers, add 3 points for every G; 1 point for each R; and none for B.

If your total is 9 points: the chakra in question is working well for you. You just need a little upkeep.

If your total is between 3 and 7 points: your chakra is working regular. You need to tone and balance it.

If your total is between 0 and 3 points: your chakra is working poorly. You need to work on raising your energy level, do breathing exercises, and use gemstones, colors, and massage.

## CHAKRA POINTS ON THE BODY

Below, you will find a short list of pressure points on the meridians for each chakra. But above all, remember:

- Just as with shiatsu, each point is worked on by applying pressure.
- These points are directly related to each chakra.
- Do not mix methods for the chakras: use a single technique for at least a couple of sessions, then switch.

### Muladhara chakra
FRONT: SP 12, SP 13; ST 42; IG 4.
BACK: GV 1, GV 2, GV 3, GV 8; GB 31; CV 1; SP 4.

### Swadisthana chakra
FRONT: CV 2, GV 7, GB 28, GB 29; C 6; SP 6, SP 10, SP 11; KI 11.
BACK: BL 22, BL 23, BL 31, BL 34, BL 36, BL 46, BL 55, BL 57, BL 62, BL 67; GV 4; KI 3, KI 6.

### Manipura chakra
FRONT: GB 16; KI 17, KI 19; LI 14; CV 10, CV 11, CV 12, CV 13; LU 14; HT 4; ST 19, ST 25, ST 36.
BACK: GV 5, GV 6, GV 7, GV 8, GV 9.

### Anahatta chakra
FRONT: GV 22; KI 25, 26, KI 27; CV 17, CV 22; LU 1, LU 2, LU 9; GB 22; HT 7, HT 9; CS 3.
BACK: SI 10; GV 10 GV 13.

### Vishudda chakra
FRONT: ST 9, ST 10, ST 11; CV 22.
BACK: BL 10; GB 12, GB 20; GV 20, GV 21; SI 10; TH 5, TH 15; LI 14.

### Ajna chakra
FRONT: GB 1, GB 14; BL 1, BL 2; TH 23.

### Sahasrara chakra
FRONT: GV 16, GV 17, GV 18, GV 19, GV 20, GV 24, GV 25; GB 5.

# REFLEXOLOGY

Foot reflexology is an ancient therapeutic method to restore balance in the body's energy through foot massage.

As we saw in chapter 2, this effective ancient treatment is based on stimulating nerve endings. These nerve endings are connected to all body organs. In reality, it is estimated that there are about 7,200 nerve endings on the soles of the feet.

Egyptians used this technique, as shown in the papyri and the tomb murals for Ankhmahor, who was a renowned physician of the Sixth Dynasty (circa 2300 BC). These paintings depict a man who appears to be massaging the feet of one of his patients. So they used it to relax the body, but physicians also used it as a healing therapy.

Reflexology was also practiced in China, Japan, and India, where numerous sculptures of Buddha with engravings on the soles of the feet have been found.

In the West, the nervous system began to be explored during the nineteenth century, but therapeutic treatment was not discovered until years later. In 1917, Vladimir Bekhterev coined the term reflexology. In the '30s, Eunice Ingham developed techniques to match the different organs in the body to the points on the soles of the feet.

Moreover, in 1930, Dr. William H. Fitzgerald discovered zone therapy consisting of ten bundles of ten horizontal vertical nerves that correspond to each axis of the body. Human beings are a great mystery of energy.

How could we determine who was the first person to discover that the feet are connected to the whole body? And furthermore, not just the feet, but also the meridians, the points of the ears and hands, etc. I think an event like the following story describes could have started the first study into reflexes in the body, as well as its healing properties.

> There once was a very powerful king with a serious problem: he suffered a constant headache that did not let him live in peace.
>
> Tormented, he had visited many healers but no one could take away his pain.
>
> One day, the king was walking through a forest when he saw a man practicing archery. The man was about to shoot an arrow into a tree but he saw the king, became fearful, and inadvertently diverted his bow, sending the arrow into the king's foot.
>
> This enraged the king, but then he very quickly calmed down as he felt that his headache was now gone.
>
> In the end, the fortunate man was rewarded by the king.

## THE BENEFITS OF REFLEXOLOGY IN THE BODY

### Skin

Skin is the body's largest organ. Reflexology stimulates blood circulation and activity of the sebaceous glands, which helps eliminate waste substances that are present on the skin, as well as opening the pores, and breathing.

Reflexology also protects against the effects of free radicals and allows skin to regain its natural glow.

## The muscular system

Reflexology reduces muscle tension, relaxing the entire body. Muscles are exposed on a daily basis to pressure, force, and poor posture, so this therapy restores the correct amount of tension and stretch.

## The cardiovascular system

Applying pressure to reflexology points improves and accelerates blood circulation. This effect is particularly important for the legs and arms, where circulation is often poor due to inactivity and other problems, and where a large number of toxins tend to accumulate, causing swelling. Furthermore, massage helps reduce high blood pressure and regulates heartbeat.

## The lymphatic system

It is responsible for collecting toxins generated by muscle movement and taking them to the lymph nodes for elimination.

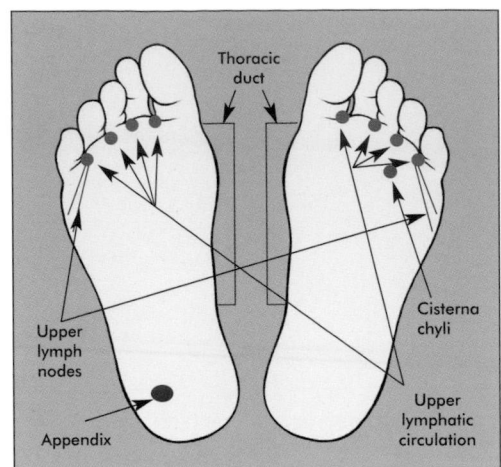

*Map of the foot: the lymphatic system.*

Massage stimulates drainage, prevents toxins from accumulating in the ganglia, and facilitates cleaning our bodies.

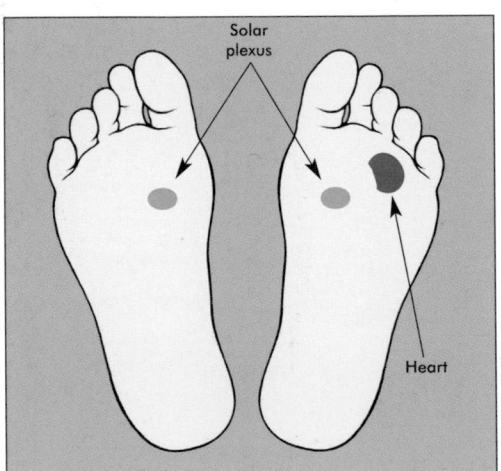
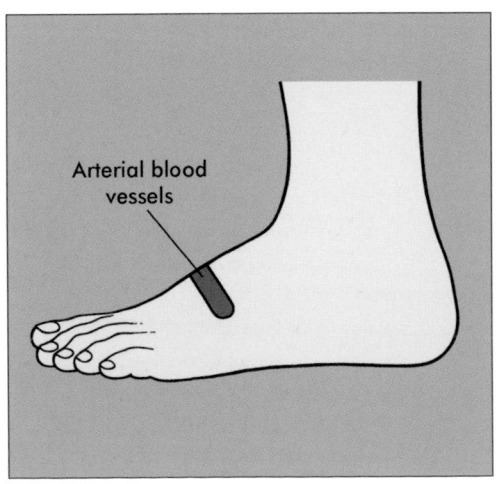

*Map of the foot: the circulatory system.*

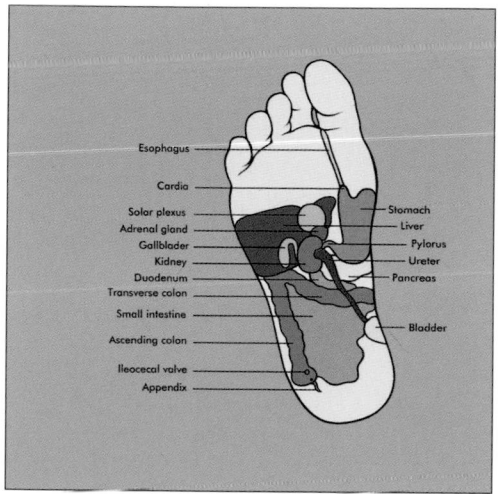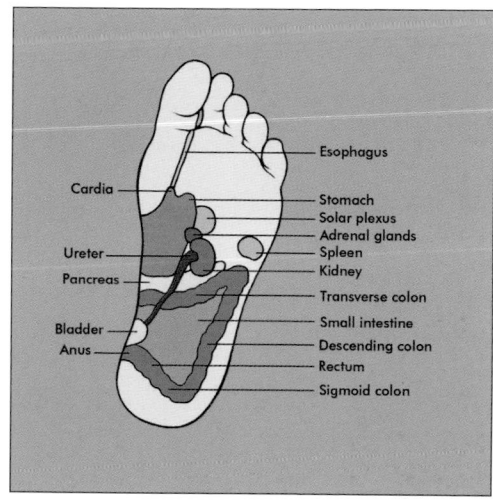

Map of the foot: Digestive and urinary system. The illustration on the left corresponds to the right foot and the illustration on the right corresponds to the left foot.

## The digestive and urinary systems

Some areas and points on the feet let you stimulate the peristaltic activity of the colon and gastric juice secretion, which in turn promotes the functioning of these organs and the elimination of waste and fluids.

## The urogenital system

The urinary and genital systems produce urine that removes waste and toxins from the body. The kidneys, ureters, bladder, and urethra form the urinary system, while the gonads and testes or ovaries make up the reproductive system.

The kidneys process urine: filter, reabsorb, and eliminate substances. In people who eat a lot of meat but do not drink enough water, their kidneys are overloaded.

The ureters are tubes that expand like a funnel and carry urine to the bladder. The bladder is a muscular organ where the distended ureters end. It stores urine until it is time to release it through the urethra, a tube that measures about 1.5 inches (4 cm) in women and 8 inches (20 cm) in men.

For people with fluid retention, the bladder is inflamed.

## The nervous system

Eliminating toxins and creating muscular relaxation causes a calming effect on the body. Also, if reflexology is done regularly, it can eliminate disorders such as insomnia, irritability, or headaches.

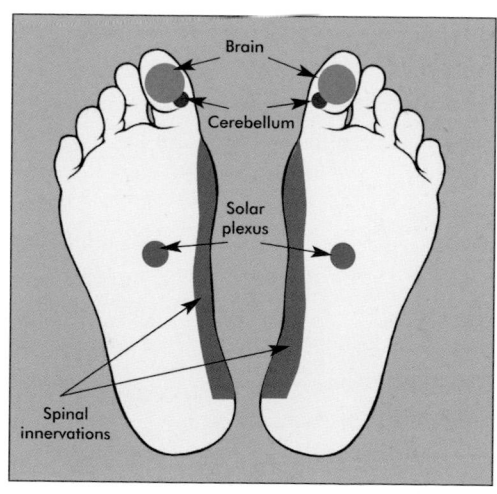

Map of the foot: the nervous system.

## The skeletal system

The following illustrations show a map of the foot's skeletal system.

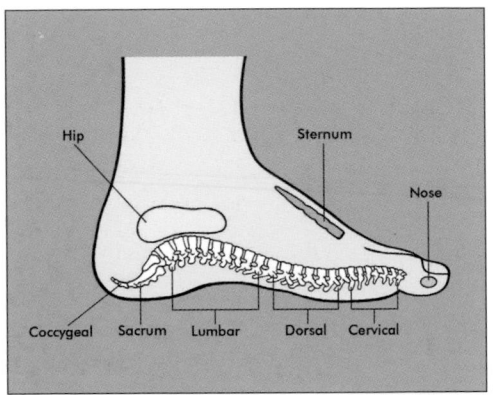

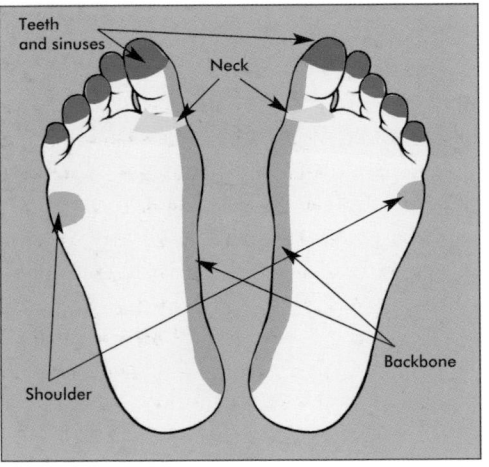

## The endocrine system

Endocrine glands secrete hormones (derived from the Greek word *hormón*, meaning "to set in motion") that enter the bloodstream and then spread throughout the body. The endocrine system, along with the nervous system, regulates cellular activities.

The endocrine system is closely related to a chakra: if there is any psycho-emotional dysfunction, the corresponding gland will also be affected.

The areas are a lot more sensitive when there is dysfunction. Reflexology can help improve the regular functioning of the glands. However it is advisable to consult an endocrinologist and work with a team. (Reflexology is well known among many professionals, and a high percentage of physicians use this technique.)

### Pituitary or hypophysis:

This is the main gland and it is located in the hypothalamus. It consists of two lobes that produce hormones that are necessary for thyroid function, the reproductive system, and the production of melanin. It is related to the seventh chakra, at the top of the head.

### Pineal or epiphysis:

This is a sensory organ and it is influenced by light. This gland's secretion is related to sexuality. It is related to the third eye chakra.

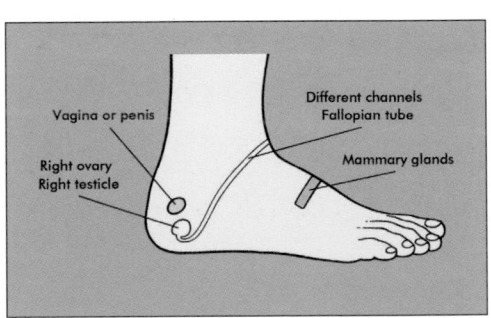

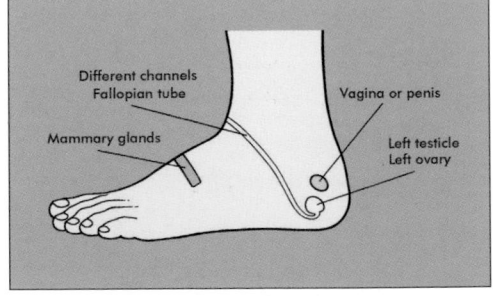

*Map of the foot: the urogenital system.*

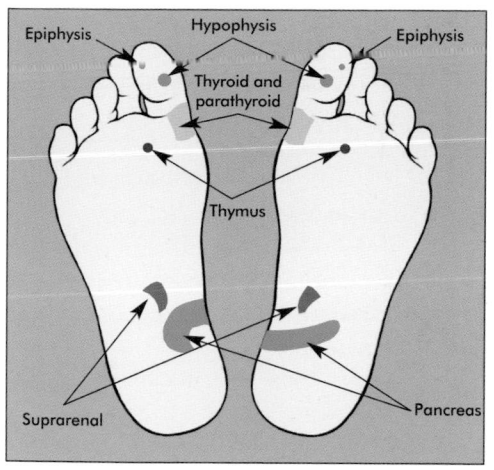

*Map of the foot: the endocrine system.*

### Thyroid:

Formed by two joined lobes at the sides of the trachea and larynx. Produces hormones that stimulate cell metabolism and growth. Hyperthyroidism increases intracellular combustion, but hypothyroidism slows down the metabolic rate. It is linked to the fifth chakra.

### Parathyroid:

The secreted hormone is related to the metabolizing of calcium. Its hyper function results in calcium deposits on the wall of the vessels, forming kidney stones.

### Thymus:

Located between the sternum. In youth it is highly developed, but it starts to regress as we get older. Related to the immune system and emotions and connected to the fourth chakra.

### Pancreas:

This gland produces insulin and glucagon. The overproduction of insulin is known as hypoglycemia, whereas low production of insulin causes diabetes. Linked to the third chakra.

### Adrenal gland:

Their name comes from their position on the kidney. They produce corticosteroids and important substances. Related to the second chakra.

### Testicles:

Male sex glands that make hormones or androgens that develop spermatogenesis, sperm production. They bring on the development of the genitals and body hair as well as bone growth and voice tone. In men, it is connected to the first chakra.

### Ovaries:

Female glands that regulate the menstrual cycle. This cycle is maintained by association with the hypothalamus and pituitary. In women, it is connected to the first chakra.

## The immune system

The feeling of wellbeing that results from a foot massage releases endorphins, the body's natural painkillers, whose presence in the blood reduces stress hormones that can weaken the immune system. Our defenses are thus indirectly strengthened. Furthermore, by improving the functioning of various organs and systems, massage produces a very healthy invigorating effect on the entire body. This is especially noticeable in breathing, which becomes slower and deeper: oxygen flows throughout the body and relaxes the mind.

## The spine

The spine is the basis of support for the human body; it has thirty-three or thirty-four vertebrae. It is shaped like an S, and these curves provide flexibility for physical body movement.

The spine is very important to Eastern energy traditions because, on an astral level, the seven chakras are in it.

The spine consists of seven cervical vertebrae, twelve thoracic vertebrae, five lumbar vertebrae, five sacral vertebrae, and five coccygeal vertebrae. The sacral and coccygeal vertebrae are fixed and give rise to the sacrum (sacred) and the coccyx.

The spine can have defects which can be divided into three types: cervical lordosis or parrot beak; dorsal kyphosis as a hunchback; and lumbar lordosis when the buttocks stick out while the lumbar region pushes inward.

Reflexology treats spinal problems by targeting the pain that these problems cause.

Ladder and circular movements on specific areas provide excellent relief to the whole spine.

---

### CONTRAINDICATIONS TO THE APPLICATION OF REFLEXOLOGY

Although reflexology is harmless, stop treatment at once for those individuals with high blood pressure, pregnant women, menstruating women, recent heart surgery patients, or after lengthy travel.

---

## MAP OF THE FOOT

The various maps in the previous pages will show us all the points we can work, as well as all the nerve endings that are directly related to a particular organ or body part. The reflex action of the nervous system transmits the impulses of all the stimuli that occur within the body.

Organs that are located on the right side of the body correspond to the right foot, and those that are located on the left side correspond to the left foot. Moreover, the head is reflected on the big toe, the shoulders on the outside of the foot, under the little toe, and the spine on the inner part of both feet.

Through experience, you will have the opportunity to encounter different types of feet. Some individuals have longer toes, flat feet, or archless feet that affect the spine. There are also feet with blisters, calluses, moles, or ingrown toenails. All this has to be observed and further analyzed because it will help us determine the condition of the glands or organs.

For example, if an individual has bunions or corns on the area that correspond to the throat, they probably have difficulty expressing themselves. On the other hand, scars from surgeries or deformities will affect the rest of the body's functions.

### Getting to know the body through the feet

Self-knowledge, so valued by all Eastern disciplines, scholars, and seekers of the divine, must be based first on self-awareness of the body.

It is well known that emotions affect the organs, that weather affects mood, and that thoughts influence a person's present and the future. Therefore, it is important that we get to know our entire body, using it, caring for it, nurturing it, allowing it to rest, giving it pleasures, and above all, knowing the relationships and partnerships between the different organs, as well as their different functions, and possible symptoms.

## FOOT MASSAGE TECHNIQUES

The foot can be stimulated and worked on in these different ways:

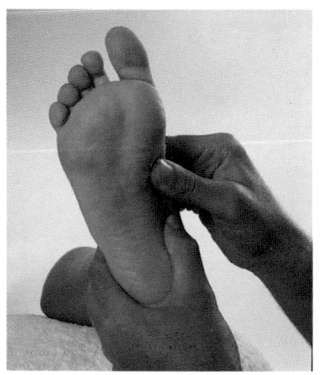

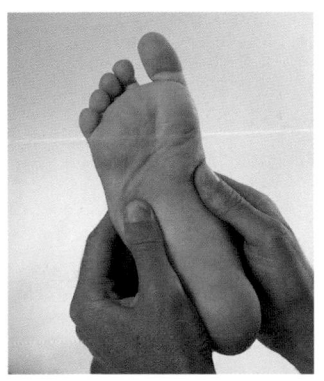

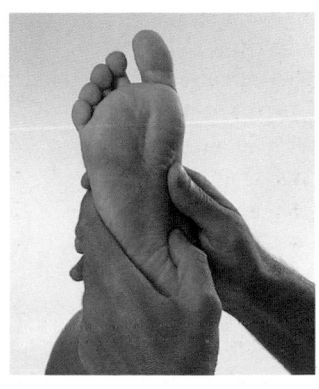

**1. Push and pull:** *This technique is based on the balance between our breathing and the pressure we apply to the area. Inhale as we loosen and exhale as we press. The weight of the pressure will vary according to the recipient, but it is generally six to thirteen pounds (three to five kilograms).*

**2. Ladder with both thumbs:** *This technique consists of gliding one thumb after the other over a specific area. This technique is very useful along the spine, for instance.*

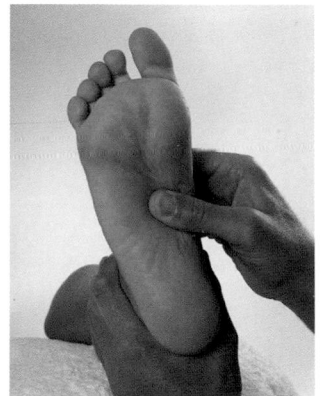

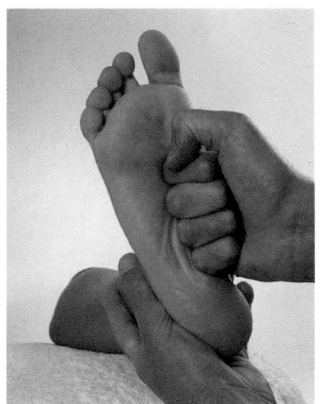

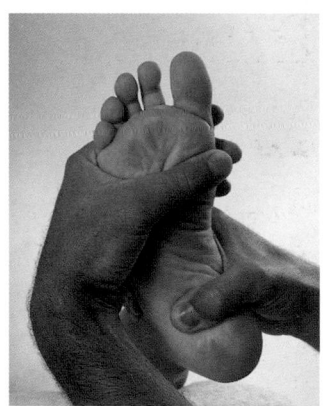

**3. Rotations:**
*Just as in shiatsu, use both thumbs and go counterclockwise to sedate, and clockwise to tone up.*

**4. Knuckles:** *Use your knuckles to rotate and glide over the entire sole of the foot or specific areas. For example, applying this technique to the intestinal area is very beneficial.*

**5. Squeezing:** *Finally, this technique keeps feet warm, so do it after you finish massaging one area and before you start massaging the next. It is also very pleasant.*

## How long should you work on each point and area?

Give each person a different treatment, depending on their needs. Regardless of what you choose, always begin by working on the solar plexus and, in addition to working on the particular area of emphasis, in each session work on their digestive system, circulatory system, and skeletal system.

The time varies from one to three minutes per area, but you can come back and work on a particular spot after a break or at the end of the session.

For example, a case that I remember with great affection and satisfaction is that of a thirty-nine-year-old woman whose menstrual flow had stopped for six months. I asked her if she had experienced some sort of strong emotional event or a problem with someone at work or at home. The woman replied that six months ago she had lost her mother and she felt helpless.

During a reflexology session, I stimulated the corresponding points and areas. She called me the next day with good news saying her menstruation was back to normal.

### Crystals

Sometimes deposits can be felt inside our feet. These are called crystals or sand, and they are made up of uric acid residue and other waste products. When touched, they feel like hardened deposits on the nerve endings.

When these deposits are treated, they can cause severe pain and when pressed they turn from light red to dark red. In uric acid deposits, these crystals may feel as though they were "ground glass" or small balls of hardened sand.

| CIRCULATORY SYSTEM | DIGESTIVE SYSTEM | SKELETAL SYSTEM |
| :---: | :---: | :---: |
| Solar plexus | Solar plexus | Solar plexus |
| Pituitary gland | Lungs and bronchi | Top of the head |
| Thyroid | Liver | Frontal and nasal cavities |
| Ears | Gallbladder | Maxillary cavity |
| Eyes | Stomach | Trigeminal nerve |
| Uterus | Kidney | Neck, cervical vertebrae |
| Prostate | Urethra | Shoulder |
| Ovaries or gonads | Bladder | Spine |
| Tonsils | Intestine | Sciatic nerve |
| Thorax | Pancreas | Hip |
| Lymph and circulatory area | Small intestine | Knee |
| | Spleen | |
| *Finally, a relaxing massage on the foot for about ten minutes.* | Heart (very briefly) | *Relaxing massage on the entire foot for about ten minutes.* |
| | *Relaxing massage on the entire foot for about ten minutes.* | |

These crystals appear because diseases that are not completely cured by the body's immune system leave their mark on the corresponding reflex zones.

The inadequate functioning of organs that eliminate body waste (kidneys, intestines, lungs, and skin) may also be the cause of metabolic waste deposits.

When a drug treatment is followed, its residues are often found in blood and throughout the cells, and they can form organic waste deposits in the nerve endings, especially close to the spine.

The reflex zones can determine every disease that a person has had from their birth since most diseases do not heal naturally, but are immediately stopped with the use of medication.

Pain is an even clearer sign alerting us that there is something wrong in our bodies. The body uses pain to guide our attention to the problem. And the crystals hurt, but after several sessions they disappear along with the pain.

## TIPS FOR BEFORE AND AFTER THE SESSION

Before the session, make a personal routine (meditation, concentration, protective light for your aura, and breathing).

Then, focus on the work that you will perform with the recipient and accept the recipient as an individual, with specific problems, body type, emotions, etc.

Advise the recipient to wear comfortable shoes because many people "strangle" their feet with trendy shoes. Our feet need to be comfortable as they bear the full weight of the body throughout the day.

After the session ends, the recipient should drink plenty of water to help eliminate toxins through urination.

A shower is a good soothing tonic that you should do too, let the water run over your head, spine, chakras, and hands so that no energetic and astral impurity remains "attached" to your aura.

Eat very lightly before the session (which should be done at least an hour and a half before or after eating) and after you are done, eat some fruits or food that will give you energy.

Finally, let there be at least twenty-four hours between any sessions.

# SENSITIVE MASSAGE

Sensitive massage is based on the importance and quality of touch and the union between body and mind.

This technique allows the recipient to experience a state of total surrender, traveling inwardly beyond the normal state of wakefulness, and awakening the conscious into a deeper fusion with the inner self. It dissolves tension by letting the individual feel protected and free.

Small babies who are cared for, touched, held, and ultimately loved are vastly different from those who are left unprotected and lacking physical contact. It is well known that a caress, a hug, and sensitive massage have a therapeutic effect.

Human beings have to live, survive, investigate, accept, surrender, and positively connect with their loneliness. We are surrounded by others but we are alone in our existence. It is a universal mystery that is simultaneously an individual struggle.

At the moment of birth, when we are totally unprotected and alone, we receive the first messages and hints of companionship. Massage, at its most profound, encourages love, the warmth of being served by another person, and accepting oneself. According to Zen, tao, and tantra, existence is a big emptiness that holds everything. Similarly, by becoming void, the individual can connect to the Whole, with the True Self, and become one with That.

How can we explain a feeling? How can we know what water tastes like unless we try it? Sensitive massage invites you to leave your personality and mind far behind, and let the loving hands of another person cradle you.

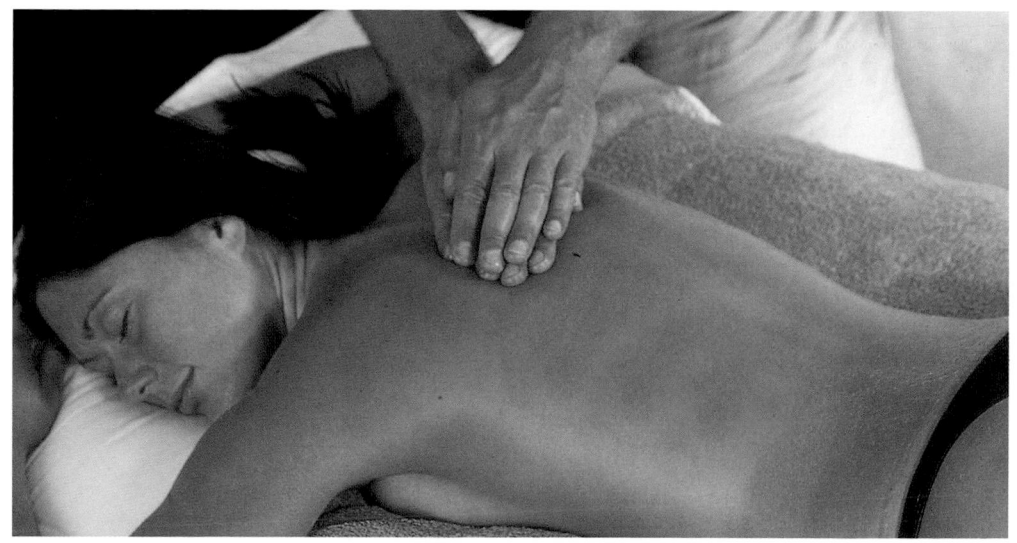

Unlike tantric massage or shiatsu, the main principle of sensitive massage is slowness. Almost all movements are smooth, long, slow, and coupled with conscious breathing to decompress dormant energies and contracted muscles.

## BASICS OF SENSITIVE MASSAGE

### Body perception

The recipients will perceive themselves as "energy in motion" because they will slowly move away from pain and physical perception to feeling more like energy and less like matter. Above all, they will feel that their physical body is united.

For example, people who are too intellectual or brainy tend to neglect their legs, joints, and pelvis because they carry all their energy in the head. Here, the recipients will feel that the therapist's hands glide over their entire bodies, and they will experience a sensation of overall wellbeing.

### Skin and sensations

Work on this entire organ using "waves and energy vibrations." When a body area is blocked, sensitive massage will make it flow again.

The skin externalizes an internal state of lightness, erotic energy, tingling, affinity, mystical oneness with the universe, and much more. Sensations vary according to each person and where they may be in their own personal lives.

Sensitive massage will make skin appear "tan" as it heals it with love.

### Releasing blockages

Energy moves whenever a previously existent blockage gets removed. Every blockage is stagnant energy, and sensitive massage techniques aim to let that energy flow again.

Eliminating emotional and energetic blockages is so beneficial, restorative, renewing, and transformative that, just as in Robert Fischer's book *The Knight in Rusty Armor*, contact with the divine essence and inner silence destroy these blockages completely.

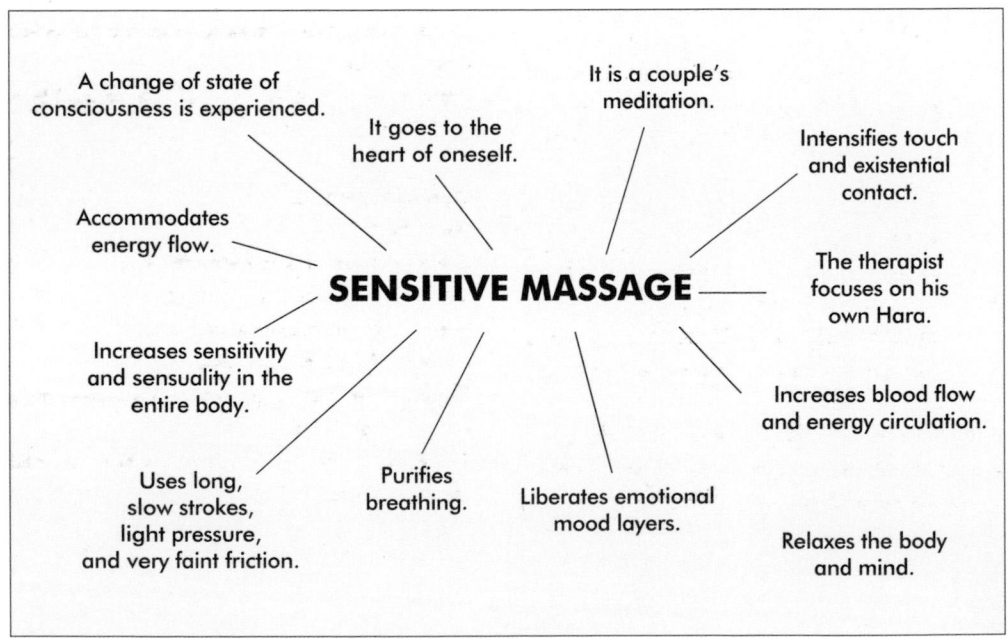

## Meeting the inner core

This rebirth is a very valuable internal event. Many people live lost, asleep, unaware of their fate, without using their talents, ignoring the magical present.

Massage is a spiritual bell, an invitation to awake (although recipients fall asleep very often during the session).

## Security and surrender

The first contact between therapist and recipient is very important. Pay attention to your physical appearance and your choice of words. Look at the recipient directly in the eyes. Regard the recipient as though you were meeting a "messiah": someone unique, individual, and different. You are not feeding anyone's ego; this is about providing attention and service, and loving their essence, which will result in a mutual feeling of security and trust.

We are used to control and are reluctant to trust. Trusting divinity and relying on your personal God is what counts. Trusting means releasing a little ego into a sea of consciousness.

Security is what allows for this release. Sense of security can be transmitted in several ways: hygiene and decoration of your workspace, sensory stimuli, the therapist's honesty and energy level, to name a few.

## Life vision

As odd as it may seem, many people do not pay attention to the lifestyle they have until they get sick, injured, or suffer an accident. Massage serves as a wakeup call that initiates inner mechanisms to "start paying attention."

Realization or insight is a dynamic experience of self-realization that comes from the depths of the unconscious. It is the fact of being aware. You can be living in the wrong way, disregarding your health, welfare, and fulfillment of your destiny, and this event can transform you.

Massage lets you reset a natural rhythm of living by connecting to the laws of nature, because when our body is deeply relaxed, we can travel inside ourselves to the soul. It is as if a race car was traveling at 155 miles (250 kilometers) per hour: we would not be able to see the details in its bodywork, the power of its tires, or engine technology. It would go by very fast. But when it is parked, we can see all its features in detail.

Through massage, when the vehicle (the physical body) is at ease and rest, each person has the opportunity to look within and observe how the current situation is being experienced.

# SENSITIVE MASSAGE FOR DIFFERENT TYPES OF PEOPLE

Every human being is its own world. Some have rigid bodies and personalities; the cerebral and intellectuals, for whom logical reason is most important; or the dominant ones who always want to be in control.

Next, we will see five personality types and how to work on them.

## Dependent person
### Characteristics:

- Fears isolation and abandonment.
- Craves recognition from others.
- Slim body with very little muscle.
- Body tends to bend forward.
- Physically immature: narrow pelvis, sparse hair, weak feet, and legs.
- Tends to lean on others; does not know how to fend for himself.

- Needs contact with others; seeks warmth and support.
- Low energy level.
- Some feeling of deprivation due to lack of contact with the mother.
- Feelings of emptiness and emotional deprivation.
- Likely born by C-section, which drives him to seek help from others.

**Massage therapy:**

Help the recipient become aware of their own worth and their individuality by strengthening and massaging the arms and legs in particular.

Emphasize their contact with the earth by using reflexology.

Use oils to massage the entire body to help them feel as though they are back in the womb, and softly bring energy to the palms of the hands and the soles of the feet.

## Submissive person
**Characteristics:**

- Suffers and cries, or hardly speaks.
- Usually forgoes his rights and needs.
- Unable to change situations.
- Afraid to express feelings, especially boredom, hostility, and superiority.
- Represses deep anger, and can only show it through an explosion of aggression.
- Builds up a strong muscular structure capable of handling anger and aggression.
- Creates walls around himself.
- May have been raised by a mother who was smothering, oppressive, particularly with regards to food. Resulting in bottled up feelings.
- Blocked by retention in the arms and legs.
- Probably humiliated as a child.
- Blocked energy in the neck, shoulders, and pelvis.

- Fears feeling genital arousal and, therefore, retains energy in the pelvic organs and buttocks.

**Massage therapy:**

Requires strong techniques to dissolve blockages and release whatever is repressed within.

Use breathing and sound techniques: the recipient will inhale deeply and exhale with an open mouth, using vowel sounds to release the blockages.

The massage will be strong and slow.

## Dominant or controlling person
**Characteristics:**

- Characterized by musculature suitable to scare away fear of failure.
- Inhales by lifting up the chest.
- Needs to feel superior to others.
- Denies feelings and emotions.
- Wants to have power over others: either arrogantly or by means of seduction.
- Disproportionately heavier on the upper body.
- Wants power more than pleasure, to be able to control.
- Has problems with his father; an unloving father forced him into a confrontation.

**Massage therapy:**

Dominant recipients need to balance their energy by making it flow from the top to the bottom.

That is, they need to ease their cervical, scapular, thoracic, and diaphragmatic tensions, so that they can exhale freely.

Work by applying rhythmic pressure on the chest, increasing exhalation. This will undo some of the chest's tendency to rise up, and it will relieve tension down the neck, chest, and jaw.

## *Rigid or structured person*
**Characteristics:**

- Feels the need to control own emotions and not be mean to others.
- Head up high and straight back.
- Neck is hard, chest is full and narrow.
- Afraid of falling, venturing out.
- To a rigid or structured person, submission is equivalent to death.
- Usually ambitious and active.
- Sexually, the man is narcissistic, while the woman is not open.
- The body is physically balanced, but unyielding with a shield or armor.

**Massage therapy:**

Make direct, clear, precise, and neutral movements that are not emotional as they may be bothersome. Use controlled pressure, stretching, rhythmic shaking, and rocking.

This massage has to provide elasticity and smoothness in every muscle of the back, chest, rib cage, and heart.

Lastly, it will be essential to mobilize the joints.

## *Cerebral and rational person*
**Characteristics:**

- Works like a computer, always thinking and calculating.
- Shows a tendency to rationalize everything.
- Keen observer of what happens around them.
- All the energy gets stored in the head, forgetting the limbs, joints, and lower body.
- Reason and thought are at his center so he simply denies or criticizes anything that he cannot understand.
- More prone to stress due to energy congestion.

**Massage therapy:**

Start at the head to release tension by "decapitating" the recipient energetically so that they no longer feel like they are just a brain.

The movements will spread out.

Guide the recipient through cleansing breaths, and focus on massaging the arms, as well as the pelvis, hands, legs, and feet.

Stimulate the area of the spine by making figure eights.

## TEST TO DETERMINE PERSONALITY

Almost all of us can be categorized in at least one of the aforementioned personalities. So to better determine what type of person we are and what techniques to combine, I made the following test. By using it, you will learn whether your recipient is dominant and cerebral, or submissive and dependent, in which case you will do a twenty-minute massage for former personality and another thirty-minute massage for the latter. Make note of any positive responses because they will help you determine which traits are most predominant, but do not forget to observe their physical structure.

### DEPENDENT PERSONALITY

1. Were you born by C-section?
2. Do you avoid being alone and always look for company?
3. Do you feel that your mother gave you little affection?
4. Do you run each new project by friends or relatives?
5. Are you always seeking recognition from others?

### SUBMISSIVE PERSONALITY

1. Do you take on the role of a victim and think that others are out to hurt you?
2. Do you feel a lump in your throat because you cannot say what you feel and think?
3. Do you always prioritize the needs of others and leave yours aside?
4. Was your mother manipulative or controlling towards you?
5. When you feel sexual desire, do you suppress it or express it?

### DOMINANT AND CONTROLLING PERSONALITY

1. Do you like all things to be done your way?
2. Whether in sports or work, do you feel the need to be the best, to excel, and to compete?
3. Among your group of friends, are you the one who decides where to go or what movie to see?
4. Are you reluctant to falling in love for fear of losing power and control?

5. Did you lack affection and protection from your father?

### RIGID AND STRUCTURED PERSONALITY

1. Do you have a set personal routine with strict schedules?
2. If you had the opportunity to go and live in another country, would you be afraid of adventure?
3. Are you ambitious and act decisively to pursue your goal?
4. Do you hide behind an emotional shield to avoid expressing what you feel?
5. Do you want your opinions to always be right and do not see the full worth of other points of view?

### BRAIN AND RATIONAL PERSONALITY

1. If you feel affinity and attraction toward someone, do you analyze the situation first and push aside what is in your heart?
2. Do you analyze and rationalize all your experiences?
3. Do you live with stress and does your head hurt often?
4. When you do not understand something, do you tend to deny it and criticize it?
5. Do you spend most of your time reading, studying, and using your intellect?

## TECHNIQUES FOR DIFFERENT PERSONALITY TYPES

### 1. Techniques for a dependent personality

#### Face down

OIL: Geranium or lemon.
TIME FOR EACH TECHNIQUE: One to two minutes.
OBJECTIVE: Awaken the "I can."

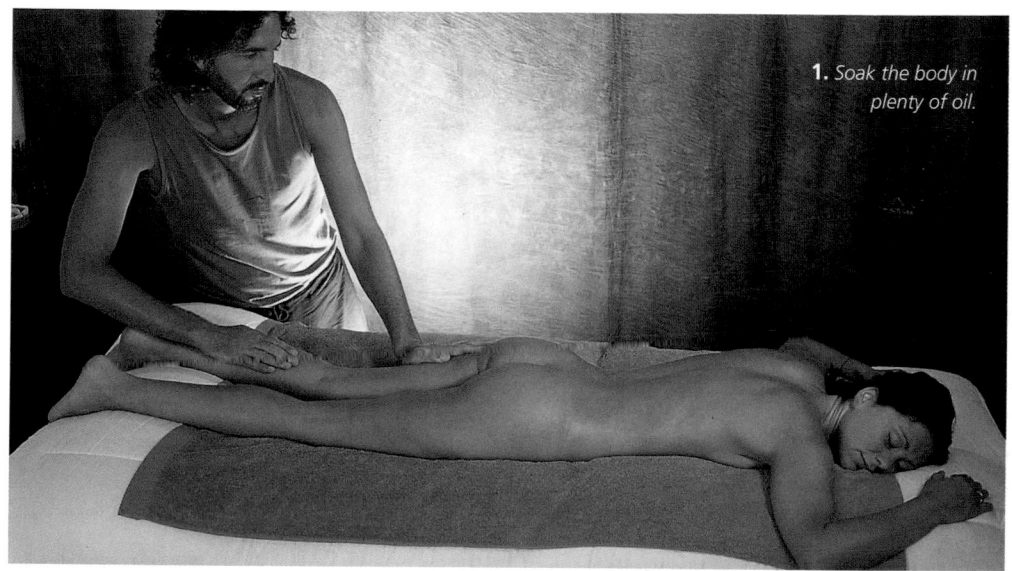

**1.** Soak the body in plenty of oil.

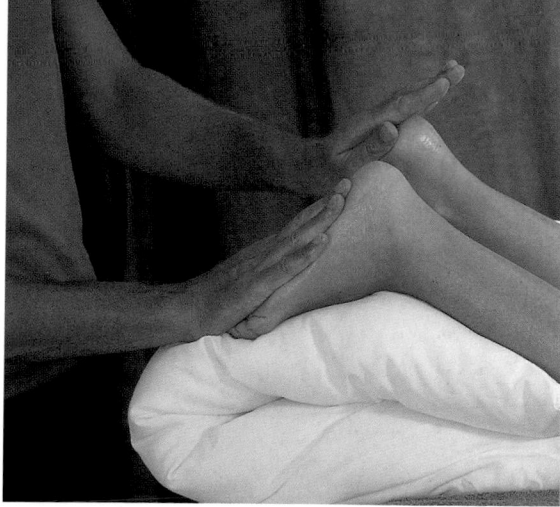

**2.** Glide your open hands very gently from the feet up to the head.

**3.** Strongly stimulate the soles of the feet with the palm of your hand.

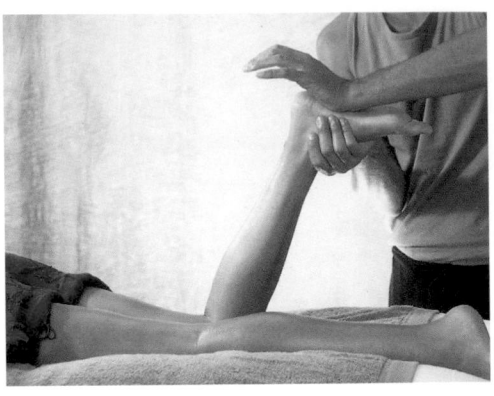

**4.** *Tap on the soles of the feet (mostly on the heel) with clenched fists to activate the bases. This way they can feel self-assured and not dependent on others.*

**5.** *Make circles across the foot with your hand.*

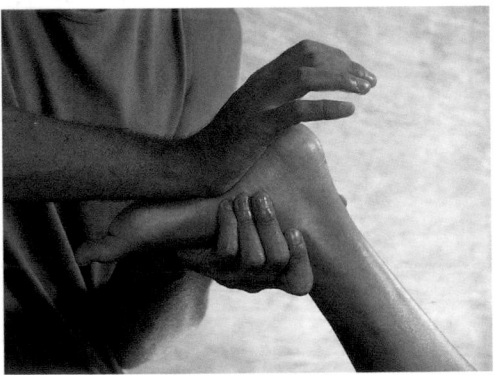

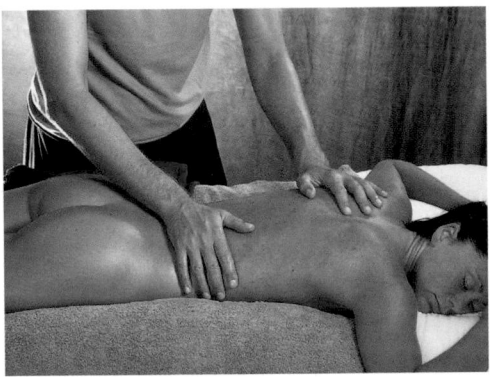

**6.** *Knead the ankle with both hands.*

**7.** *Glide your hands across the entire body, moving freely and using the entire palm of the hand, giving a sense of protection.*

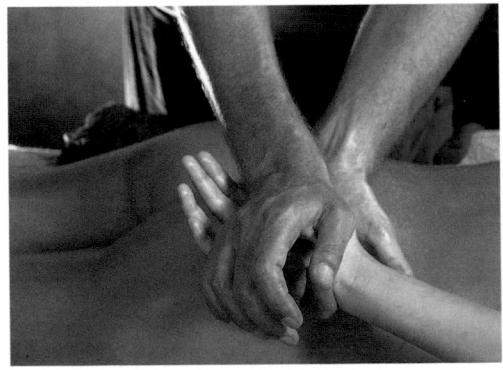

**8.** *Make circular motions at the base of the hand.*

**9.** *Stimulate the hand by pressing with both thumbs.*

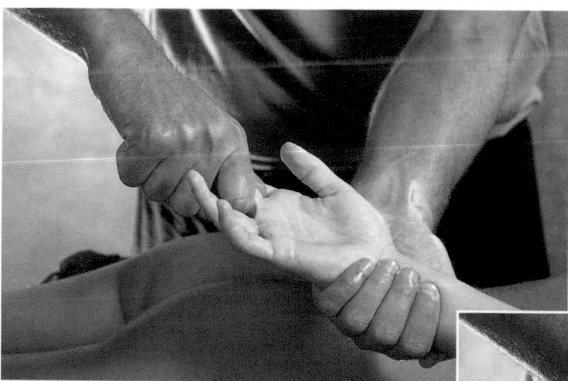

**10.** *Squeeze one finger at a time.*

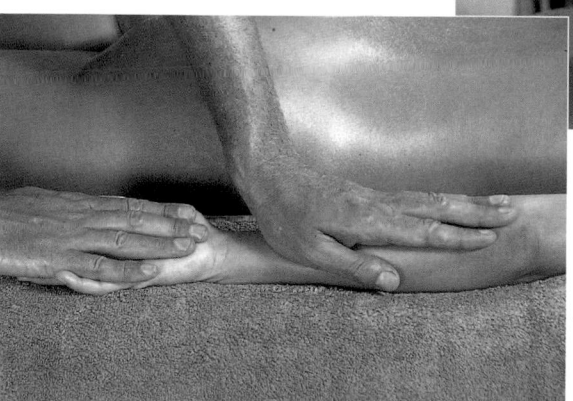

**11.** *Stamp with clenched fists, rotating at the base of the hand.*

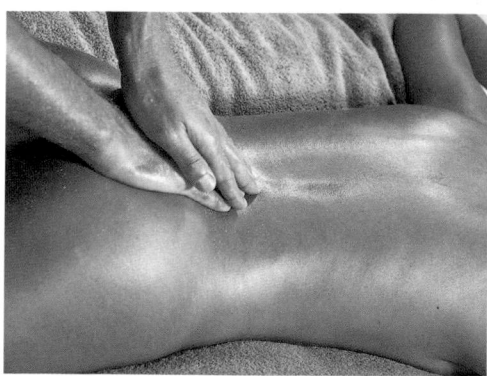

**12.** *Gently glide one hand after the other.*

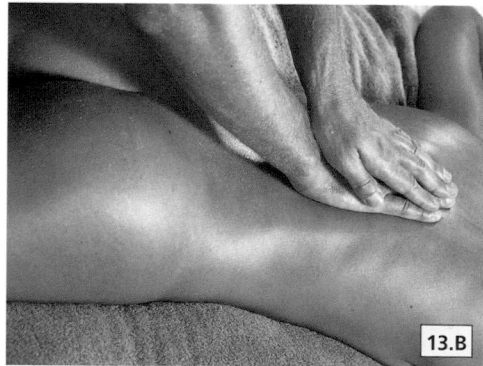

**13.** *With one hand over the other, go up and down vigorously to stimulate the entire spine. This technique helps raise energy levels, generates heat, and provides protection to the recipient.*

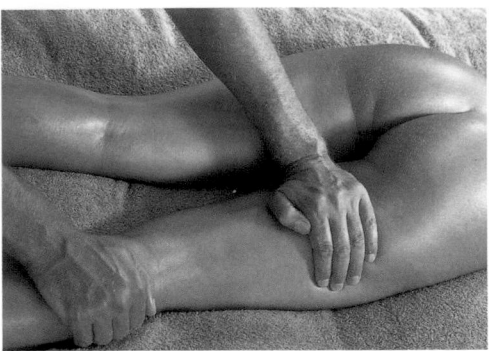 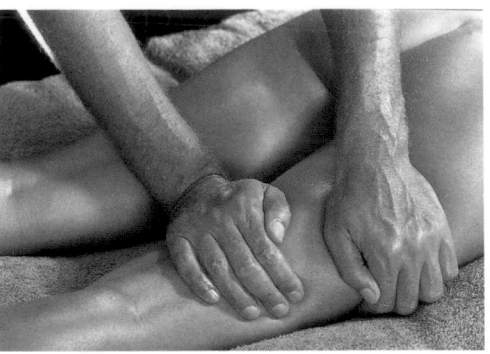

**14.** *Press and hold as you move up the entire leg. Move up and down applying enough force.*

**15.** *Glide and press as you stimulate the entire leg.*

**16.** *Make six-inch-wide (fifteen centimeter) circles with one palm over the other, moving clockwise on the middle of the back (the fourth chakra that holds emotions, affection, and protection) to generate a lot of heat.*

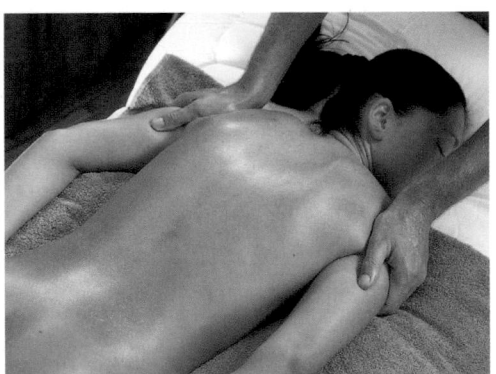 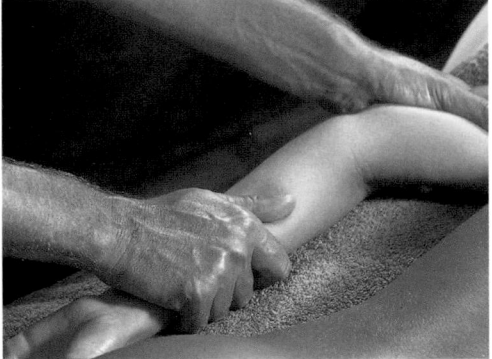

**17.** *Stimulate the shoulder through pressure and kneading to activate the sense of "I can fend for myself."*

**18.** *Stimulate both hands, by applying pressure to both arms, to activate the feeling of "I act."*

## Face up

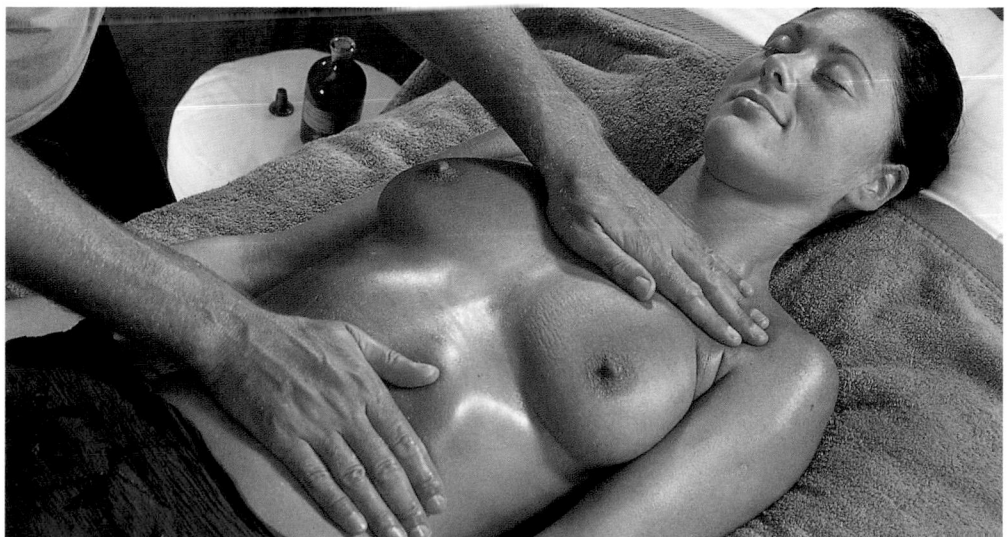

**19.** Soak the body in oil and spread it with a sense of protection (slowly and consciously).

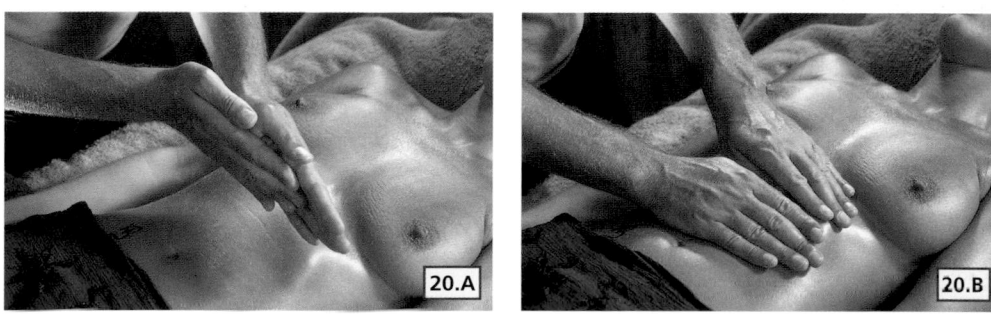

**20.** Rub both hands until you create heat and then apply it to the solar plexus (third chakra that holds self-esteem and willpower).

**21.** Make clockwise circles at the center of the chest or the fourth chakra.

**22.** Placing the recipient's arms above their head, massage from their shoulders to their hands by applying the glove technique.

**23.** *Make semicircular and continuous movements up and down. Join the solar plexus to the cardiac plexus and finish at the shoulders.*

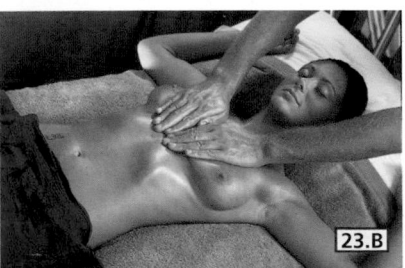

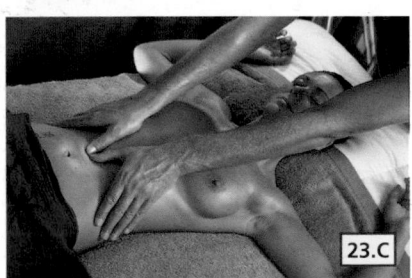

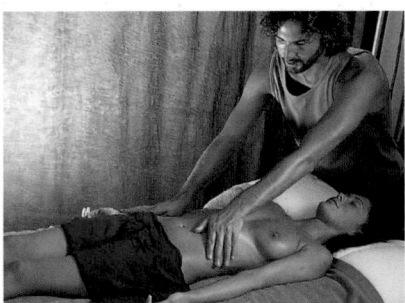

**26.** *Lastly, make the final relaxation by gliding your hands in a surrounding manner over the entire body.*

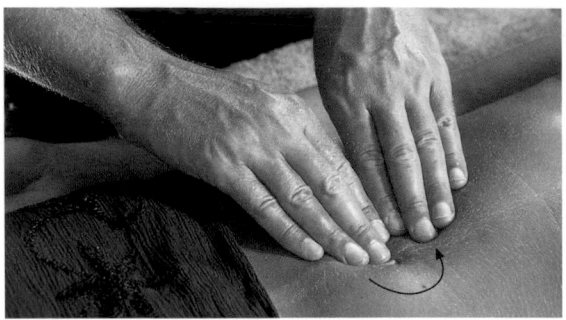

**24.** *With your fingertips, make small circles around the navel to awaken the feeling of having cut the psychological umbilical cord or dependence on the mother.*

**25.** *Rub the knees because they are linked to the flexibility of personality, the fear of death and, in men, loss of vitality by uncontrolled ejaculation.*

Let the recipient enjoy the effects and changes brought on by the massage, play soft background music, and guide them through the following meditation:

> *Breathe deeply and slowly, as if you were a baby. Visualize yourself walking barefoot through a dark tunnel that leads toward a burst of warm and familiar light that you can see at the end. Feel the attraction to this light; feel how you are able to proceed on your own. You can go into the light. You are tenderness and power at the same time. You have the power within yourself. The light surrounds you, protects you, and fills you with affection.*
>
> *You discover that you are a seed of light that begins to germinate until it becomes a tree. Feel the roots in the ground; the balance in its trunk; opening and expression of the branches that grow. You are its roots, trunk, branches, and fruits. Feel secure and firm, but also flexible enough to dance with the wind.*
>
> *Return to feeling your whole body with every sensation that this meditation has given you.*

## 2. Techniques for a submissive personality

> OIL: Mint and Eucalyptus.
> TIME FOR EACH TECHNIQUE: Three to four minutes.
> OBJECTIVE: Awaken the "I express myself."

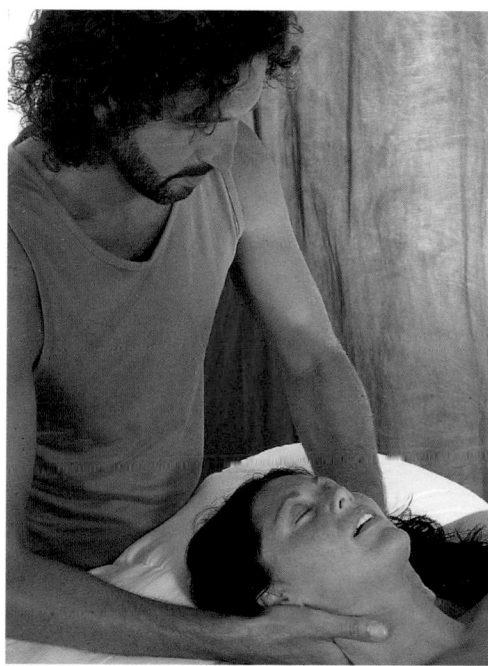

**1.** Stretch the neck with both hands with soft and alternative movements while the recipient exhales loudly through the mouth.

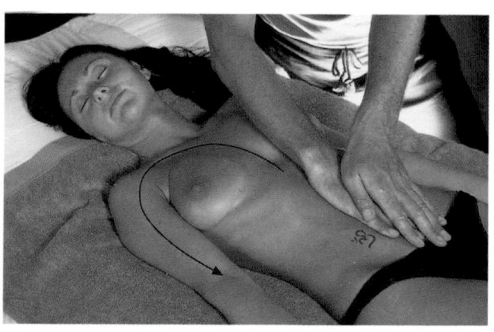

**2.** Cleanse the energy by starting at the hara and moving up with both hands (one on each side) toward the center of the chest, shoulders, arms, ending at both hands.

**3.** Apply moderate pressure to the center of the chest while the recipient says each vowel aloud with each exhalation: aaaaaaaaa, eeeeeeeee, iiiiiii, ooooooo, uuuuu. (Sometimes this technique causes laughter, so it is twice as therapeutic.)

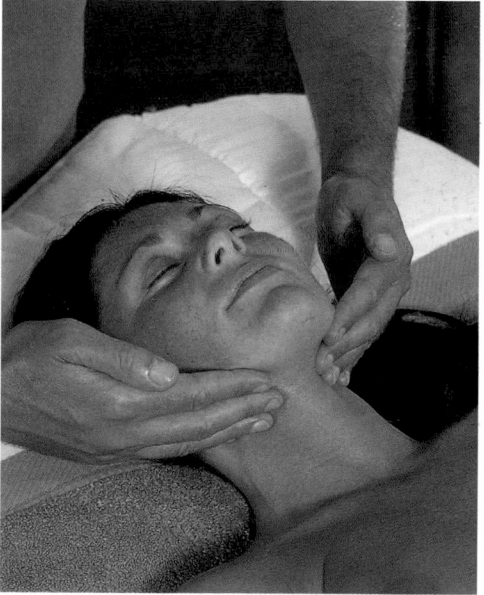

**4.** Make opening moves in the throat area (laryngeal plexus, fifth chakra). Peppermint oil or eucalyptus oil will open up this area by releasing repression and lack of self-expression.

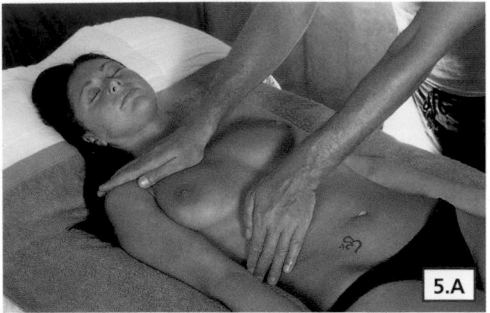
5.A

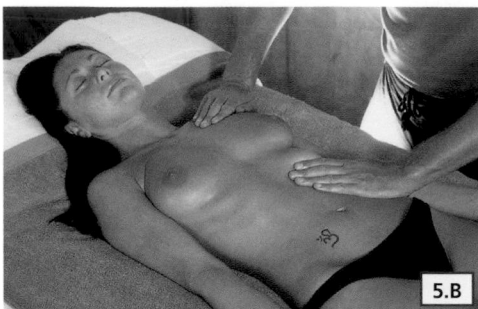
5.B

**5.** *Work with both hands at once, so that one hand works to open the area from the collarbone to the shoulder, while the other hand opens up the stomach area.*

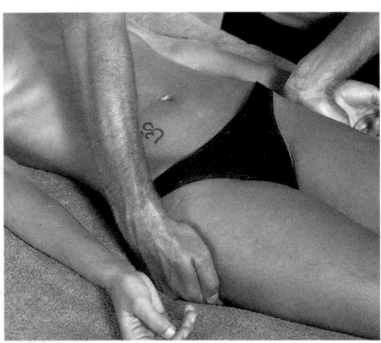

**6.** *Knead upward on the hip, waist, and lower buttocks. This area is very suppressed in women and massaging it will help them recover the sense of "I feel my life energy."*

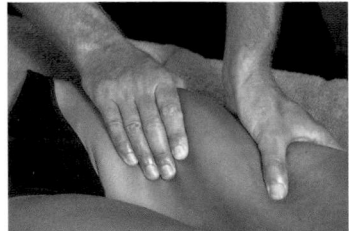

**7.** *Knead the upper area of the quadriceps, one hand on the inside and one on the outside.*

**8.** *Place your hands below the middle of the back, moving them to-and-fro (spreading about six inches). This movement lets the chest expand through deep breaths, and it mobilizes emotionally dormant energy.*

**9.A**

Keep in mind that when you breathe through your mouth, you can connect directly to the fourth chakra, allowing emotional blockages to dissolve, and you open up that oceanic feeling of unity with life. On the other hand, nasal breathing only connects you to the brain, which stimulates the third eye and intellect.

After a break, have the recipient return to deep breathing, play soft background music, and guide them through the following meditation:

> *Breathing very gently, see yourself diving into an ocean of calm and clear water. See the fish, coral reefs, seaweed, and all the mystery of the underwater world. Very calmly, imagine all the people that do not let you express yourself; look at them straight in the eye and let them know who you are. Make them feel that you were born free and you want to use your creative energy. Dance in the water and show them what you can do: move, express, flow.*
>
> *Then go up to the surface together where you can breathe the air, and look at the sun in the sky. Looking straight into the eyes of people who try to repress you, tell them how you feel and what you want to do. Let them know that you will be yourself because you allow yourself to be who you truly are. You have a gift to communicate and you will always do it with love by trusting your inner power. God is within you.*

**9.B**

**9.** *Apply tight pressure to the entire body, zone by zone, for ten minutes. It is important that the pressure be strong enough without causing pain. This technique is accompanied by "breathing" of the heart which consists of inhaling and exhaling through the mouth at a steady pace and depth.*

### 3. Techniques for a controlling or dominant personality

#### Face up

OIL: Lavender.
TIME FOR EACH TECHNIQUE: Two to three minutes.
OBJECTIVE: Awaken the sense of "I surrender to the love and wisdom of the Universe."

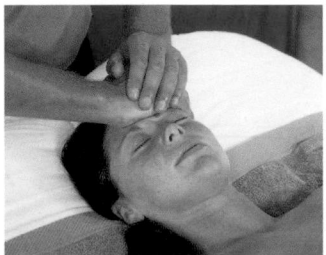

**1.** Make counterclockwise circular motions on the recipient's forehead with one hand over the other.

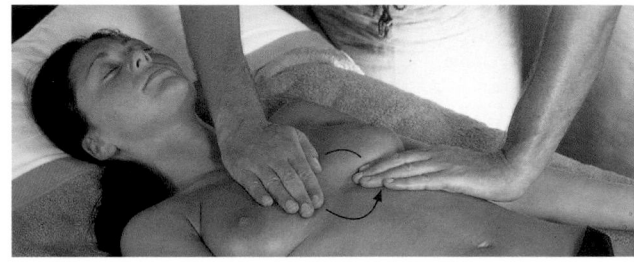

**2.** Make calming rotational movements on the chest and rib cage. Guide the recipient to exhale slowly through the mouth and awaken their sense of "surrender."

**3.** Relieve cervical tension using the technique of the ladder (alternating one hand after the other), gently shaking the head.

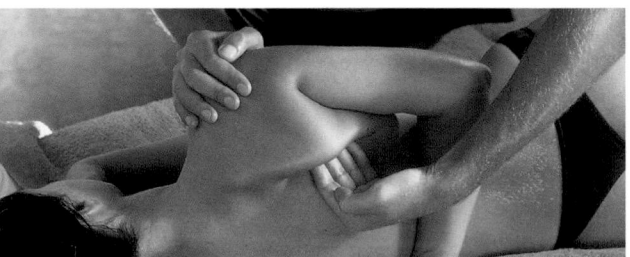

**4.** Work on opening the shoulder sideways with the thumbs and then with the whole hand. This is an area where we tend to deposit emotional repression and build up our defenses as a protective armor to guard our emotions.

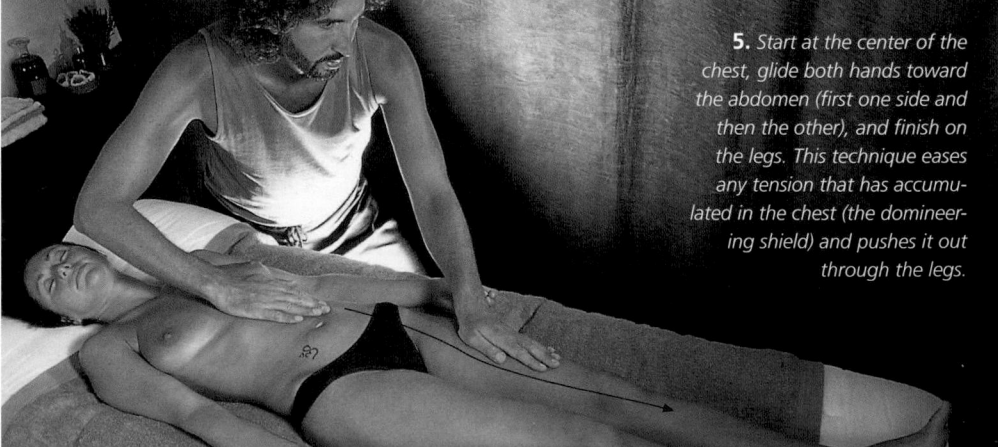

**5.** Start at the center of the chest, glide both hands toward the abdomen (first one side and then the other), and finish on the legs. This technique eases any tension that has accumulated in the chest (the domineering shield) and pushes it out through the legs.

## Face down

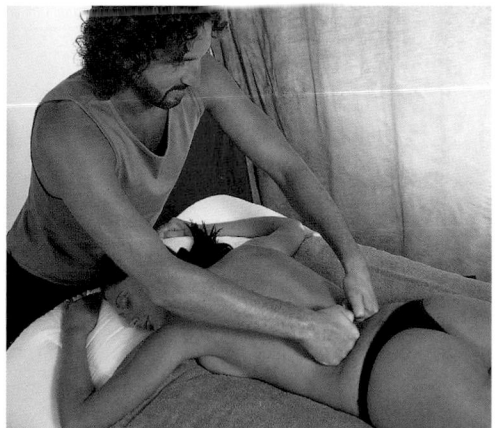

**6.** *As if you were a tractor sowing a field, slide your knuckles from the neck along the entire back to restore blood flow.*

**7.** *Place one hand over the other and massage from the neck to the shoulder.*

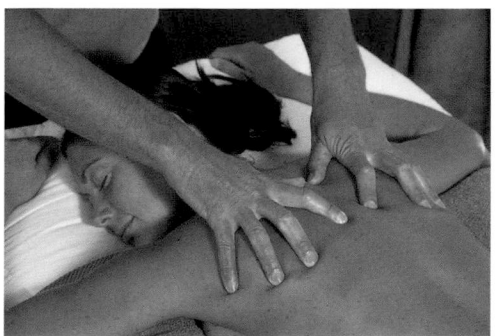

**8.** *Rake your fingers down the back to the sacrum.*

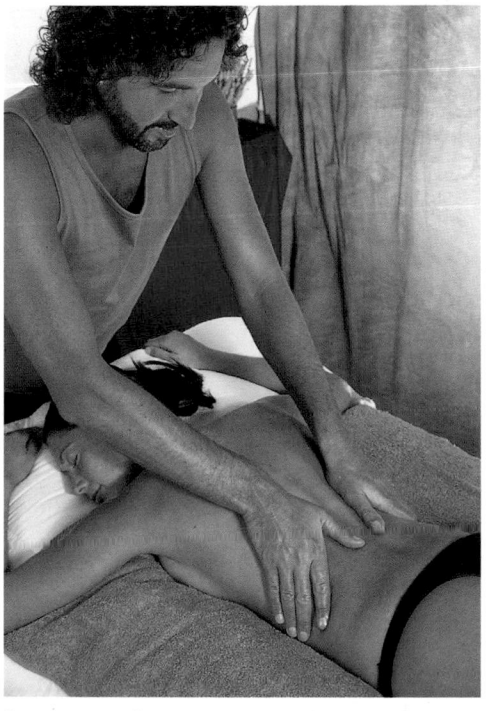

**9.** *Press very softly along the sides of the entire spine.*

Let the recipient enjoy the effects and changes brought on by the massage, play soft background music, and guide them through the following meditation:

> *Breathe very softly and feel as though you were a baby. Someone very dear to you rocks and cradles you. Your whole being is protected and safe, bathed in pleasure itself. You are pleasure and you are one with everything that exists. Everything is in harmony for you to calmly and sweetly surrender to your destination.*
>
> *Quietly, doing nothing, spring comes and grass grows by itself. At this moment, you do not have to be anything. Just imagine that you are water coming down from the mountain, and deeply relax. Everything is in order. Everything is ready for you to fly, so float and give in to this moment of profound peace.*

## 4. Techniques for a rigid and structured personality

### Face down

> OIL: Sandalwood.
> TIME FOR EACH TECHNIQUE: One to two minutes.
> OBJECTIVE: Awaken the idea of "I trust the flow and the natural change of life."

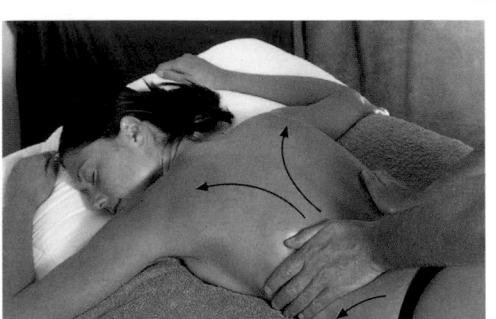

**1.** *"Open" the back with ample movements from the center of the sacrum outward and upward.*

**2.** *Move and release the tension in the shoulders with semicircular movements.*

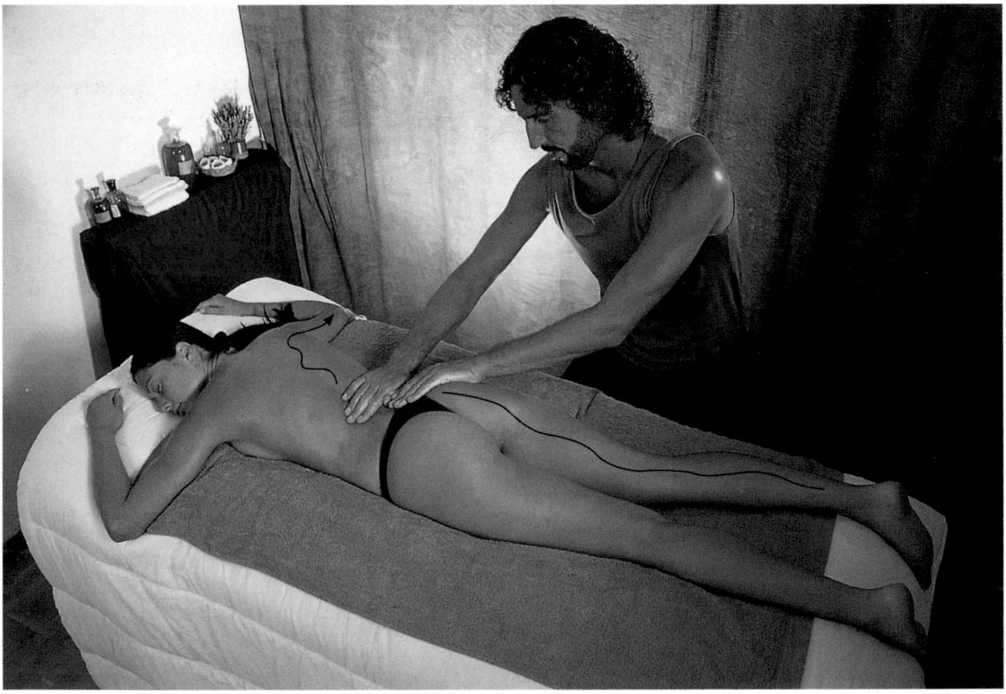

**3.** *With one hand over the other, go up from the legs to the back making undulating movements, akin to what a snake would do.*

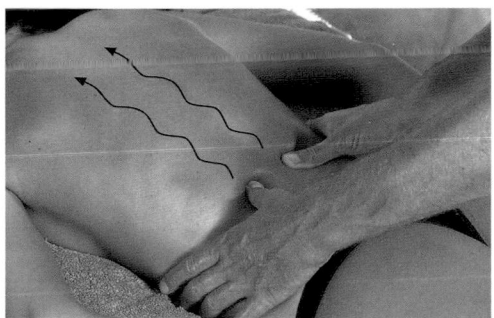

**4.** *With both thumbs, move up, making undulating movements along the vertebrae but without touching them.*

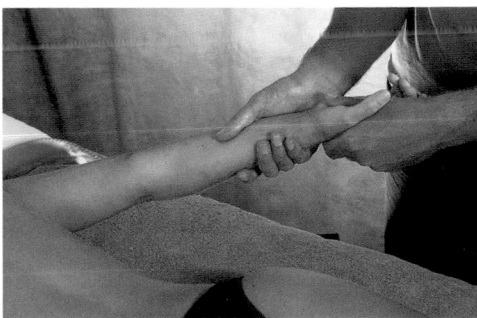

**5.** *Grab the recipient's hands and shake the arms (one at a time).*

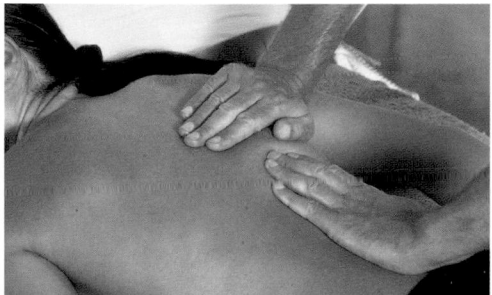

**6.** *Apply sustained pressure across the entire back and arms.*

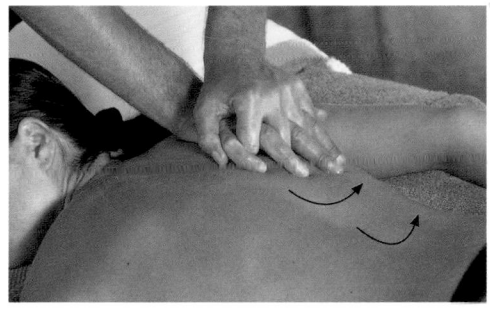

**7.** *With one hand over the other, apply slow but strong movements to ease tension in the back area.*

**8.** *Loosen the neck. One hand goes up and the other goes down.*

**9.** *Grab the ankles and shake the whole body at a slow pace.*

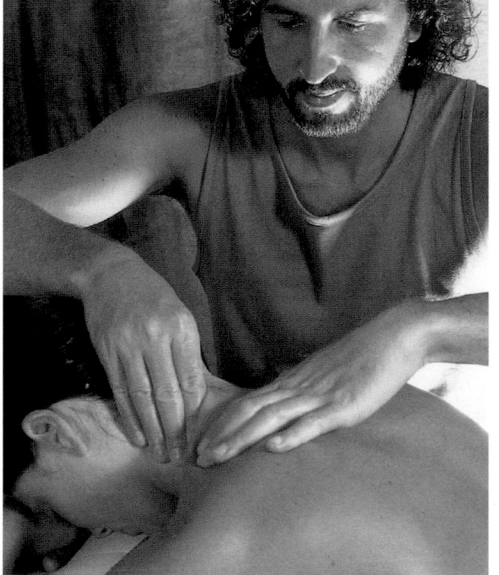

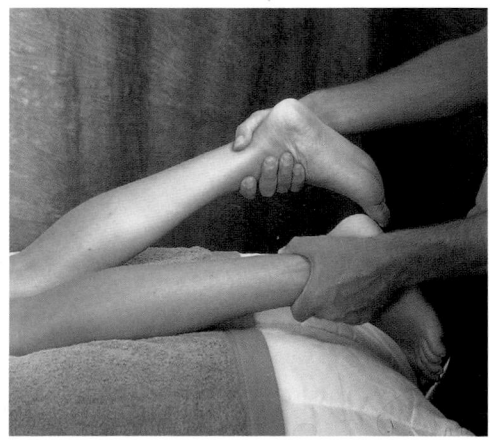

## *Face up*

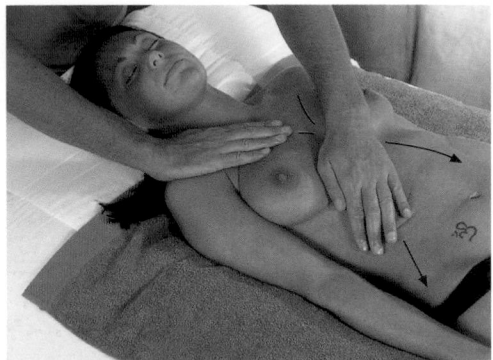

**10.** *Trace "X" figures at the center of the chest.*

**11.** *Stretch the shoulders down.*

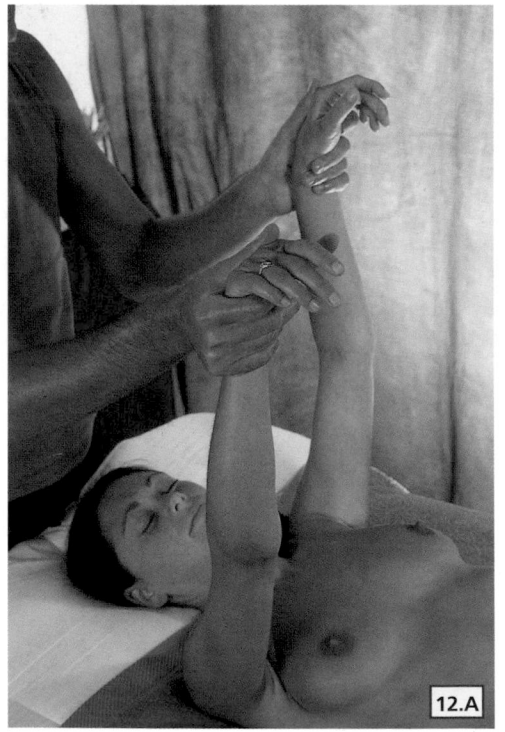

12.A

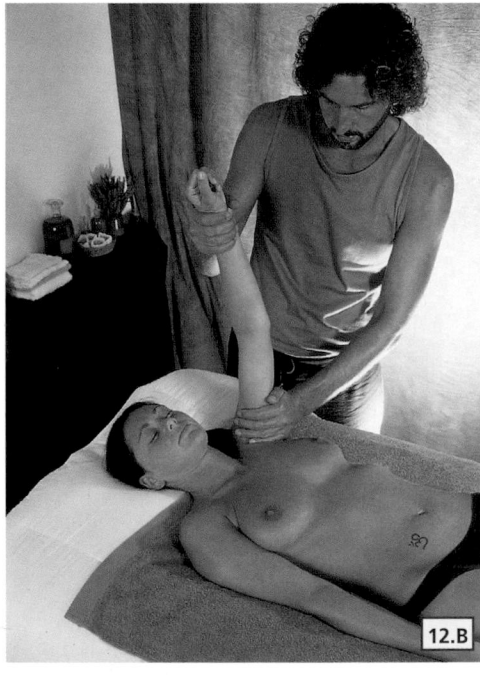

12.B

**12.** *Shake the arm vertically in an "L" shape, making a smooth motion.*

## *Work on the joints*

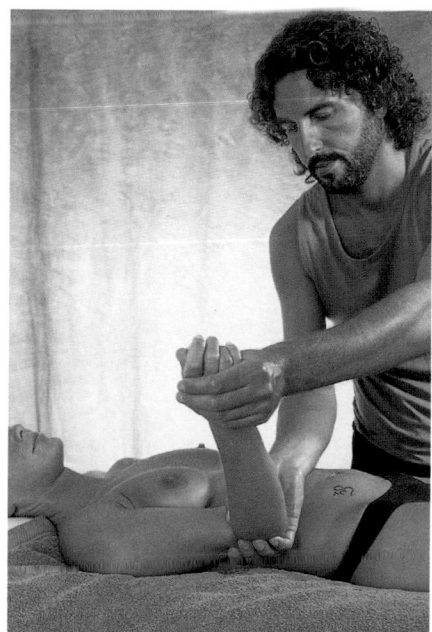

**13.** *Rotate the forearm.*

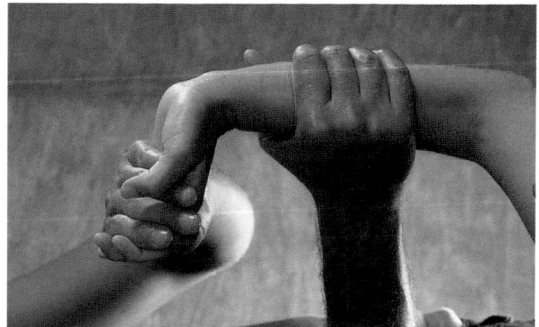

**15.** *Move the hip to and fro.*

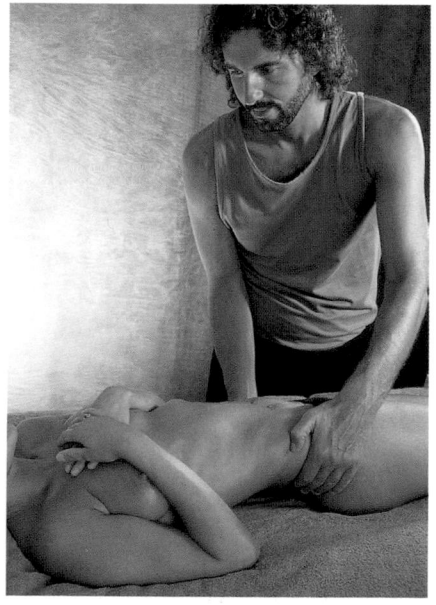

**14.** *Move the wrist.*

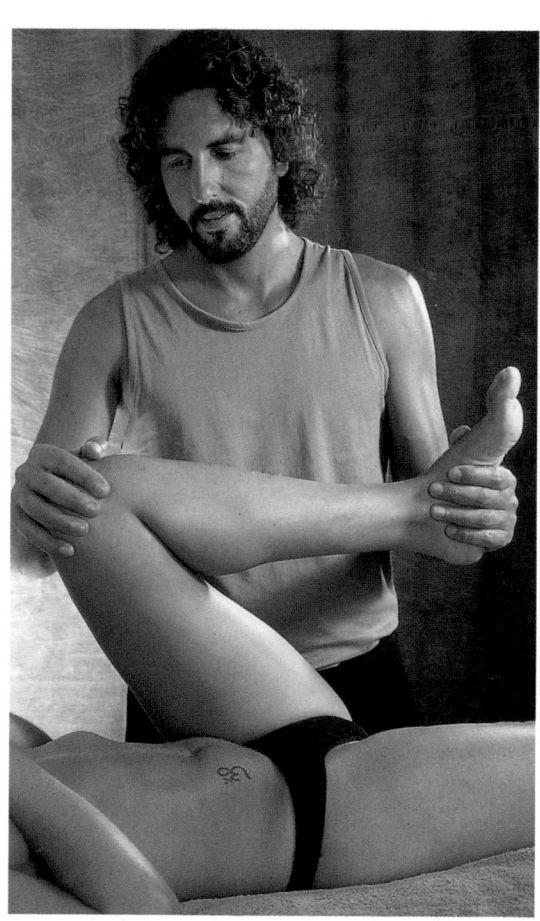

**16.** *Move the knees up to the chest.*

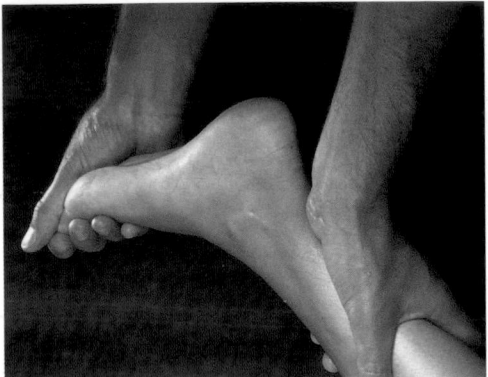

**17.** *Rotate the ankles.*

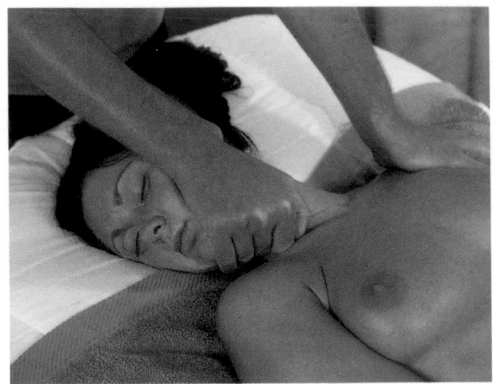

**18.** *Gently stretch the neck.*

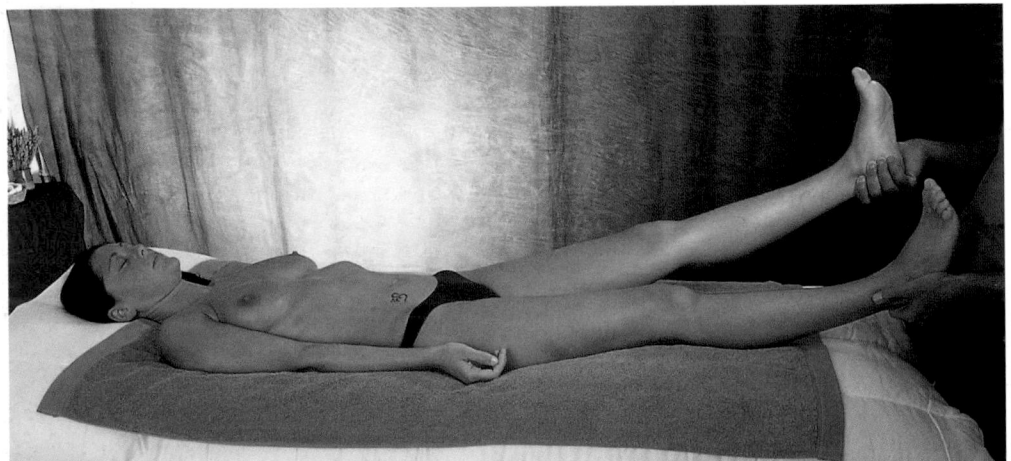

**19.** *Grab both ankles and shake the legs simultaneously.*

Let the recipient enjoy the effects and changes brought on by the massage, play soft background music, and guide them through the following meditation:

> *Breathe very softly, and imagine a green, leafy tree. The wind caresses it and the tree sways slowly. You can feel it moving from side to side. It is flexible, young, and full of life. It adapts to the rhythm of the wind, to the movement, and the new. What is more, you can see how the tree does not move but it just swings. It dances with the sun and the sky. It dances and it celebrates that, although it is grounded, it can still move.*
>
> *You feel it because you are a dragonfly and you are about to undergo your own transformation from dragonfly to butterfly. Feel how you move by leaning on the tree. You go from one stage to another; you are changed, you are reborn, and you develop your wings . . . and you fly freely in space. Everything flows in your being as a butterfly. Feel the joy of flying, changing, and getting carried away by the wind. Enjoy your flight . . .*

### 5. Techniques for a rational or cerebral personality

Guide the recipient toward breathing through the mouth to make contact with the heart (inhalation and exhalation).

> OIL. Rose with chamomile.
> TIME FOR EACH TECHNIQUE: Three to four minutes.
> OBJECTIVE: Open up to feelings and calming the mind.

### Face up

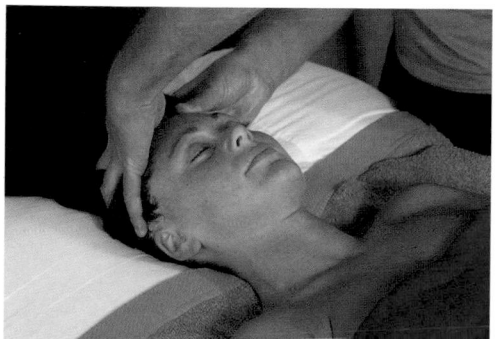

**1.** *Massage the head for some time (four to five minutes).*

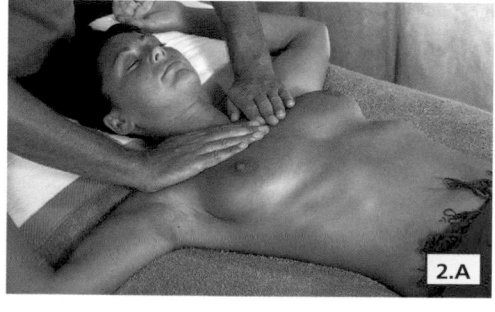

2.A

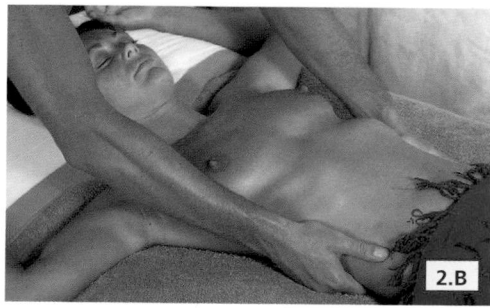

2.B

**2.** *Make an ample movement from the collarbones and chest to the belly. Then go up along the sides.*

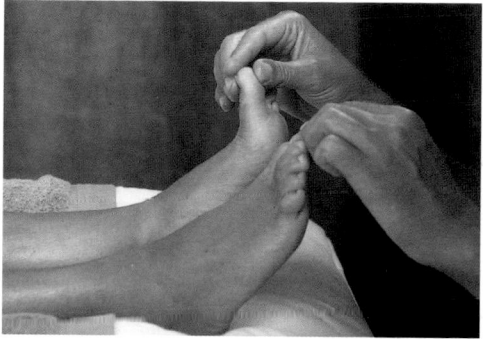

**3.** *Move the big toes with unequal numbers of circles (for instance, do five on the left, then three on the right, then two on the left). This technique lowers the energy in the head and "forces" the recipient to release control. The abrupt change from the head to the foot helps the recipient to start feeling with other parts of the body besides the head.*

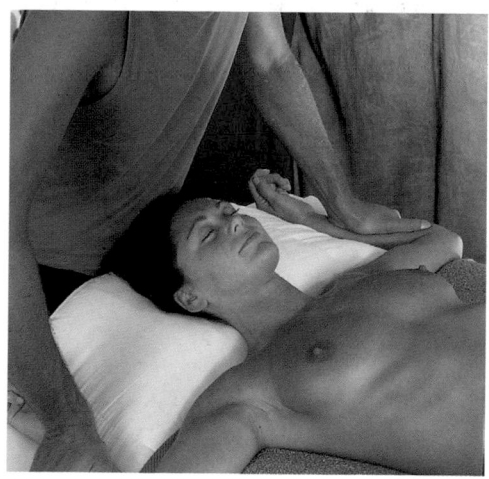

**4.** *Squeeze the arms firmly so the recipient becomes aware of other areas and unites body and mind.*

**5.** *Massage the hands by gliding your hands over the recipient's.*

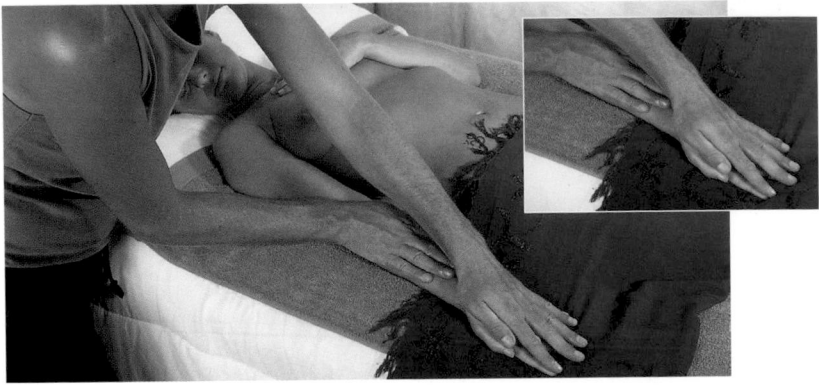

**6.** *Gently massage all around the eyelids (without using oil). Eye movements are linked to the mind: still eyes, calm mind; shifting eyes, restless mind.*

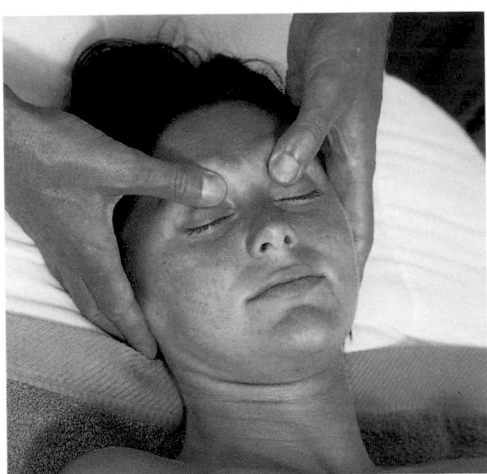

**7.** *Release tension in the pelvic walls with undulating movements, like a belly dancer.*

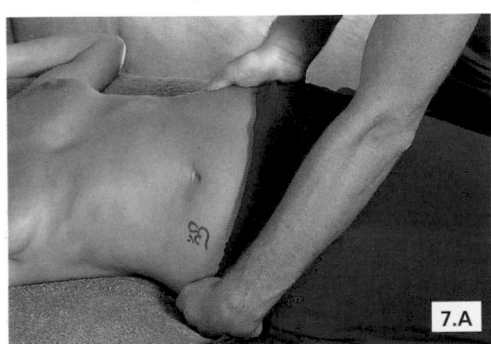

7.A

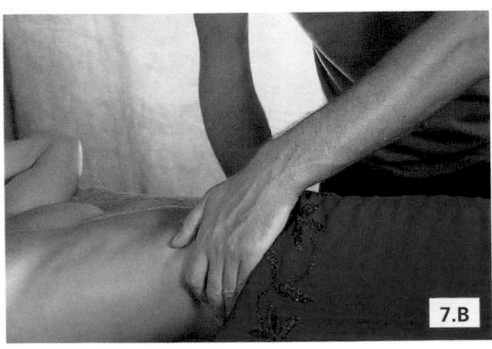

7.B

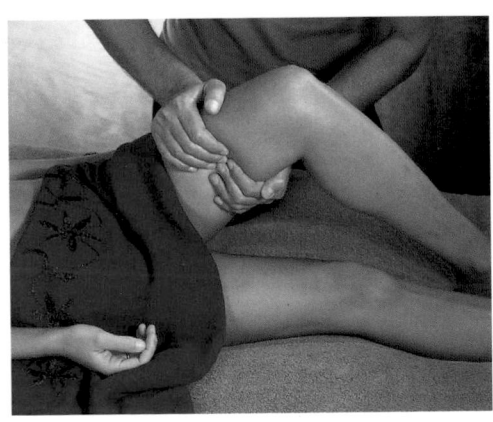

**8.** *Apply pressure to the legs.*

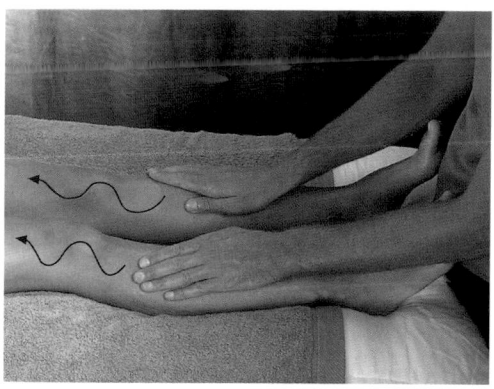

**9.** *Make a zigzag motion down the legs.*

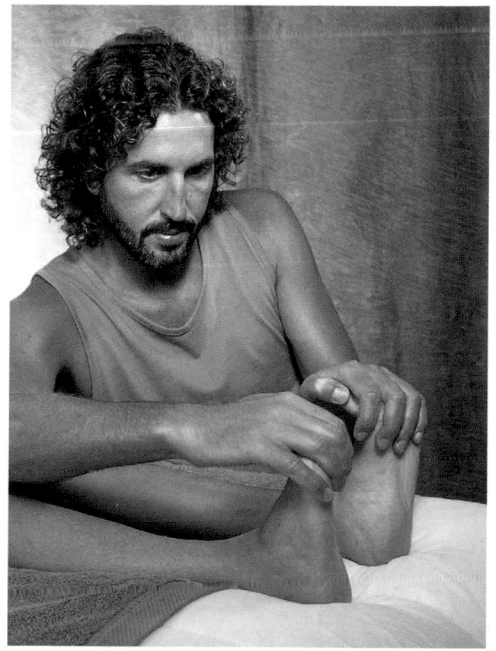

**10.** *Stretch the feet.*

## *Face down*

Breathing is to be done only through the nose.

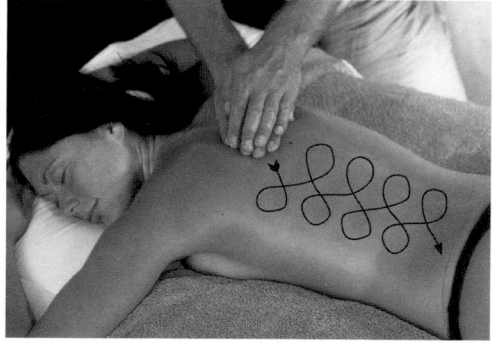

**11.** *Draw five small figure eights sideways across the entire back, from the neck to the sacrum.*

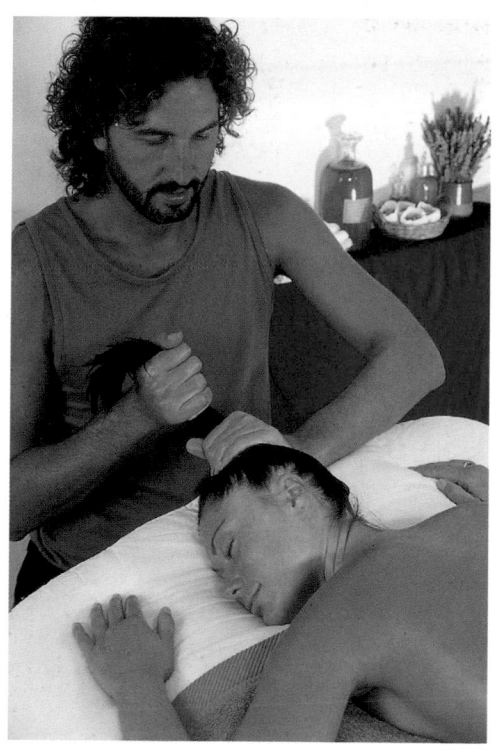

**12.** *Pull the hair and then shake the hands.*

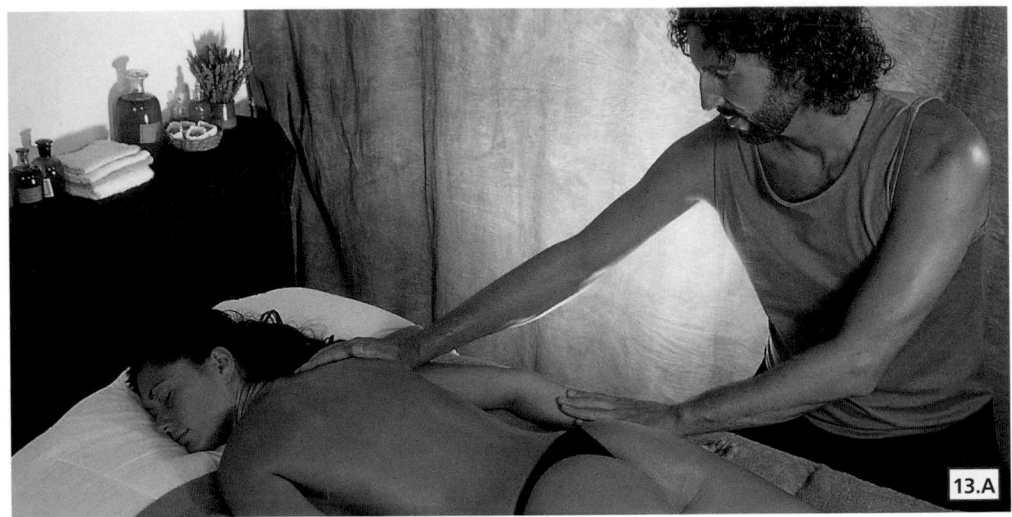

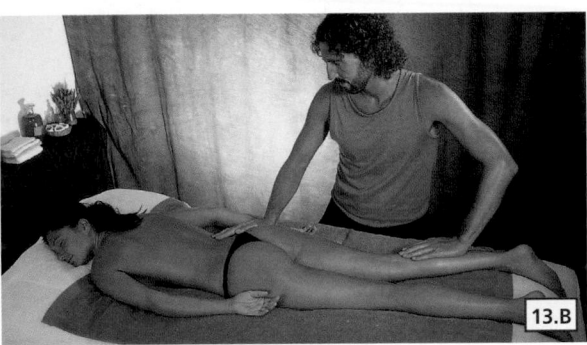

**13.** *Glide and move your hands several times, going up from the legs to the shoulders. Then do it again in reverse.*

Let the recipient enjoy the effects and changes brought on by the massage, play soft background music, and guide them through the following meditation:

> *Breathe very gently and visualize a very powerful green and pink circle in the center of your chest. The green is deep and the pink is sweet. Imagine a circle that spins on your chest with these beautiful colors. Your chest grows bigger and the colors get more intense, and at the same time you feel that the image of your head disappears, vanishes, becomes blurred.*
>
> *You do not feel your head, but you do feel your chest. You allow something different to reveal itself. You feel comfortable in your chest. You feel safe, as if a secret code began to open within. You feel pleasure and the circle spins; your conscience is in that circle without thinking, without analyzing, without worrying. You are in your internal home. The heart that you had when you were a child has returned. Do you remember when you used to dream? Do you remember when you used to live to play?*
>
> *Listen again how that voice inside you returns. Do you feel the child you once were, who did not worry about tomorrow? Enjoy this reunion and enjoy the moment. You have no head, you are pure heart. This experience is your own. Live it, feel it . . .*
>
> *Listen to your heart-to-heart conversation with the child you used to be. It is time to embrace that child again . . .*

# EPILOGUE

## I HAVE A MESSAGE FOR YOU

I hope that your journey through this book is like climbing a tree that is bearing fruit.

I hope that you learn and practice the different techniques and apply them as if each person who will be receiving them is a very dear person to you.

Treat every recipient with grace and care, just as you would have them massage you, because they possess the same essence as you.

There are a variety of options at your disposal: use them, test their effectiveness, and enjoy. Whether you are giving or receiving a massage, let it help you understand that we are energy that is evolving toward the supreme power, toward the spiritual sun that stays alive for eternity.

---

### TO GET IN TOUCH WITH THE AUTHOR

You may connect with Guillermo Ferrara at:
tantra09@hotmail.com
www.guillermoferrara.org
www.facebook.com/guillermoferrarainUSA
www.twitter.com/GuilleFerrara

---

## ABOUT THE AUTHOR

Guillermo Ferrara is an artist, therapist, and philosopher, as well as the author of twenty-two books, including several bestselling novels and works on personal development. His books have been translated into Spanish, English, Greek, French, Chinese, German, Portuguese, Serbian, Russian, and Romanian. His books are valuable tools for people to improve their quality of life. A researcher of ancient civilizations and cultures, Ferrara also specializes in holistic philosophy and transpersonal psychology. He teaches about spirituality, tantra, quantum physics, meditation, yoga, alchemical sexuality, emotional healing, and advances in the field of consciousness, from a spiritual-scientific angle.

Ferrara has been an instructor of tantric yoga since 1991. Thousands of people have taken his personal transformation workshops, both in person and online. He has taught courses and conferences in Mexico, the United States, Spain, Greece, London, Germany, Argentina, Colombia, Costa Rica, and several countries where he is contracted to share his extensive experience and his revolutionary method of spiritual enlightenment. He writes articles for newspapers and is frequently invited to present on television and radio.

He is the author of these books, also from Skyhorse Publishing: *The Art of Tantra* (Skyhorse, 2015), *The Ultimate Guide to Tantric Sex* (Skyhorse, 2016), and *Yoga for Couples* (Skyhorse, 2016). He lives in Miami Beach with his wife Sandra.